VISUAL QUICKSTART GUIDE

MySQL

Larry Ullman

 Peachpit Press

MySQL: Visual QuickStart Guide

Larry Ullman

Peachpit Press

1249 Eighth St.
Berkeley, CA 94710
510/524-2178
800/283-9444
510/524-2221 (fax)

Find us on the Web at www.peachpit.com.
To report errors, please send a note to errata@peachpit.com.

Peachpit Press is a division of Pearson Education.
Copyright © 2003 by Larry Ullman

Editor: Rebecca Gulick
Production Coordinator: Connie Jeung-Mills
Copy Editor: Brenda Benner
Technical Reviewer: Adam Nelson
Compositor: Owen Wolfson
Indexer: Karin Arrigoni
Cover Design: The Visual Group

Notice of Rights

Notice of Liability

Trademarks

ISBN 0-321-12731-5

9 8 7 6 5 4

Printed and bound in the United States of America

For Jess, my one and only.

A lifetime supply of thanks to:

The wonderful people at Peachpit Press. My sincerest thanks to everyone there (and at Pearson) for their dedication to putting out quality books, for giving me these opportunities to publish, and for everything else they do. Specifically, I would like to thank Nancy Aldrich-Ruenzel, Marjorie Baer, Kim Lombardi, Gary-Paul Prince, and the other two dozen people whose names and jobs I may not know but should.

This book's editor, Rebecca Gulick. My job is easier and the book is better when I have the pleasure of working with you. I am very fortunate to have had that opportunity once again.

Brenda Benner, for her spot-on copy editing and attention to detail.

Connie Jeung-Mills, Production Coordinator Extraordinaire, for turning a disparate collection of text files and images into a usable, physical book, and for being so nice about it, too!

Owen Wolfson, Compositor; Karin Arrigoni, Indexer; and Adam Nelson, Technical Reviewer.

John O'Malley, programmer to the stars and all-around smart person, for his help on the Java chapter. You're one of my top-ten, all-time favorite people, even if you aren't a veteran.

As always, everyone at DMC Insights, Inc., for lots of reasons.

The readers of my previous books who took the time to let me know how much they appreciated them (even if they followed that up with a support question) and for requesting that I write a MySQL book. I hope it's everything you were looking for.

Finally (whew!), thanks to everyone in the MySQL community—from those at MySQL AB to the participants of the various mailing lists. MySQL is yet another example of how great open source technology can be!

For Jess, my one and only.

A lifetime supply of thanks to:

The wonderful people at Peachpit Press. My sincerest thanks to everyone there (and at Pearson) for their dedication to putting out quality books, for giving me these opportunities to publish, and for everything else they do. Specifically, I would like to thank Nancy Aldrich-Ruenzel, Marjorie Baer, Kim Lombardi, Gary-Paul Prince, and the other two dozen people whose names and jobs I may not know but should.

This book's editor, Rebecca Gulick. My job is easier and the book is better when I have the pleasure of working with you. I am very fortunate to have had that opportunity once again.

Brenda Benner, for her spot-on copy editing and attention to detail.

Connie Jeung-Mills, Production Coordinator Extraordinaire, for turning a disparate collection of text files and images into a usable, physical book, and for being so nice about it, too!

Owen Wolfson, Compositor; Karin Arrigoni, Indexer; and Adam Nelson, Technical Reviewer.

John O'Malley, programmer to the stars and all-around smart person, for his help on the Java chapter. You're one of my top-ten, all-time favorite people, even if you aren't a veteran.

As always, everyone at DMC Insights, Inc., for lots of reasons.

The readers of my previous books who took the time to let me know how much they appreciated them (even if they followed that up with a support question) and for requesting that I write a MySQL book. I hope it's everything you were looking for.

Finally (whew!), thanks to everyone in the MySQL community—from those at MySQL AB to the participants of the various mailing lists. MySQL is yet another example of how great open source technology can be!

TABLE OF CONTENTS

INTRODUCTION

In the midst of the Information Age, where more and more data is being stored on computers, the need for high-speed, reliable databases has increased dramatically. For years, certain companies, such as Oracle, have been providing data warehousing applications used primarily by Fortune 500 companies, which can afford the cost and personnel demands of high-end software for mission-critical work. Meanwhile, within the open source community—which has blossomed particularly in the past decade, a new wave of small, reliable, and inexpensive database applications came to the market. Such software, such as mSQL, MySQL, and PostgreSQL, gave common users and developers on a budget a practical database choice.

MySQL, fortunately, has left its modest beginnings in the dust, turning into a robust, reliable, and easy-to-manage database application. More astounding, MySQL has managed to retain its open source roots, continuing to be available for use or modification without any cost. MySQL's capabilities today explain why major operations such as Yahoo!, the United States Census Bureau, and NASA use it within their organizations. Its low cost and accessibility explain why you, too, can incorporate MySQL into your projects. With *MySQL: Visual QuickStart Guide*, you will be doing just that in no time!

What Is MySQL?

MySQL is the world's most popular, and some might argue best, open source database. In fact, more and more, MySQL is a viable competitor to the pricey goliaths such as Oracle and Microsoft's SQL Server.

MySQL was created and is currently supported by MySQL AB, a company based in Sweden (www.mysql.com, **Figure i.1**). MySQL, to some degree, grew out of an existing open source database, mSQL, which is still developed, although its popularity has waned. Amusingly enough, one thing neither this book nor any other can tell you is what MySQL stands for. The latter part, SQL, refers to Structured Query Language—the language used to interact with most databases, but the "my" preface is officially unaccounted for even within the MySQL AB company.

MySQL is a database management system (DBMS) for relational databases (therefore, MySQL is an RDBMS). Technically, MySQL is an application that manages files called databases, but you will commonly hear the term "database" applied equally to both. A database is simply a collection of interrelated data, be it text, numbers, or binary files, that are stored and kept organized by the DBMS.

There are many types of databases, from the simple flat-file to relational and object-oriented. A relational database uses multiple tables to store information in their most discernable parts. Prior to the early 1970s, when this concept was developed, databases looked more like spreadsheets with single, vast tables storing everything. While relational databases may involve more thought in the designing and programming stages, they offer an improved reliability and data integrity that more than makes up for the extra effort.

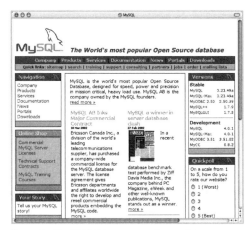

Figure i.1 The MySQL home page, located at www.mysql.com, is where you can obtain the software, view the manual, and more.

Pronunciation Guide

Trivial as it may be, I should clarify up front that MySQL is technically pronounced "My Ess Que Ell," just as SQL should be said "Ess Que Ell," as this is a question many people first have.

MySQL is an open source application, like PHP and some variants of Unix, meaning that it is free to run or even modify (the source code itself is downloadable). There are occasions in which you should pay for a MySQL license, though, especially if you are making money from the sales or incorporation of the MySQL product. Check MySQL's licensing policy for more information on this.

The MySQL software consists of several pieces, including the MySQL server (*mysqld*, which runs and manages the databases), the MySQL client (*mysql*, which gives you an interface to the server), and numerous utilities for maintenance and other purposes. You can interface with MySQL using most popular programming languages, including PHP, Perl, and Java, all of which will be demonstrated in this book.

MySQL was written in C and C++, and it functions equally well over several different operating systems. MySQL has been known to handle databases as large as 60,000 tables with more than 5 billion rows. MySQL can work with tables as large as 8 million terabytes (since version 3.23) on some operating systems and generally a healthy 4 GB otherwise.

MySQL, at the time of this writing, is on version 3.23.49a, and the much-anticipated Version 4 will be out later in 2002. Version 4 of MySQL takes the technology to the next level, incorporating a number of features developers have been requesting for years. Throughout the course of the book I will attempt to specify at every point which features are new to MySQL 4 and therefore will not work on earlier versions.

WHAT IS MYSQL?

Primary MySQL Resources

Because MySQL is a free application, most of your questions will need to be answered by members of the MySQL mailing lists rather than by MySQL AB itself. The company is, however, available for contractual support, consulting, and training, which you might want to consider if you are using MySQL on a larger scale or in a corporate environment.

MySQL has a solid online manual (available at www.mysql.com/documentation/, **Figure i.2**), which includes the occasional user-submitted comment. It's searchable, thorough, and able to answer most of the questions you'll come across. At the time of this writing, the manual covered up to version 4.0.2-alpha of the software.

The MySQL mailing lists, while not as active as some others, are populated by users and the MySQL people themselves, who are very informative and responsive. You'll also find specific mailing lists dedicated to the database on Windows and interacting with MySQL from Java, among other topics. Because of the popularity of the mailing lists, there are currently no strong MySQL newsgroups as you might encounter with other technologies.

For links to these and other MySQL references, see Appendix C, "Resources."

Figure i.2 The online version of the MySQL manual is highly detailed and well organized. You can also download other versions for immediate access from your computer.

Figure i.3 MySQL is available in versions designed to run on almost every operating system, including various types of Unix and Windows.

Figure i.4 Mac OS X comes with the Terminal application, which allows you to interact with the computer on a command-line level.

Technical Requirements

In order to follow the discussions in this book, there are a few, though not too restricting, technical requirements. The first, naturally, would be the MySQL software itself. Fortunately, this is freely available and runs on most operating systems (**Figure i.3**). Chapter 1, "Installing MySQL," will cover the fundamentals of installing MySQL on three popular operating systems: Windows, Linux, and Macintosh.

The bulk of the chapters involve administering and interacting with the database from a command-line perspective. Whichever application on your operating system gives you this access is acceptable, be it a DOS prompt on Windows, a Linux shell, or the Mac OS X Terminal (**Figure i.4**).

Lastly, the programming chapters covering PHP, Perl, and Java—Chapters 6, 7, and 8, respectively—will require a text editor, a Web browser, and so forth. The specific requirements will be discussed in the pertinent chapter.

TECHNICAL REQUIREMENTS

About This Book

In this book I have attempted to explain the fundamentals of MySQL, teaching the information that most MySQL users might require. In keeping with the format of the Visual QuickStart series, the information is taught using a step-by-step approach with corresponding images. The demonstrations in the book will be geared toward specific knowledge as opposed to developing in-depth MySQL-based applications (such as a programming text might have).

Most of the examples in the book will be executed from a command-line interface (**Figure i.5**), although the three programming chapters plus Chapter 9, "Database Programming Techniques," will function differently. In those chapters, I will go through writing the scripts in detail and then test them using the most applicable technique (be it a Web browser or whatever).

The structure of the book is fairly linear. It begins with basic installation and administration of the software. After that, database design and SQL—elements common to most database applications—will be covered, followed by some MySQL-specific functions. The three programming chapters will come next, and I will conclude with some specific database-application techniques as well as MySQL-related utilities with which you should familiarize yourself. The appendices discuss troubleshooting techniques and provide a reference section along with where to turn for more information.

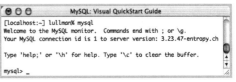

Figure i.5 Most of the chapters will demonstrate techniques by accessing the MySQL client (or other MySQL utilities) from a command line.

Is This Book For You?

This book was written for a wide range of
people within the beginner to intermediate
range. Obviously, this book is for anyone
wanting to use MySQL in some capacity, but
I specifically had in mind those who have
never used any database before, those who
have used other databases and want to know
how MySQL specifically operates, and those
who are currently using MySQL in a limited
capacity and would like to elevate their skills
to a more professional level. I should note
that I will not be teaching any programming
languages here but rather demonstrate how
to use those languages with MySQL.

Companion Web Site

I have developed a companion Web site specifically for this book, which you may reach at
www.DMCinsights.com/mysql. There you
will find every script from this book (for the
programming chapters), text files containing
lengthy SQL commands, and a list of errata
that occurred during publication. (If you
have a problem with a command or script,
and are following the book exactly, check
the errata to ensure there is not a printing
error before driving yourself absolutely mad.)
At this Web site you will also find useful
Web links, a forum where readers can ask
and answer each others' questions (related
to the material herein or not), and more!

Questions, Comments, or Suggestions?

If you have any MySQL-specific questions, you can turn to one of the many Web sites, mailing lists, and FAQ repositories already in existence. Appendix C, "Resources," lists the most popular of these options. You can also direct your questions, comments, and suggestions to me directly, via email, at: mysql@DMCinsights.com. I do try to answer every email I receive, although there is no guarantee as to my alacrity. (Preference and more detailed responses will be given to emails pertaining to the content of this book; more prompt and thoughtful replies with other issues are best sought through the mailing lists or the book's online reader forum.)

INSTALLING MySQL

Because MySQL is an open source database, you have more options when it comes to installation than you would with a commercial application. These options range from the very simple execution of an installer to customizing and compiling your own installation using MySQL's source files (the code MySQL is written in).

In this chapter I will cover installation on the Windows, Macintosh, and Linux operating systems. These three platforms cover a large portion of the MySQL audience, but the database is available on many other platforms as well. Between the Windows binary and the Linux source installation instructions, you should have a good sense of the various issues regardless of the operating system you are using.

There are a number of considerations when deciding which product to download and install, the first being whether you choose a stable or development release (frequently marked alpha or beta). MySQL is thoroughly tested both within MySQL AB (the company that develops MySQL) and by users around the world, so installing a stable version of MySQL should always result in reliable performance. The development versions are best left to the experts who can clearly distinguish between bugs (or "features") and user errors.

Version 4 of MySQL Server is currently at an alpha development stage and is expected to be released as a stable version before the end of 2002. This version will have plenty of long-awaited features, including increased speed (for an already fast database server); direct use of InnoDB tables, which allow for transactions; and support for secure transactions via SSL (Secure Sockets Layer). After 4.0's successful release, version 4.1 of MySQL Server will incorporate nested subqueries (the ability to have a query contain another query), stored procedures, and foreign key recognition. Once these capabilities have been included, MySQL will be comparable to even the largest, most expensive database management systems. If you would like to get a sense of what the future of MySQL will be, install version 4, but it would be best not to use this for critical purposes until it's final.

This chapter covers downloading the software, installing the server, and creating the initial MySQL databases. If you have problems with any of the installation steps described here, see Appendix A, "Troubleshooting," or the relevant sections of the MySQL manual.

INSTALLING MySQL

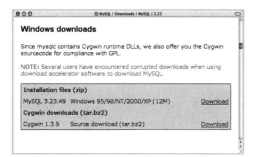

Figure 1.1 After clicking on this link, I will be given the choice of which mirror Web site closest to me to use for downloading.

Installing MySQL on Windows

There are two primary ways of installing the MySQL software on a Windows operating system: using a precompiled distribution or compiling your own binary from the MySQL source files. The former is significantly easier than the latter and will be the technique I use here.

MySQL will run on most Windows operating systems (specifically those that are 32-bit, such as Windows 95, 98, Me, NT, 2000, and XP). If you're using an NT OS such as Windows NT, 2000, or XP (either the Home or Professional version), you can run MySQL as a service, which I'll demonstrate in the next chapter. For my example here, I'll be installing the latest stable release of MySQL on Windows XP Home.

To install MySQL on Windows:

1. Download the Zip file from the MySQL Web site (**Figure 1.1**).

   As of the time of this writing, the most current stable release of MySQL is version 3.23.49.

2. Unzip the downloaded file.

   It doesn't really matter where you choose to unzip the files in this step, but when installing MySQL (step 3), it would be best to install MySQL into the C:\mysql directory, so plan accordingly.

   continues on next page

3. Run the `setup.exe` application by double-clicking on the file (**Figure 1.2**).

If you are using a version of Windows NT, you must be logged in as an administrator-level user with the permission to install software. Follow through the various steps, selecting a destination (**Figure 1.3**) and installation type (Typical, Compact, or Custom) when prompted. In my case I chose the Typical installation into the `C:\mysql` directory.

4. Open the newly created `C:\mysql\bin` directory in Windows Explorer.

Assuming that you choose `C:\mysql` as the destination of the software, all of the applications you will be running will be stored in its `bin` subdirectory.

5. Run the WinMySQLadmin utility (**Figure 1.4**) by double-clicking on the file.

The WinMySQLadmin application will finish setting up the necessary files that MySQL needs to run. This step will also create a MySQL service for NT operating systems and place a stoplight icon in the System Tray indicating MySQL's status. Be sure to remember your MySQL user name and password, as it is entered here.

✔ Tips

■ You are not required to install MySQL into the `C:\mysql` directory, but it is a good idea. If, for some reason, you would prefer to install the software elsewhere, specify the correct directory when `setup.exe` prompts you.

■ That being said, you will have an easier time running MySQL as a service in an NT environment if you use the default `C:\mysql` directory.

Figure 1.2 After you have unzipped the installation files, install MySQL by double-clicking the `setup.exe` application (the file with the computer icon).

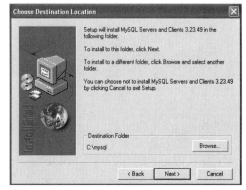

Figure 1.3 The MySQL `setup.exe` installer takes you through a couple of steps, including the preferred destination of the software.

Figure 1.4 Running the WinMySQLadmin utility is the last step for installing MySQL. It will also be used to manage the server.

Figure 1.5 Marc Liyanage's Web site offers great details about using MySQL on Mac OS X, as well as the installation files themselves.

Installing MySQL on Macintosh

Mac OS X uses a FreeBSD foundation with a Macintosh graphical user interface, meaning that it has the usability and stability of any Unix operating system but the appearance and interface of a Mac. The implication of this is that, now more than ever, there is an Apple operating system that programmers and developers are actively using. Furthermore, most software that installs and runs on a Unix system, such as MySQL, will also work with Mac OS X.

At the time of this writing, there are two primary ways to install MySQL on Mac OS X: install from the source, as I will demonstrate with Linux next; or use Marc Liyanage's precompiled package, available through his Web site at www.entropy.ch/software/macosx/mysql (**Figure 1.5**). Marc has done an excellent job with his MySQL installation package, so I would advocate—and will demonstrate here—using his system.

Being the Root User

Unix-based operating systems, including Max OS X and Linux, rely on the concept of users for security purposes. The ultimate user, *root*, can do virtually anything within the operating system, including destroy it. For this reason the root user should be handled gingerly, but it is also a necessary evil when installing new software.

If a root user account has already been established (with a password), you can become root by typing **su root** within the Terminal application. You will then be prompted for the root user's password. You can also preface every line with **sudo**, like **sudo ./scripts/mysql_install_db**, after which time you will be prompted for the root password.

To establish a root user password on Mac OS X, type **sudo passwd root**, press Return at the first prompt, and then enter the new password twice.

To install MySQL on Mac OS X:

1. Download the current package from the Web site.

   At the time of writing, Marc had a 3.23.49 version compiled. The name of the file to be downloaded will be something like *mysql-3.23.49.pkg.tar.gz*.

2. Unpack the file.

   Using a utility such as StuffIt Expander, unpack the downloaded file until you are left with the MySQL package itself (**Figure 1.6**).

3. Install MySQL.

   Double-click on the MySQL package and follow through its steps.

4. Open the Users control panel through the System Preferences (**Figure 1.7**).

   I will create a specific user for running the MySQL software, which is a safety precaution you ought to take.

5. Add a new user named *mysql* (**Figure 1.8**).

   To do this, click on the *New User* button, then add a user with the name and short name of *mysql*, and use whatever you would like for the password. Finally, click *Save* and close out of the Users control panel.

Figure 1.6 Mac OS X, like Unix, can install software using the .pkg package files, whose icon looks like this.

Figure 1.7 The Users panel (under System Preferences) is Apple's current tool for managing system users.

Figure 1.8 The details of the *mysql* user are not pertinent as long as you use an easy-to-remember unique name and make note of the password, should you establish one.

INSTALLING MySQL ON MACINTOSH

Figure 1.9 To finish up the installation process, use the Terminal application as the *root* user.

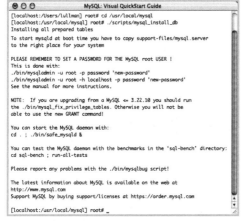

Figure 1.10 The mysql_install_db script will create the initial pair of databases, *mysql* and *test*.

6. Open up the Terminal application and log on as the *root* user (**Figure 1.9**).

   For most of these steps it will be easier if you can log on as the *root* user. If you have not yet established *root* access, you can preface each of the following commands with sudo, then enter the administrator's password when prompted (see the sidebar *Being the root User* earlier in this chapter).

7. Move to the /usr/local/mysql directory.

   cd /usr/local/mysql

8. Install the initial databases (**Figure 1.10**).

   ./scripts/mysql_install_db

9. Change the permissions on the directory.

   chown –R mysql /usr/local/mysql/*

   If you decide to establish a specific user for running MySQL, change the permissions of the MySQL files to this user's account. After this final step you will be ready to start and use MySQL.

✔ Tips

■ Marc has also created an installer that will ensure that MySQL automatically starts every time your computer is booted. You can find this on his Web site as well.

■ If you decide to install MySQL using the source files—which is very manageable, you may need to install Apple's developer tools. These files are available through Apple's Web site (go to http://developer.apple.com) or on the Developer Tools CD-ROM that may have come with your OS.

Installing MySQL on Linux

MySQL AB advises that the best way to install MySQL on Linux is to use an RPM (Red Hat Package Manager) and the MySQL Web site provides a number of RPMs in case, for example, you want to install only the server or the client (**Figure 1.11**). Most likely you will want to install at least the server and the client, but if you only want to access a MySQL server running on another machine, the MySQL client alone will suffice.

The RPMs, by default, will install the applications within the /var/lib/mysql directory. Further, the RPM will add the requisite data to the /etc/rc.d/ directory so that the MySQL server daemon will be automatically started when the computer is booted. Installing an RPM is straightforward enough that I will not cover it here; it's very similar to installing any other RPM or running the Windows setup.exe executable.

Two other options you have are to install precompiled binary versions or compile the source yourself. In either case, the steps overlap quite a bit so I will describe both simultaneously.

To install MySQL on Linux:

1. Access the server via a command-line interface (**Figure 1.12**).

   In my example here, I will be installing MySQL on Red Hat Linux 6.1, using the Terminal application. You will need to have permission to manipulate files and create new directories within the /usr/local directory, so you may need to switch to the *root* user (see the sidebar *Being the Root User* earlier in this chapter for more information).

Figure 1.11 If you want the easiest way to install MySQL on a Linux system, download the appropriate files from MySQL's Web site and install them as you would any other RPM.

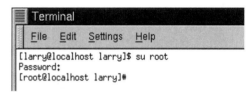

Figure 1.12 If you are installing a binary or source distribution of MySQL, you will need to work with the server from the shell (preferably as the *root* user).

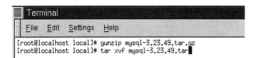

Figure 1.13 The first step in installing either the binary or source distributions is to unpack the files in the /usr/local directory.

Figure 1.14 Making a symbolic link to your MySQL files can save time—and errors—later but is not required.

2. Go to the /usr/local directory.

cd /usr/local

The /usr/local directory is where I prefer to install MySQL and where the MySQL manual recommends as well. Naturally you can choose another location, as long as you stay within the accepted parameters of your operating system.

3. Download the MySQL binary or source distribution.

You have several options here; the two easiest may be:

▲ Download the file from www.mysql.com using your Web browser, then move it to the /usr/local directory.

▲ Use wget or curl to immediately download the file to the current directory.

4. Unpack the files (**Figure 1.13**).

gunzip mysql-3.23.49.tar.gz
tar xvf mysql-3.23.49.tar

The source versions use a naming convention like *mysql-VERSION.tar.gz*. A binary download will be named *mysql-VERSION-PLATFORM.tar.gz*, for example, mysql-3.23.49a-pc-linux-gnu-i686.tar.gz. In this step, and in those following, be sure to change your commands appropriately if you are using a different version than I am here.

5. Create a link referring to this directory (**Figure 1.14**).

ln –s /usr/local/mysql-3.23.49 mysql

This step is not required, but it does allow the MySQL files to be linked from the easier-to-type /usr/local/mysql directory rather than, for example, /usr/local/mysql-3.23.49a-pc-linux-i686.

continues on next page

INSTALLING MySQL ON LINUX

6. Create a new MySQL user and group.

`groupadd mysql`

`useradd –g mysql mysql`

This step will allow you to run and manage MySQL as the *mysql* user, rather than *root*, which adds extra security to your system.

7. Move into the new `mysql` directory.

`cd mysql`

Because of the symbolic link created in step 5, this will really move you into the actual MySQL directory (e.g., `/usr/local/mysq-3.23.49a-pc-linux-i686/`).

8. Configure the MySQL source files (**Figure 1.15**).

`./configure --prefix=/usr/local/mysql`

If you are using the MySQL source, as opposed to the binary, you will need to configure it yourself, then make and install the files (steps 9 and 10). If you are using a precompiled binary, you can skip this and the next two steps.

For more information on configuring MySQL, see "Configuration Options" later in this chapter or the pertinent sections of the MySQL manual. The `prefix` option is very important, as it specifies where MySQL, and therefore the actual binary files to be executed, will be found.

9. After the configuration has run (**Figure 1.16**), make and install the files.

`make`

`make install`

These two steps will take some time, depending upon the operating system and processor speed of your server. If you encounter problems with `make`, do not proceed to the `make install` step. If you continue to have difficulties with this part of the installation, check the MySQL manual or Appendix A, "Troubleshooting," for more information or consider using a binary version instead of the source.

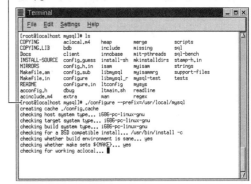

Figure 1.15 If you are using the source files of MySQL, you'll need to configure it yourself. At the very least, be sure to specify the `prefix` in your configuration statement.

Figure 1.16 If the configuration step (Figure 1.15) worked, you should see a message like this, meaning you are ready to make and install the files.

INSTALLING MySQL ON LINUX

Figure 1.17 Before running the server for the first time, you will need to install the default databases, accomplished by running the mysql_install_db script.

Figure 1.18 After installing the databases, you will see these lines, telling you what steps to take to run the server.

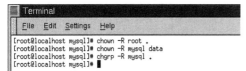

Figure 1.19 By giving the *mysql* user permissions over your files, you can avoid the security risk of running MySQL as *root*.

10. Install the default databases (**Figure 1.17**).

scripts/mysql_install_db

This step will create the database MySQL needs to function properly (called *mysql*) along with an appropriately named test database (called *test*). This will need to be done whether you are installing MySQL from the source or from the binary. Once the script has run, you will see a number of messages regarding the software (**Figure 1.18**).

11. Change the permissions on the new files (**Figure 1.19**).

chown –R root /usr/local/mysql/.

chown –R mysql /usr/local/mysql/data

chgrp –R mysql /usr/local/mysql/.

This final step allows the MySQL server to run under the guise of the newly created *mysql* user.

✔ **Tip**

■ Depending upon your operating system, you may have to add the *mysql* user and group using different terminology (like **adduser** and **addgroup**) than the example here. With Red Hat, the Linuxconf panel may be the easiest method.

INSTALLING MySQL ON LINUX

Configuration Options

Because MySQL is open source and very flexible in how it runs, there are numerous ways you can configure the software. By installing MySQL from the source files, as I did with Linux, you can establish certain parameters at the time of installation, which affects how the software functions.

At the time of installation, you can set the location of the binary files using the `prefix` option (as I did in my Linux example), choose whether or not to install the MySQL server (leaving only the client), and select what language to use. These are just examples; the full listing of options is available by typing `./configure --help` at the command line from within the MySQL root directory (e.g., `/usr/local/mysql`) (**Figure 1.20**).

After you have installed MySQL, you can do a fair amount of configuration by editing the `my.cnf` file, found in the `/etc/my.cnf` directory (depending upon your installation). To see what possibilities there are, open this file in your text editor. If it doesn't exist, you can create your own, which will be read by MySQL. After making any changes, be sure to restart the MySQL server for them to take effect. (Stopping and starting MySQL is covered in Chapter 2, "Running MySQL.")

On Windows, your best bet for altering how MySQL runs is to use the WinMySQLAdmin utility (**Figure 1.21**), briefly introduced during the installation process. This utility has the effect of editing the `my.ini` or `my.cnf` files that MySQL uses. The former is stored in the Windows directory (`C:\WINDOWS` or `C:\WINNT`), while the latter resides under the root MySQL directory (`C:\mysql`). They can also be manually edited using a text editor such as Notepad.

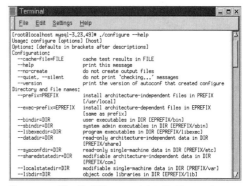

Figure 1.20 The MySQL manual details the most common configuration options, while `./configure --help` gives the entire list.

Figure 1.21 For Windows operating systems, the WinMySQLAdmin application is the best and easiest way to alter the way MySQL operates.

✔ Tip

■ For more information on configuring MySQL on various platforms, see www.mysql.com/doc/c/o/configure_options.html.

Figure 1.22 The mysqladmin utility can be used to stop a running MySQL server.

Upgrading MySQL

Once you have MySQL successfully installed and running, you might later decide to upgrade MySQL to a new version, particularly once version 4 is released. Upgrading MySQL is no more challenging than installing it for the first time, but it's best to take some precautions (such as backing up your system) in case things go awry. In fact, when installing MySQL on Windows, the installer could easily destroy existing MySQL files, data and all, if you are not careful.

The MySQL manual covers the specifics of upgrading from one version of MySQL to another in great detail so you can be best prepared as to what you might encounter. The directions I give below are more generalized recommendations.

To upgrade MySQL:

1. Stop the currently running MySQL server daemon (**Figure 1.22**).

   In general you can stop the MySQL server by typing bin/mysqladmin –u root shutdown from within the mysql directory.

   If you established a MySQL *root* user password (as you should), use this code:

   bin/mysqladmin –u root –p shutdown

   If you are running Windows, from a DOS prompt, type NET STOP MySQL if MySQL is running as a service (or use the traffic light icon in the tray, as demonstrated in the next chapter).

   I will discuss stopping the MySQL application more specifically in Chapter 2.

   continues on next page

2. Back up the existing MySQL data (**Figure 1.23**).

See Chapter 10, "MySQL Administration," for information about MySQL utilities that can back up your database or, on Linux and Mac OS X, you can run from the command line:

```
tar –cvf /tmp/mysql-data.tar data
```

which will package and store your information in the temporary directory.

3. Install the new version of MySQL.

Follow the directions in this chapter, installing MySQL as you otherwise would. Some steps you can omit here, such as creating a new user and running the `mysql_install_db` script.

4. Replace the new data directory with the files you backed up (**Figure 1.24**).

Restoring backed-up data will be covered in more detail in the Chapter 10, but if you used the Linux trick from step 2, you can just type:

```
tar –xf /tmp/mysql-data.tar
```

5. Restart the server, per the instructions in Chapter 2, "Running MySQL."

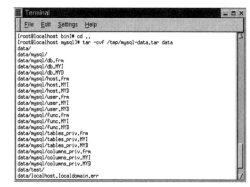

Figure 1.23 Using the `tar` command is one way to back up existing MySQL data. Chapter 2, "Running MySQL," will cover some of MySQL's utilities that also can be used.

Figure 1.24 To reinstall the data that was previously backed up (Figure 1.23), the `tar` command is used once again.

UPGRADING MYSQL

✔ Tips

- If you are running MySQL as a service on a Windows NT server and you need to change an existing service, delete it first by typing `mysqld-max-nt --remove` at the DOS prompt from within the `mysql\bin` directory.

- You need to run the `mysql_install_db` script only once, but it is always safe to run it, since it won't affect existing databases and tables.

- As an extra precaution when upgrading MySQL on Unix operating systems, you can rename the existing MySQL server (*mysqld*) to *mysqld.old* or something similar. If the new *mysqld* fails to work properly, you can revert back to the original *mysqld* easily.

- When upgrading MySQL on a Unix system, do not forget that the RPMs also create the appropriate entries in the `/etc/rc.d/` directory so MySQL starts automatically at boot time. The implication of this is that if you are upgrading MySQL using an RPM, your original startup file in the `/etc/rc.d/` directory will be overwritten unless you make a copy of it beforehand.

Patching MySQL

To fix bugs or security holes, you may need to install a patch from time to time. MySQL AB keeps a list of current patches on its Web site at www.mysql.com/downloads/patches.html (**Figure 1.25**). Keep in mind that you can patch only a source distribution of MySQL that you have compiled yourself, not a binary or RPM version.

To install a patch:

1. Shut down the running MySQL server.

2. Download the file to the same directory as your MySQL source.

3. Unpack the file, if necessary.

   `gunzip patch-file-name.gz`

   Patches are really just text files. Another way to obtain a patch is to view it in your Web browser and then export the text as a new text file.

4. Apply the patch.

   Type `patch –p1 < patch-file-name` from the command line. This will alter the source files using the information in the patch.

5. Delete the existing configuration information.

   `rm config.cache`
   `make clean`

   When you configure software on Unix yourself, a configuration file called `config.cache` is created that stores the configuration details. To create a new installation with a new configuration, you'll need to erase the existing configuration data. These two lines of code will prepare the server properly.

6. Reconfigure, make, and install MySQL, per the instructions earlier in this chapter.

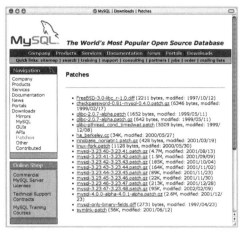

Figure 1.25 MySQL AB keeps a list of current patches on its Web site. To stay on top of your MySQL database administration, check this page for periodic updates.

RUNNING MySQL

2

Now that the MySQL software has been successfully installed (presumably), it's time to learn how to start and stop the database. Assuming that you did not install just the client software (e.g., as an RPM), you now have several different utilities installed that will aid you in running and maintaining your databases.

In this chapter I will first cover starting and stopping MySQL on the different platforms. From there I will go into creating a root user password, using the mysql monitor with your database, and adding users. Should you have any problems with a step in this section, refer to Appendix A, "Troubleshooting," or the appropriate sections of the MySQL manual.

I will demonstrate the different techniques in this chapter using a combination of Red Hat Linux, Windows 2000, and Mac OS X. Fortunately, most commands used will be identical whether you are running Linux, Mac OS X, AIX, or Windows XP from the DOS prompt. Do not fear that the technique being used will not work for you, as I will do my best to specify what alterations you may need to make to perform that task under other conditions. Also, for Windows users, most of your database administration can be managed through the WinMySQLAdmin application, which was briefly introduced in the previous chapter.

Starting MySQL

Unfortunately, you cannot truly know that MySQL has been successfully installed until you've been able to successfully start it. Starting MySQL is a frequent place of problems and confusion, especially for the beginning or intermediate user on Unix operating systems. On the bright side, MySQL is very stable and reliable once you have it running, and it can remain up for months at a time without incident. If you run into difficulties in these steps, check the "Starting MySQL" section of Appendix A, "Troubleshooting."

The MySQL server itself—the application that runs and manages the database—is called *mysqld*. On non-Windows systems, the mysqld daemon is started using the *safe_mysqld* application, which ensures that mysqld continues to run. On Windows NT systems, you can start one of several mysqld binaries that come with the installation files. The MySQL server will also run as a service (meaning it will automatically start when the operating system comes up) under NT. For other operating systems—such as Windows 98 or Me, you will need to manually start the mysqld process each time you restart your computer.

To start MySQL on Unix:

1. Log onto your system from a command-line interface.

2. Change to the MySQL directory (**Figure 2.1**).

   cd /usr/local/mysql

   Assuming you followed the installation instructions as detailed in Chapter 1, all of the relevant MySQL utilities will now be located within the bin subdirectory of the /usr/local/mysql directory. Red Hat Linux users may find these utilities in /usr/bin instead.

[localhost:/Users/lullman] root# cd /usr/local/mysql
[localhost:/usr/local/mysql] root# _

Figure 2.1 Practically all of the steps within this chapter will be executed from a command-line interface within the mysql root directory.

STARTING MYSQL

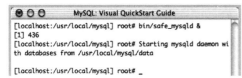

Figure 2.2 If the mysql daemon started properly, you'll see messages like those here.

3. Start safe_mysqld so that it runs in the background (**Figure 2.2**).

`bin/safe_mysqld &`

This line tells the server to keep safe_mysqld running constantly. What the safe_mysqld application does is check to see if mysqld is running and, if it is not, start up the daemon. The very first time you start safe_mysqld, it will immediately realize that mysqld is not up and will therefore start it.

Unix systems can be difficult with respect to where you can and cannot start applications. If the above line does not work, either try `./bin/safe_mysqld &` or go into the **bin** directory and type `safe_mysqld &` or `./safe_mysqld &`.

If mysqld fails to start, make note of the error message displayed and refer to Appendix A, "Troubleshooting," for more help, as this is a most common occurrence.

4. Begin administering your database.

See the remainder of this chapter for information on accessing MySQL, creating users, and so forth.

STARTING MySQL

Starting MySQL on a Windows operating system is far easier than it is with Unix. After you've decided which version of mysqld to run—there are several options—you should not have a problem booting it. Also, if you are using an NT version of Windows (NT, 2000, or XP), you have more choices and would presumably run mysqld as a service. The steps below detail how to start MySQL on Windows should you not use the WinMySQLAdmin utility as described in Chapter 1 (the WinMySQLAdmin application will automatically start the server for you as a service).

To start MySQL on Windows:

1. Decide which server you will use (**Figure 2.3**).

The MySQL distribution includes different versions of the MySQL server that you can use, depending upon your needs. The options are

▲ mysqld, the standard server.

▲ mysqld-opt, a version for optimized performance.

▲ mysqld-nt, similar to mysqld except more specific to the NT family of Windows.

▲ mysqld-max, like the mysqld-opt, but made to support the InnoDB and DBD table types. These other table types will be discussed in Chapter 11, "Advanced MySQL."

▲ mysqld-max-nt, a cross between mysqld-nt and mysqld-max.

For the average user, you may not see a remarkable difference among the above. When making your decision, I'd recommend starting with the most basic option—mysqld or mysqld-nt—and then making changes later to fine-tune MySQL's performance. Which MySQL server you use does not affect the data stored in the database in any way.

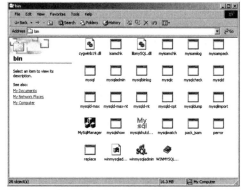

Figure 2.3 The Windows version of MySQL comes with several preconfigured binaries, all found within the `mysql/bin` directory.

STARTING MYSQL

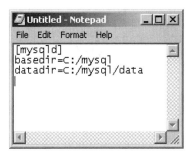

Figure 2.4 You can manually create the my.ini file with Notepad or another text editor.

2. Open Notepad or another text editor to create a configuration file.

There are some instances in which a configuration file for MySQL is required, and if you are not using the WinMySQLAdmin utility, you'll need to manually create one. You must do this step if you change the location of MySQL, if you want to use the mysql, mysql-max, or mysqld-max-nt servers (see step 1), or if you want to otherwise change how the MySQL server runs.

With Windows, you can create and edit a file called either my.ini, located in the **WINDOWS** or **WINNT** directory, or my.cnf, located in C:\. You should use one or the other but not both, and I would recommend going the my.ini route.

That being said, if you followed the directions in Chapter 1 and ran the WinMySQLAdmin tool, the configuration file will automatically be created for you.

3. Type the following in your text editor (**Figure 2.4**):

```
[mysqld]
basedir=C:/mysql
datadir=C:/mysql/data
```

This is just the basis of a configuration file. These two important pieces of information tell the MySQL server both where the MySQL files are located (basedir) and where the database files are (datadir). If you chose to alter your setup during installation, or if you otherwise require nonstandard configurations, adjust these lines appropriately.

You can add comments to this file—such as a creation date and creator name—by preceding the line with the number sign (#).

4. Save the file as my.ini.

Be certain to save this file within your Windows root directory (e.g., C:\WINDOWS or C:WINNT).

continues on next page

STARTING MYSQL

5. Start the server (**Figure 2.5**).

From the DOS prompt, enter the following lines:

```
cd C:\mysql\bin
mysqld --standalone
```

If you are not using an NT version of Windows, you can start MySQL with just the mysqld command (the --standalone option is NT-specific).

6. Begin administering your database.

See the remainder of this chapter for information on accessing MySQL, creating users, and so forth.

✔ Tips

■ The mysqld-nt and mysqld-max-nt applications, which are intended to run under Windows NT, 2000, or XP, can be run on Windows 95, 98, or Me, assuming that you also have TCP/IP installed.

■ To get to the DOS prompt from Windows, go to Start > Run > and then enter cmd.

■ Some Red Hat users have experienced problems starting MySQL using the directions above. If you installed MySQL using an RPM, then it may be already established as a service. If so, you can start mysqld using either service mysqld start or the linuxconf control panel. A last option would be to use the line /etc/rc.d/init.d/mysqld start

■ You should notice that Windows uses the backward slash (\) in file paths while other operating systems use the forward slash (/).

■ The mysqld daemon (and, therefore, the safe_mysqd script) can take a number of arguments to adjust how it runs. The average user will not need to tinker with these, but the complete listing can be found at www.mysql.com/doc/C/o/Command-line_options.html.

Figure 2.5 To start the mysqld server within Windows (and without using WinMySQLAdmin), type mysqld at the DOS prompt in the mysql\bin directory (with --standalone option for NT users).

Stopping MySQL

Once you've been able to successfully start the MySQL process, it's a snap to stop it. Stopping MySQL is not something you'll need to do with any frequency; you'll need to stop it primarily only before upgrading the software or performing some other serious level of maintenance (the application as a whole was created with the intention of running continuously without issue).

The instructions for stopping the server are the same for Windows and Unix/Linux/Mac OS X, except for those using the WinMySQLAdmin utility. I'll go through the generic instructions first, then indicate how to use WinMySQLAdmin, and finally, in the Tips below, list a couple of other methods.

To stop MySQL:

1. Log onto your system from a command-line interface.

   You should not have to be logged on as an administrative-level user (root or otherwise) for this step.

2. Move to the mysql/bin directory using either:

   cd /usr/local/mysql/bin *(Unix)*

   or

   cd C:\mysql\bin *(Windows)*

   Again, some systems differ as to where you can and cannot execute applications. Change this line and the next accordingly if you run into problems. For example, under some versions of Linux, you should go to the /usr/local/mysql directory and then precede the next command with bin/. Under other versions of Linux, like Red Hat, you'll need to be in the /usr/bin directory.

   continues on next page

3. Type `mysqladmin shutdown` (**Figure 2.6**).

If your system already has a root password assigned, you'll need to add the user name and password options by typing

`mysqladmin -u root -p shutdown`

After pressing Return, enter the root user's password at the prompt (**Figure 2.7**).

To stop MySQL using WinMySQLAdmin:

1. Click on the traffic light icon in the system tray (**Figure 2.8**).

Since the WinMySQLAdmin tool runs MySQL as a service, it will place a little traffic light icon in your system tray (the lower-right side of your screen as a default). When you click on the icon, you'll be presented with a menu of choices.

2. Move over the Win NT text (**Figure 2.9**).

If you are using a non-NT version of Windows, naturally, the wording here will be different.

3. Click on *Stop the Service* (Figure 2.9).

4. Click *Yes* at the prompt (**Figure 2.10**).

Unlike its Unix counterparts, the Windows version of MySQL will first warn you that shutting down the service kills all existing connections (i.e., current users will be disconnected).

Figure 2.6 If you have not yet established a root user password, you can stop the mysql server with the command `mysqladmin shutdown`.

Figure 2.7 If the root user requires a password, add the code `-u root -p` to your shutdown command.

Figure 2.8 Clicking on the traffic light icon gives you access to the WinMySQLAdmin utility.

Figure 2.9 Moving your mouse over the Win NT text creates a menu of options, including a method of stopping the MySQL server.

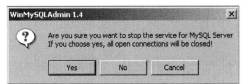

Figure 2.10 The prompt window gives you one more chance to reconsider before shutting down mysqld.

Figure 2.11 A red traffic light indicates that MySQL is not running. Green means that it is, and yellow that it is stopping.

5. Confirm that MySQL has shut down by looking at the traffic light icon again (**Figure 2.11**).

When MySQL is running as a service, the traffic light is green. While it is shutting down, it becomes yellow. Finally, when MySQL is no longer running, the traffic light is red.

✔ Tips

■ On Unix systems (particularly Red Hat Linux), you might also have luck stopping MySQL with /etc/rc.d/init.d/mysqld stop.

■ If MySQL is running as a service on Windows NT, you can also stop the process using NET STOP mysql from the command line (you do not have to be within a particular directory).

■ Most Windows systems will save you a step by allowing you to directly type, for example, C:\mysql\bin\mysqladmin shutdown from the DOS prompt without moving to the actual directory first.

STOPPING MySQL

Using mysqladmin

The mysqladmin utility, as the name might imply, is used to perform administrative-level tasks on your database. This includes stopping MySQL (as you saw in the previous section), setting a user's password, and more. A number of the functions of the mysqladmin application are replicated on Windows operating systems with the ubiquitous WinMySQLAdmin. Further, some of the things you can do with mysqladmin can also be accomplished more directly within the mysql monitor, which you'll see in the next section of this chapter.

One of the first uses of mysqladmin is to assign a password to the root user. When MySQL is installed, there is no such value established. This is certainly a security risk that ought to be remedied before you begin to use the server. Just to clarify, your databases can have several users, just as your operating system might. The MySQL users are different from the operating system users, even if they share a common name. Therefore, the MySQL *root* user is a different entity than the operating system's *root* user, having different powers and even different passwords (preferably but not necessarily).

Most importantly, understand that the MySQL server (mysqld) must be running in order for you to use mysqladmin. If MySQL is not currently running, start it now using the steps outlined earlier in the chapter.

Figure 2.12 Because I cannot run mysqladmin from within the bin directory, I had to use the bin/mysqladmin code instead (from the mysql directory) to change the root user's password.

Figure 2.13 To change an existing root user's password, add the -p option to your mysqladmin line (Figure 2.12) so that you can enter the current password.

To assign a password to the root user:

1. Log onto your system from a command-line interface.

2. Move to the mysql/bin or just mysql directory, depending upon your operating system using either:

cd /usr/local/mysql/bin *(Unix)*

or

cd C:\mysql\bin *(Windows)*

3. Enter the following, replacing *thepassword* with the password you want to use (**Figure 2.12**):

mysqladmin –u root password
→ 'thepassword'

Keep in mind that passwords within MySQL are case-sensitive, so *Kazan* and *kazan* are not interchangeable. The term **password** that precedes the actual quoted password tells MySQL to encrypt that string.

Once you've established the root user's password, it's only slightly more complicated to change it.

To change the root user's password:

1. Log onto your system from a command-line interface.

2. Move to the mysql/bin or just mysql directory, depending upon your operating system.

3. Enter the following, replacing *newpassword* with the password you want to use (**Figure 2.13**):

mysqladmin –u root -p password
→ 'newpassword'

Because it has already been established, the password is required to use the mysqladmin tool from here on out. The -p argument will make mysqladmin prompt you for the current password.

USING MYSQLADMIN

There are a number of other uses of the mysqladmin application, including the creation and deletion of databases. These will be covered more directly with the mysql monitor in Chapter 4, "SQL." One last use of mysqladmin, which I'll demonstrate here, is to confirm the operation of the server by checking its status.

To check the current status of MySQL:

1. Log onto your system from a command-line interface.

2. Move to the mysql/bin or just mysql directory, depending upon your operating system.

3. Enter the following (**Figure 2.14**):

   mysqladmin –u root -p status

At the password: prompt, enter the current root user password. If you are successful, you should see how long the mysql daemon has been running (in seconds) as well as other statistics.

✔ Tips

■ To see what version of MySQL you are running, type mysqladmin –u root -p version.

■ To check if MySQL is running without viewing all the status details, try mysqladmin –u root -p ping (**Figure 2.15**).

■ It can, and unfortunately does, happen that you forget or misplace the root user password, essentially locking the most important user out of the database. To fix this when it does happen, see Appendix A, "Troubleshooting," where I'll walk you through the solution.

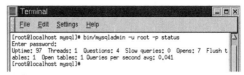

Figure 2.14 The status option for mysqladmin displays pertinent information about the current state of the mysqld process.

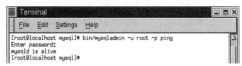

Figure 2.15 The ping option for mysqladmin shows only whether or not MySQL is currently running (i.e., alive).

```
● ○ ○        MySQL: Visual QuickStart Guide
mysql> START OF QUERY
    -> CONTINUE QUERY
    -> ADD QUOTATION MARK '
    '> CLOSE SINGLE QUOTE AND ADD DOUBLE ' "
    "> CLOSE DOUBLE "
    -> END QUERY (EXPECT TROUBLE);
ERROR 1064: You have an error in your SQL syntax near 'START
OF QUERY
CONTINUE QUERY
ADD QUOTATION MARK '
CLOSE SINGLE QUOTE AND ADD DO' at line 1
mysql> _
```

Figure 2.16 The mysql client will indicate what it thinks you are doing by using different prompts.

mysql **Monitor Prompts**	
PROMPT	MEANING
mysql>	Ready
->	Continuing a command
'>	Need to finish a single quote
">	Need to finish a double quote

Table 2.1 These four prompts, also represented in Figure 2.16, are used to clue you in as to what the mysql monitor is expecting.

Using the mysql Client

The most common way to interface with the mysqld application—aside from a programming perspective—is to use the *mysql client* (or *mysql monitor*, as it is also called). This application can be used to connect to mysqld running on the same machine, or even on another. Most of the examples throughout the rest of this book will be accomplished via mysql (the lowercase word *mysql* will refer to the client, as opposed to MySQL, which refers to the software as a whole).

The mysql client can take several arguments up front, including the user name, password, and hostname (computer name). You establish these arguments like so:

```
mysql -u username -p -h hostname
```

The -p option will cause mysql to prompt you for the password, just as the mysqladmin tool did. You can specify the password on this line if you prefer, by typing it directly after the -p prompt, but it will be visible, which is insecure.

Within the mysql monitor, every statement (SQL command) needs to be terminated by a semicolon. This means that you can continue the same statement over several lines, to facilitate typing. With this in mind, you will also see a few different prompts when working, as illustrated in **Figure 2.16** and listed in **Table 2.1**.

As a quick demonstration of accessing and using the mysql client, I will show you how to start mysql, select a database to use, and quit the monitor. As always, the MySQL daemon (mysqd) must be running to use the mysql client.

To use the mysql monitor:

1. Log onto your system from a command-line interface.

2. Move to the mysql/bin or just mysql directory, depending upon your operating system:

   cd /usr/local/mysql/bin *(Unix)*

   or

   cd C:\mysql\bin *(Windows)*

3. Enter the following text (**Figure 2.17**):

   mysql -u username -p

   The -h hostname argument described above is optional, and I tend to leave it off unless I cannot get into mysql otherwise. If you set a password for the root user, as detailed earlier in this chapter, you can use the root user name and password now.

4. Select which database you want to use (**Figure 2.18**).

   USE test;

   The USE command tells MySQL which database you want to deal with from here on out (saving typing the database name over and over again later). The mysql_install_db script run during the installation process creates two starter databases—*mysql* and *test*.

   If you know in advance which database you will want to use, you can simplify matters by starting mysql with

   mysql -u username -p databasename

5. Quit out of mysql (**Figure 2.19**).

   exit

   You can also use the command quit to leave the monitor. This step—unlike most other commands you enter—does not require a semicolon at the end.

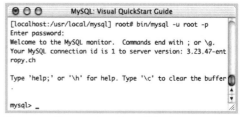

Figure 2.17 The mysql monitor will be the most commonly used method to access databases throughout this book.

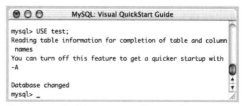

Figure 2.18 The first step you will normally take within the mysql client is to choose the database with which to work.

Figure 2.19 The commands exit or quit will get you out of the mysql monitor.

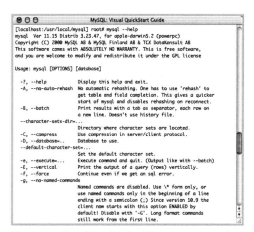

Figure 2.20 For all the details of how to start mysql, type mysql --help.

✔ Tips

■ To see what else you can do with the mysql utility, type mysql --help (**Figure 2.20**).

■ The mysql client makes use of the Unix readline tool, allowing you to use the up and down arrows to scroll through previously entered commands. This can save you oodles of time later on.

■ You can also expedite your work within the mysql monitor by pressing the TAB key to complete words (type a single # and press Return to see what words can be completed), using CTRL + A to move your cursor to the beginning of a line, and using CTRL + E to move the cursor to the end of the line.

■ If you are in a long statement and make a mistake, cancel the current operation by typing \c and pressing Return. If mysql thinks a closing single or double quotation mark is missing, you'll need to enter it first.

■ Even though you terminate commands within mysql with the semicolon, queries being sent to the server from a script (PHP, Perl, etc.), should not have semicolons. This is a common (and albeit minor) mistake to make.

■ Depending upon how MySQL is installed on your system, some Windows users can run the mysql monitor—and other utilities described in this chapter—simply by double-clicking on the executable file found within the mysql/bin folder. You can also directly run the mysql monitor from the Start > Run menu.

■ To be particularly safe when using mysql, start the application using the --i-am-a-dummy argument. And, no, I am not making this up (the argument limits what you can and cannot do).

Users and Privileges

After you have MySQL successfully up and running, and after you've established a password for the root user, it's time to begin adding other users. To improve the security of your databases, you should always create new users for accessing your databases, rather than continuing to use the root user at all times.

The MySQL privileges system was designed to ensure proper authority for certain commands on specific databases. This technology is how a Web host, for example, can securely have several users accessing several databases, without concern. Each user within the MySQL system can have specific capabilities on specific databases from specific hosts (computers). The root user—the MySQL root user, not the system's—has the most power and is used for creating sub-users, although sub-users can be given rootlike powers (inadvisably so).

When a user attempts to do something with the MySQL server, MySQL will first check to see if the user has the permission to connect to the server at all (based upon the user name, the user's password, and the information in the user table of the *mysql* database). Secondly, MySQL will check to see if the user has the permission to run the specific SQL statement on the specific databases—for example, to select data, insert data, or create a new table. To determine this, MySQL uses the db, host, user, tables_priv, and columns_priv tables, again from the *mysql* database. **Table 2.2** lists the various privileges that can be set on a user-by-user basis. Most of these privileges will be demonstrated as an SQL query in Chapter 3, "SQL."

MySQL Privileges

PRIVILEGE	ALLOWS
SELECT	Read rows from tables.
INSERT	Add new rows of data to tables.
UPDATE	Alter existing data in tables.
DELETE	Remove existing data in tables.
INDEX	Create and drop indexes in tables.
ALTER	Modify the structure of a table.
CREATE	Create new tables or databases.
DROP	Delete existing tables or databases.
RELOAD	Reload the grant tables (and therefore enact user changes).
SHUTDOWN	Stop the MySQL server.
PROCESS	View and stop existing MySQL processes.
FILE	Import data into tables from text files.
GRANT	Create new users.
REVOKE	Remove the permissions of users.

Table 2.2 This is the list of available privileges that can be assigned to MySQL users on a case-by-case basis.

There are a handful of ways to set users and privileges within MySQL, but I prefer to do it manually, using the mysql monitor and the GRANT command. The syntax goes like this:

GRANT privileges ON database.* TO username
➝ IDENTIFIED BY 'password'

For the privileges aspect of this statement, you can list specific privileges from the list in Table 2.2, or you can allow for all of them using *ALL* (which is not prudent). The database.* part of the statement specifies which database and tables the user can work on. You can name specific tables using database.tablename syntax or allow for every database with *.* (again, not prudent). Finally, you can specify the user name and a password.

The user name has a maximum length of 16 characters. When creating a user name, be sure to avoid spaces (use the underscore instead) and note that user names are case-sensitive. The password has no length limit but is also case-sensitive. The passwords will be encrypted within the mysql database, meaning they cannot be recovered in a plain text format. Omitting the IDENTIFIED BY 'password' clause results in that user not being required to enter a password (which, once again, should be avoided).

Finally, there is the option of limiting users to particular hostnames. The hostname is either the name of the computer on which the MySQL server is running (*localhost* being the most common value here) or the name of the computer from which the user will be accessing the server. This can even be an IP address, should you choose. To specify a particular host, change your statement to

GRANT ALL ON database.* TO username@
➝ localhost IDENTIFIED BY 'password'

continues on next page

To allow for any host, use the hostname wildcard character (%).

GRANT ALL ON database.* TO username@ '%'
→ IDENTIFIED BY 'password'

As an example of this process, I will create two new users with specific privileges.

To create new users:

1. Log onto your system from a command-line interface.

2. Move to the mysql/bin or just mysql directory, depending upon your operating system (I'll use mysql with Red Hat Linux and append bin/ to the next line of code).

3. Log into the mysql monitor.

   mysql -u username -p

4. Create two new databases (**Figure 2.21**).

   CREATE DATABASE alpacas;
   CREATE DATABASE movies;

   Although I have not formally discussed creating databases before now, the syntax is obvious and having two example databases already created will allow for better examples in these steps.

5. Create a user that has administrative-level privileges on the *alpacas* database (**Figure 2.22**).

   GRANT SELECT, INSERT, UPDATE, DELETE,
   → CREATE, DROP, ALTER, INDEX, FILE ON
   → alpacas.* TO llama@localhost
   → IDENTIFIED BY 'camel';

   This user, *llama*, will be able to create tables, alter tables, insert data, update data, and so forth, on the *alpacas* database. This essentially constitutes every administrative-level capability aside from creating new users. Be certain to use a password—perhaps one more clever than this—and, preferably, specify a particular host.

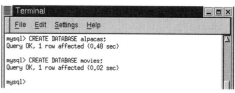

Figure 2.21 Before adding new users, I created a couple of extra databases using the CREATE DATABASE *databasename* SQL command.

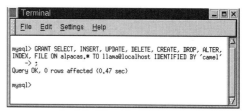

Figure 2.22 The first user I have created will have every requisite privilege for manipulating the *alpacas* database.

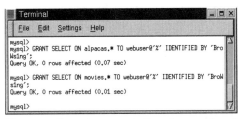

Figure 2.23 The webuser created here is a generic and safe user for selecting data from tables.

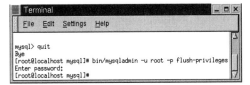

Figure 2.24 For privilege modifications to take effect, you must use mysqladmin to flush the existing privileges.

6. Create a user that has browsing-level access to both databases (**Figure 2.23**).

   GRANT SELECT ON alpacas.* TO webuser@
   → '%' IDENTIFIED BY 'BroWs1ng';

   GRANT SELECT ON movies.* TO webuser@'%'
   → IDENTIFIED BY 'BroWs1ng';

   Now the generic *webuser* can browse through records (SELECT from tables) but cannot modify the data therein. A more direct way of creating this user for every database would be to use the code GRANT SELECT ON *.* TO webuser@'%' IDENTIFIED BY 'BroWs1ng'; except that would also give this user permission to select from the *mysql* database, which is not a good idea. When establishing users and privileges, work your way from the bottom up, allowing the bare minimum of access at all times.

7. Exit out of mysql.

   quit

8. Apply the changes using mysqladmin (**Figure 2.24**).

   bin/mysqladmin -u root
   → -p flush-privileges

   The changes just made will not take effect until you have told MySQL to reset the list of acceptable users and privileges, which is what this command will do. This is the same as typing bin/mysqladmin -u root -p reload (you'll frequently see either). Forgetting this step and then being unable to access the database using the newly created users is a common mistake.

   continues on next page

USERS AND PRIVILEGES

9. Test your new user (**Figure 2.25**).

`bin/mysql -u llama -p alpacas`

This command should let you into the mysql monitor to begin creating the *alpacas* tables.

✔ Tips

- Any database whose name begins with *test_* can be modified by any user who has permission to connect to MySQL. Therefore, be careful not to create databases named like so unless it truly is experimental.

- If you are not comfortable modifying users and privileges manually as I have here, try using the mysqlaccess utility (it's actually a Perl script), located within the `bin` directory. Refer to the manual or use `mysqlaccess --howto` for more information.

- There is an even more manual way to create new users: by running `INSERT` commands on the user and other mysql database tables. This is only for the more experienced users who fully comprehend the relationships among the *user*, *db*, and other *mysql* tables.

- You can also enact user changes by typing the command `FLUSH PRIVILEGES` from within the mysql monitor.

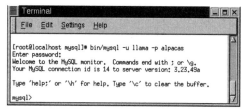

Figure 2.25 Once the new user has been given permission, I can now access the *alpacas* database through the mysql monitor with this account.

USERS AND PRIVILEGES

3

DATABASE DESIGN

Whenever you are working with a relational database management system such as MySQL, the first step in creating and using a database is to establish its structure. Database design, aka *data modeling*, is crucial for successful long-term management of your information. Using a process called *normalization*, you carefully eliminate redundancies and other problems that will undermine the integrity of your data.

The techniques you will learn in this chapter will help to ensure the viability, performance, and reliability of your databases. The example I will use—a record of business transactions such as invoices and expenses—will be referred to in later chapters, but the principles of normalization apply to any database application you might create.

Normalization

Normalization was developed by an IBM researcher named E.F. Codd in the early 1970s (he also invented the relational database). A relational database is merely a collection of data, organized in a particular manner, and Dr. Codd created a series of rules called *normal forms* that help define that organization. In this chapter I will discuss the first three of the normal forms, which is sufficient for most database designs.

Before you begin normalizing your database, you must define the role of the application being developed. Whether it means that you thoroughly discuss the subject with a client or figure it out for yourself, understanding how the information will be accessed dictates the modeling. Thus, this chapter will require paper and pen, rather than the MySQL software itself (for the record, database design is applicable to any relational database, not just MySQL).

Database design texts commonly use examples such as music or book collections (indeed, I used the latter in my book *PHP Advanced for the World Wide Web: Visual QuickPro Guide*), but I will create a more business-oriented accounting database here. The primary purpose of the database will be to track invoices and expenses, but it could easily be modified to log work hours on projects and so forth. I have created a preliminary listing of the data to record in **Table 3.1**.

✔ Tips

- One of the best ways to determine what information should be stored in a database is to clarify what questions will be asked of it and what data would be included in the answers.

- Although I will demonstrate manual database design, there are ready-made applications for this express purpose listed in Appendix C, "Resources."

Accounting Database	
ITEM	EXAMPLE
Invoice Number	1
Invoice Date	4/20/2002
Invoice Amount	$30.28
Invoice Description	HTML design
Date Invoice Paid	5/11/2002
Client Information	Acme Industries, 100 Main Street, Anytown, NY, 11111, (800) 555-1234
Expense Amount	$100.00
Expense Category & Description	Web Hosting Fees-Annual contract for hosting www.DMCinsights.com
Expense Date	1/26/2002

Table 3.1 Based on my intended usage of this database, all of the requisite information to be recorded is listed here.

Keys

Keys are pieces of data that help to identify a row of information in a table (a row is also called a *record*). There are two types of keys you will deal with: *primary* and *foreign*. A primary key is a unique identifier that has to abide by certain rules. They must

◆ Always have a value (it cannot be NULL)

◆ Have a value that remains the same (never changes)

◆ Have a unique value for each record in the table

The best real-world example of a primary key is the U.S. Social Security number. Although I have heard stories of duplicate numbers being assigned, the principle is that each individual has a unique Social Security number and that the number never changes. Just as the Social Security number is an artificial construct used to identify people, you'll frequently find creating an arbitrary primary key for each table to be the best design practice.

The second type of keys are foreign keys. Foreign keys are the representation of the primary key from Table A in Table B. If you have a *movies* database with a *movie* table and a *director* table, the primary key from *director* would be linked as a foreign key in *movie*. You'll see better how this works as the normalization process continues.

Currently, MySQL formally implements foreign keys only when using the InnoDB table type (see Chapter 11, "Advanced MySQL," for more information on the different table types) but generally ignores their existence otherwise. Hence, foreign keys in MySQL are more of a theoretical presence than a binding one, although this should change in later versions of the software.

KEYS

The *accounting* database is just a simple table as it stands, but to start off the normalization process, I'll want to ensure at least one primary key (the foreign keys will come in later steps).

To assign a primary key:

1. Look for any fields that meet the three tests for a primary key.

   In this example, the only data that will always be unique, have a value, and whose value will never change should be the *Invoice Number*. Mark this field as the primary key using the *(PK)* notation (**Figure 3.1**).

2. If no logical primary key exists, invent one.

   Frequently you will need to create a primary key because no good solution presents itself. Even with Social Security numbers and book ISBNs (International Standardized Book Number)—which ought to meet the criteria—creating a dummy field expressly for being the primary key is a solid idea.

✔ Tips

- MySQL allows for only one primary key per table, although you can base a primary key on multiple columns (which is beyond the scope of this book).

- Ideally, your primary key should always be an integer, which results in better MySQL performance. This is another reason why Social Security numbers and ISBNs, which contain hyphens, would not be the best possible primary key.

Accounting Database
Invoice Number **(PK)**
Invoice Date
Invoice Amount
Invoice Description
Date Invoiced
Client Information
Expense Amount
Expense Category & Description
Expense Date

Figure 3.1 The first step I took in normalizing my database was to create the initial primary key—the *Invoice Number*.

Relationships

When I speak of database relationships, I specifically mean how the data in one table relates to the data in another. A relationship between two tables can be *one-to-one*, *one-to-many*, or *many-to-many*.

The relationship is one-to-one if one and only one item in Table A applies to one and only one item in Table B (e.g., each U.S. citizen has only one Social Security number, and each Social Security number applies to only one U.S. citizen; no citizen can have two Social Security numbers, and no Social Security number can refer to two citizens).

A relationship is one-to-many if one item in Table A can apply to multiple items in Table B. The terms *female* and *male* will apply to many people, but each person can be only one or the other. A one-to-many relationship is the most common one between tables in databases.

Finally, a relationship is many-to-many if multiple items in Table A can apply to multiple items in Table B. For example, a record album can contain songs by multiple artists and artists can make multiple albums. You should try to avoid many-to-many relationships in your design because they lead to data redundancy and integrity problems.

Relationships and keys work together in that a key in one table will normally relate to a field in another, as I mentioned earlier. Once you grasp the basics of unique identifiers and relationships, you can begin to normalize your database.

continues on next page

RELATIONSHIPS

✔ Tips

- Database modeling uses certain conventions to represent the structure of the database, which I'll follow through a series of images in this chapter. The symbols for the three types of relationships are shown in **Figure 3.2**.

- The process of database design results in an ER (Entity Relationship) Diagram, using boxes for tables and the symbols from Figure 3.2.

- The term "relational" in RDBMS actually stems from the tables, which are technically called *relations*.

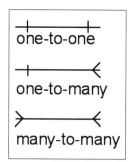

one-to-one

one-to-many

many-to-many

Figure 3.2 These three stick figures (or variations on these) are used to represent relationships between tables in database modeling.

```
┌─────────────────────────────────────┐
│  Accounting Database                 │
│  Invoice Number (PK)                 │
│  Invoice Date                        │
│  Invoice Amount                      │
│  Invoice Description                 │
│  Date Invoiced                       │
│  Client Name                         │
│  Client Street Address               │
│  Client City                         │
│  Client State                        │
│  Client Zip                          │
│  Client Phone                        │
│  Expense Amount                      │
│  Expense Category                    │
│  Expense Description                 │
│  Expense Date                        │
└─────────────────────────────────────┘
```

Figure 3.3 After running through the 1NF rules, I've separated two fields into more logical subfields.

First Normal Form

For a database to be in First Normal Form (1NF), each column must contain only one value (this is sometimes described as being *atomic*). A table containing one field for an address would not be in 1NF because it stores the street address, city, state, ZIP code, and possibly country—five different bits of information—in one field. Similarly, a field containing a person's first and last name would also fail this test (although some would suggest that a person's full name is sufficiently atomic as is).

I'll continue the normalization process by checking the existing structure for 1NF compliance.

To make a database 1NF compliant:

1. Identify any field that contains multiple pieces of information.

   Looking back at Table 3.1, two columns are not 1NF compliant: *Client Information* and *Expense Category & Description*. The date fields contain a day, month, and a year, but subdividing past that level of specificity is really not warranted.

2. Break up any fields found in step 1 into separate fields (**Figure 3.3**).

   To fix this problem, I'll separate *Client Information* into *Client Name*, *Client Street Address*, *Client City*, *Client State*, *Client Zip*, and *Client Phone*. Next, I'll turn *Expense Category & Description* into *Expense Category* and *Expense Description*.

3. Double-check that all new fields created in step 2 pass the 1NF test.

Second Normal Form

In simplest terms, for a database to be in Second Normal Form (2NF), the database must already be in 1NF (you must normalize in order), and every column in a table that is not a key has to relate only to the primary key. The most obvious indication that a database is not 2NF is if multiple records in a table might have the exact same value for a column. As an example, if you listed a producer along with each record album, this value could be repeated over the course of the album's table.

Looking at the *accounting* database (Figure 3.3), there are a number of problems. For starters, the client information will not necessarily be particular to any one invoice (a client could be billed several times). Second, the expense information is not tied to the invoices either.

To put this database into 2NF, I'll need to separate out these columns into their own tables, where each value will be represented only once. In fact, normalization could be summarized as the process of creating more and more tables until potential redundancies have been eliminated.

To make a database 2NF compliant:

1. Identify any fields that do not relate directly to the primary key.

   As I stated above, all of the client information and expense information are not invoice-particular.

2. Create new tables accordingly (**Figure 3.4**).

   The most logical modification for the existing structure is to make separate *Clients*, *Invoices*, and *Expenses* tables. In my visual representation of the database, I create a box for each table, with the table name as a header and all of its columns (or attributes) underneath.

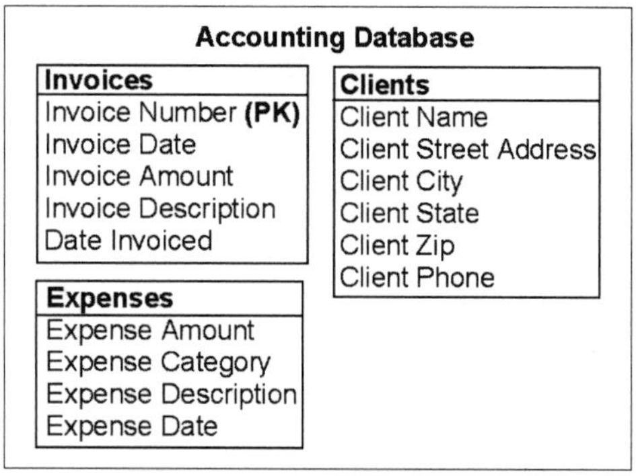

Accounting Database

Invoices
Invoice Number **(PK)**
Invoice Date
Invoice Amount
Invoice Description
Date Invoiced

Expenses
Expense Amount
Expense Category
Expense Description
Expense Date

Clients
Client Name
Client Street Address
Client City
Client State
Client Zip
Client Phone

Figure 3.4 To normalize the database, I must move redundant information—such as the client and expense data—to their own tables.

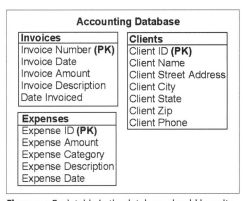

Figure 3.5 Each table in the database should have its own primary key, whether it's a dummy field such as *Client ID* or a necessary one such as *Invoice Number*.

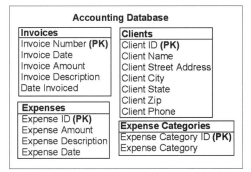

Figure 3.6 The *Expense Category* field, which was part of *Expenses*, should be its own table as well.

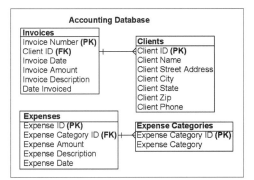

Figure 3.7 For the new primary keys, I've added corresponding foreign keys and indicated the relationships (both one-to-many).

3. Assign or create new primary keys (**Figure 3.5**).

Using the techniques described earlier in the chapter, ensure that each new table has a primary key. Because both the *Clients* and *Expenses* tables do not have good unique identifiers, I'll create artificial ones: *Client ID* and *Expense ID*. Arguably, the *Client Name* field should be unique and therefore could be the primary key, but it's always best to use integers for this purpose.

4. Repeat steps 1–3.

Since I've created new tables with new primary keys, I should double-check to see if there are any 2NF problems. In the example (Figure 3.5), there is one glaring issue—the *Expense Category* field may apply to multiple expenses. Therefore, I'll make a new *Expense Categories* table (**Figure 3.6**).

5. Create the requisite foreign keys indicating the relationships (**Figure 3.7**).

The final step in achieving 2NF compliance is to incorporate foreign keys and relationships to identify how all of the data and tables are associated. Remember that a primary key in one table will most likely be a foreign key in another. If you find that the primary key in one table is not represented as a foreign key in another, you may have missed something (but not necessarily).

✔ **Tip**

■ Another way to test for 2NF is to look at the relationships between tables. The ideal is to create one-to-many situations. Tables that have a many-to-many relationship may need to be restructured.

SECOND NORMAL FORM

Third Normal Form

A database is in Third Normal Form (3NF) if it is in 2NF and every nonkey column is independent of every other nonkey column. In other words, the fields of a table other than the keys should be mutually independent.

If you followed the first two normalization steps properly, you will not necessarily need to make any changes at this stage. However, if you made a number of changes along the way (as can happen), this could be a last check. For example, say I wanted to record a contact name and email address with each invoice (**Figure 3.8**). The problem is that this information relates not to an invoice but to the client and, therefore, the database would fail the 3NF test. The correct structure would be to add these fields to the *Clients* table (**Figure 3.9**).

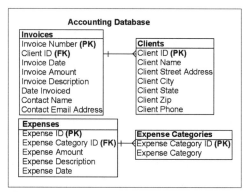

Figure 3.8 Altering the requirements of the database can muddle the design, as it is now no longer normalized with the *Contact Name* and *Email Address* additions.

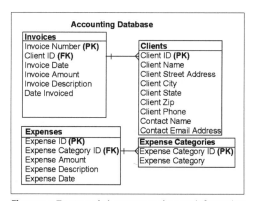

Figure 3.9 To correctly incorporate the new information (Figure 3.8), I've moved it to the *Clients* table.

✔ Tips

■ Once you've sketched out a database on paper, you could create a series of spreadsheets that reflect the design (or use an application specifically tailored to this end). This file can act both as a good reference to the Web developers working on the database as well as a nice thing to give over to the client when the project is completed.

■ Once MySQL begins enforcing the implications of foreign keys (in version 4.1 or later), normalizing your database will be even more necessary than it is currently.

Overruling Normalization

As much as ensuring that a database is in 3NF will help guarantee stability and endurance, you won't necessarily normalize every database with which you work. Before undermining the proper methods though, understand that it may have devastating long-term consequences.

The two primary reasons to overrule normalization are convenience and performance. Fewer tables are easier to manipulate and comprehend. Further, because of their more intricate nature, normalized databases will most likely be slower for updating, retrieving data from, and modifying. Normalization requires that you favor data integrity and scalability over simplicity and speed. On the other hand, there are ways to improve your database's performance but few to remedy corrupted data that can result from poor design.

THIRD NORMAL FORM

MySQL Data Types

Once you have identified all of the tables
and columns that the database will need,
you should determine each field's MySQL
data type. When creating the database, as
you will do in the next chapter, MySQL
requires that you define what sort of information each field will contain. There are
three primary categories, which is true for
almost every database software:

◆ Text

◆ Numbers

◆ Dates and times

Within each of these, there are a number
of variants—some of which are MySQL-
specific—you can use. Choosing your column
types correctly not only dictates what information can be stored and how, but also
affects the database's overall performance.
Table 3.2 lists most of the available types
for MySQL, how much space they take up,
and a brief description.

Many of the types can take an optional *Length*
attribute, limiting their size (the square
brackets, [], indicate an optional parameter
to be put in parentheses, while parentheses
themselves indicate required arguments).
Further, the number types can be UNSIGNED—
limiting the column to positive numbers or
zero—or be defined as ZEROFILL, which
means that any extra room will be padded
with zeroes (ZEROFILLs are also automatically
UNSIGNED). The various date types have all
sorts of unique behaviors, which are docu-
mented in the manual at www.mysql.com/
doc/D/A/DATETIME.html. You'll primarily
use the DATE and TIME fields without modification, so you need not worry too much about
their intricacies. There are also two extensions
of the TEXT types that result in a different
behavior—ENUM and SET—which allow you
to define a series of acceptable values when

creating the table. An ENUM field can have only one of a possible several thousand values, while SET allows for several of up to 64 possible values. There are two caveats with ENUM and SET: These types are not supported by other databases, and their usage undermines normalization.

MySQL Datatypes

Type	Size	Description
CHAR[Length]	Length bytes	A fixed-length field from 0 to 255 characters long.
VARCHAR(Length)	String length + 1 bytes	A fixed-length field from 0 to 255 characters long.
TINYTEXT	String length + 1 bytes	A string with a maximum length of 255 characters.
TEXT	String length + 2 bytes	A string with a maximum length of 65,535 characters.
MEDIUMTEXT	String length + 3 bytes	A string with a maximum length of 16,777,215 characters.
LONGTEXT	String length + 4 bytes	A string with a maximum length of 4,294,967,295 characters.
TINYINT[Length]	1 byte	Range of -128 to 127 or 0 to 255 unsigned.
SMALLINT[Length]	2 bytes	Range of -32,768 to 32,767 or 0 to 65535 unsigned.
MEDIUMINT[Length]	3 bytes	Range of -8,388,608 to 8,388,607 or 0 to 16,777,215 unsigned.
INT[Length]	4 bytes	Range of -2,147,483,648 to 2,147,483,647 or 0 to 4,294,967,295 unsigned.
BIGINT[Length]	8 bytes	Range of -9,223,372,036,854,775,808 to 9,223,372,036,854,775,807 or 0 to 18,446,744,073,709,551,615 unsigned.
FLOAT	4 bytes	A small number with a floating decimal point.
DOUBLE[Length, Decimals]	8 bytes	A large number with a floating decimal point.
DECIMAL[Length, Decimals]	Length + 1 or Length + 2 bytes	A DOUBLE stored as a string, allowing for a fixed decimal point.
DATE	3 bytes	In the format of YYYY-MM-DD.
DATETIME	8 bytes	In the format of YYYY-MM-DD HH:MM:SS.
TIMESTAMP	4 bytes	In the format of YYYYMMDDHHMMSS; acceptable range ends in the year 2037.
TIME	3 bytes	In the format of HH:MM:SS
ENUM	1 or 2 bytes	Short for enumeration, which means that each column can have one of several possible values.
SET	1, 2, 3, 4, or 8 bytes	Like ENUM except that each column can have more than one of several possible values.

Table 3.2 Here are most of the available column types for use with MySQL databases.

To choose your data types:

1. Identify whether a column should be a text, number, or date type.

   This is normally an easy and obvious step. You will find that numbers such as ZIP codes and dollar amounts should be text fields if you include their corresponding punctuation (dollar signs, commas, and hyphens), but you'll get better results if you store them as numbers and address the formatting elsewhere.

2. Choose the most appropriate subtype for each column.

   For improved performance, keep in mind two considerations:

   ▲ Fixed-length fields (such as CHAR) are generally faster than variable-length fields (such as VARCHAR), but they also take up more disk space. See the sidebar for more information.

   ▲ The size of any field should be restricted to the smallest possible value, based upon what the largest possible input could be. For example, if the largest number such as Client ID could be is in the hundreds, set the column as an unsigned three-digit SMALLINT (allowing for up to 999 values).

   You should keep in mind that if you insert a string five characters long into a CHAR(2) field, the final three characters will be truncated. This is true for any field in which the length is set (CHAR, VARCHAR, INT, etc.).

3. Set the maximum length for text and number columns as well as other attributes such as UNSIGNED (**Table 3.3**).

   Rather than going over how I defined all 21 columns and why, I've listed the properties I came up with in Table 3.3. Different developers have different preferences, but the most important factor is to tailor each

---

CHAR vs. VARCHAR

There is some debate as to the merits of these two similar types. Both store strings and can be set with a fixed maximum length. One primary difference is that anything stored as a CHAR will always be stored as a string the length of the column (using spaces to pad it). Conversely, VARCHAR strings will be only as long as the stored string.

The two implications of this are

◆ VARCHAR columns tend to take up less disk space.

◆ Unless you are using the InnoDB table types (see Chapter 11, "Advanced MySQL," for more information), CHAR columns are faster to access than VARCHAR.

Granted, the speed and disk space differences between the two types may be imperceptible in most cases and is therefore not worth dallying over.

There is also a third, minor difference between these two: MySQL trims off extra spaces from CHAR columns when data is retrieved and from VARCHAR when it's inserted.

MySQL Data Types

setting to the information at hand rather than using generic (and inefficient) TEXT and INT types at all times.

✔ Tips

■ Many of the data types have synonymous names: INT and INTEGER, DEC and DECIMAL, etc.

■ The TIMESTAMP field is automatically set when an INSERT or UPDATE occurs, even if no value is specified for the field. If a table has multiple TIMESTAMP columns, only the first one will be updated when an INSERT or UPDATE is performed.

■ There is also a BLOB type, which is a variant on TEXT, and allows for storing binary files in a table. I'll demonstrate this in action in Chapter 9, "Database Programming Techniques."

Accounting Database

Column Name	Table	Column Type
Invoice Number	Invoices	SMALLINT(4) UNSIGNED
Client ID	Invoices	SMALLINT(3) UNSIGNED
Invoice Date	Invoices	DATE
Invoice Amount	Invoices	DECIMAL(10,2) UNSIGNED
Invoice Description	Invoices	TINYTEXT
Client ID	Clients	SMALLINT(3) UNSIGNED
Client Name	Clients	VARCHAR(40)
Client Street Address	Clients	VARCHAR(80)
Client City	Clients	VARCHAR(30)
Client State	Clients	CHAR(2)
Client Zip	Clients	MEDIUMINT(5) UNSIGNED
Client Phone	Clients	VARCHAR(14)
Contact Name	Clients	VARCHAR(40)
Contact Email Address	Clients	VARCHAR(60)
Expense ID	Expenses	SMALLINT(4) UNSIGNED
Expense Category ID	Expenses	TINYINT(3) UNSIGNED
Expense Amount	Expenses	DECIMAL(10,2) UNSIGNED
Expense Description	Expenses	TINYTEXT
Expense Date	Expenses	DATE
Expense Category ID	Expense Categories	TINYINT(3) UNSIGNED
Expense Category	Expense Categories	VARCHAR(30)

Table 3.3 An often overlooked aspect of database design is defining the optimal type for each field.

MySQL Data Types

NULL and Default Values

As you have already seen, there are a few attributes you can assign when defining your data types, including UNSIGNED and ZEROFILL. Two more options are to dictate whether or not the value of a column can be NULL and to set a default value.

The NULL value, in databases and programming, is the equivalent of saying that the field has no value (or it is unknown). Ideally, every record in a database should have value, but that is rarely the case in practicality. To enforce this limitation on a field, you add the NOT NULL description to its column type. For example, a primary key might now be described as

client_id SMALLINT(3) UNSIGNED NOT NULL

Accounting Database

Column Name	Table	Column Type
Invoice Number	Invoices	SMALLINT(4) UNSIGNED NOT NULL DEFAULT 0
Client ID	Invoices	SMALLINT(3) UNSIGNED
Invoice Date	Invoices	DATE NOT NULL
Invoice Amount	Invoices	DECIMAL(10,2) UNSIGNED NOT NULL
Invoice Description	Invoices	TINYTEXT
Client ID	Clients	SMALLINT(3) UNSIGNED NOT NULL DEFAULT 0
Client Name	Clients	VARCHAR(40) NOT NULL
Client Street Address	Clients	VARCHAR(80)
Client City	Clients	VARCHAR(30)
Client State	Clients	CHAR(2)
Client Zip	Clients	MEDIUMINT(5) UNSIGNED
Client Phone	Clients	VARCHAR(14)
Contact Name	Clients	VARCHAR(40)
Contact Email Address	Clients	VARCHAR(60)
Expense ID	Expenses	SMALLINT(4) UNSIGNED NOT NULL DEFAULT 0
Expense Category ID	Expenses	TINYINT(3) UNSIGNED
Expense Amount	Expenses	DECIMAL(10,2) UNSIGNED NOT NULL
Expense Description	Expenses	TINYTEXT
Expense Date	Expenses	DATE
Expense Category ID	Expense Categories	TINYINT(3) UNSIGNED
Expense Category	Expense Categories	VARCHAR(30)

Table 3.4 I've added NOT NULL descriptions and DEFAULT values for a few of my columns to further improve the database design.

When creating a table you can also specify a default value. In cases where a large portion of the records will have the same contents, presetting a default will save you from having to specify a value when inserting new rows, unless that value is different from the norm. One example might be

```
gender ENUM('M', 'F') DEFAULT 'F'
```

Table 3.4 incorporates these two new ideas.

✔ Tips

■ Primary keys cannot contain NULL values, in accordance with proper database design and with how MySQL functions.

■ If an ENUM column is set as NOT NULL, the default value will automatically be the first of the possible allowed values.

■ Just to clarify what NULL is, understand that NULL has a different value than the number zero, an empty string (""), or a space (" ").

Indexes

Indexes are a special system that databases use to improve the overall performance. By setting indexes on your tables, you are telling MySQL to pay particular attention to that column (in layman's terms). In fact, MySQL creates extra files to store and track indexes efficiently.

MySQL allows for up to 32 indexes for each table, and each index can incorporate up to 16 columns. While a multicolumn index may not seem obvious, it will come in handy for searches frequently performed on the same set of multiple columns (e.g., first and last name, city and state, etc.)

On the other hand, one should not go overboard with indexing. While it does improve the speed of reading from databases, it slows down the process of altering data in a database (because the changes need to be recorded in the index). Indexes are best used on columns

◆ That are frequently used in the WHERE part of a query

◆ That are frequently used in an ORDER BY part of a query

◆ That have many different values (columns with numerous repeating values ought not to be indexed)

Note that, in MySQL, a primary key column is automatically indexed for efficiency.

MySQL has three types of indexes: INDEX, UNIQUE (which requires each row to have a unique value), and PRIMARY KEY (which is just a particular UNIQUE index). **Table 3.5** lists the indexes I propose for the *accounting* database.

Accounting Indexes	
COLUMN	INDEX TYPE
Invoice Number	PRIMARY KEY
Client ID	PRIMARY KEY
Expense ID	PRIMARY KEY
Expense Category ID	PRIMARY KEY
Invoice Date	INDEX
Client Name	INDEX (or UNIQUE)

Table 3.5 To improve the performance of my database, I add a few (but not too many) indexes to help MySQL access the stored information.

One final attribute a column can have that frequently works in conjunction with an index is AUTO_INCREMENT. When you define a field with this property using

`client_id SMALLINT(3) UNSIGNED NOT NULL AUTO_INCREMENT`

you are effectively telling MySQL to set the value of this column to the next logical value in the series. If the column is an integer, the next highest integer will be used when no value is set when a new record is inserted.

✔ Tips

- The AUTO_INCREMENT setting in MySQL is the equivalent of Oracle's sequences.

- Indexes are less efficient on variable-length columns, just as MySQL is generally slower dealing with fields that are not of a fixed length.

- Indexes can be named when they are created (see Chapter 4, "SQL"), but if they are not, they will take the name of the column they are applied to.

INDEXES

Final Design Steps

The final step in designing your database is to adhere to certain naming conventions. While MySQL is very flexible on how you name your databases, tables, and columns, here are some good rules to go by (some of which are required):

◆ Use alphanumeric characters.

◆ Limit yourself to less than 64 characters (this is a MySQL restriction).

◆ Use the underscore (_) to separate words.

◆ Use entirely lowercase words (this is definitely a personal preference rather than a rule).

◆ Use plural table names (to indicate multiple values stored) and singular column names.

◆ End primary and foreign key columns with id (or ID).

◆ List the primary key first in a table, followed by foreign keys.

◆ Field names should be descriptive.

◆ Field names should be unique across every table, except for the keys.

These are largely my recommendations and are therefore not absolute, except for limiting yourself to alphanumeric names without spaces. Some developers prefer to use capital letters to break up words (instead of underscores). Others like to indicate the column type in its name. The most important consideration is that you remain consistent with your conventions.

Table 3.6 shows the final database design, which will be created in the next chapter.

✔ Tips

- Database and table names are case-sensitive on Unix systems but insensitive under Windows. Column names are always case-insensitive.

- By strictly adhering to any set of database design principles, you minimize errors that could occur when programming a database interface, as you will in Chapters 6, 7, and 8.

accounting		
COLUMN NAME	**TABLE**	**COLUMN TYPE**
invoice_id	invoices	SMALLINT(4) UNSIGNED NOT NULL DEFAULT 0
client_id	invoices	SMALLINT(3) UNSIGNED
invoice_date	invoices	DATE NOT NULL
invoice_amount	invoices	DECIMAL(10,2) UNSIGNED NOT NULL
invoice_description	invoices	TINYTEXT
client_id	clients	SMALLINT(3) UNSIGNED NOT NULL DEFAULT 0
client_name	clients	VARCHAR(40) NOT NULL
client_street	clients	VARCHAR(80)
client_city	clients	VARCHAR(30)
client_state	clients	CHAR(2)
client_zip	clients	MEDIUMINT(5) UNSIGNED
client_phone	clients	VARCHAR(14)
contact_name	clients	VARCHAR(40)
contact_email	clients	VARCHAR(60)
expense_id	expenses	SMALLINT(4) UNSIGNED NOT NULL DEFAULT 0
expense_category_id	expenses	TINYINT(3) UNSIGNED
expense_amount	Expenses	DECIMAL(10,2) UNSIGNED NOT NULL
expense_description	expenses	TINYTEXT
expense_date	Expenses	DATE
expense_category_id	expense_categories	TINYINT(3) UNSIGNED
expense_category	expense_categories	VARCHAR(30)

Table 3.6 The final database design step incorporates certain naming conventions that I try to adhere to.

4

SQL

SQL, short for Structured Query Language, is a group of special words used exclusively for interacting with databases. Every major database uses SQL, and MySQL is no exception.

SQL was created shortly after E.F. Codd came up with the theory of a relational database (along with normalization). Decades later, in 1989, the American National Standards Institute (ANSI)—the organization responsible for maintaining the language—released the first SQL standard, referred to now as SQL 89. SQL2 was released in 1992 and is still the current, working version (also called SQL92 or just plain SQL).

Using the *accounting* database created in the previous chapter, this chapter will discuss and demonstrate all of the major SQL terms. Since you must use SQL to communicate with MySQL, the information presented here will be referenced throughout the remainder of this book.

Creating Databases and Tables

The first logical use of SQL will be to create a database. In Chapter 2, "Running MySQL," I quickly defined two databases to help demonstrate how to add users. (At that time you also used the GRANT SQL command.) As you may recall, the syntax for creating a new database is

CREATE DATABASE databasename

The CREATE term is also used for making tables.

CREATE TABLE tablename (column1name
→ description, column2name description …)

As you can see from the syntax above, after naming the table, you define each column—in order—within parentheses. Each column and description should be separated by a comma. Should you choose to create indexes at this time, you can add those at the end of the creation statement (you can add indexes at a later time, as well).

To demonstrate the CREATE statement, I'll establish the *accounting* database and its four tables, as prescribed by the normalization process from Chapter 3, "Database Design."

To create databases and tables:

1. Access the mysql monitor (**Figure 4.1**).

   mysql -u username -p

   Through the rest of this chapter, all of the SQL will be entered using the mysql client. Using the steps in Chapter 2, "Running MySQL," open the mysql monitor, entering the proper syntax (user name, password, etc.) for your system and configuration.

2. Create and select the new database (**Figure 4.2**).

   CREATE DATABASE accounting;
   USE accounting;

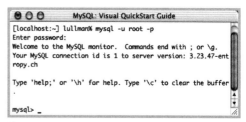

Figure 4.1 The examples in this chapter will take place entirely from within the mysql client.

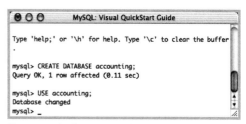

Figure 4.2 The first steps I take are to create and select the *accounting* database.

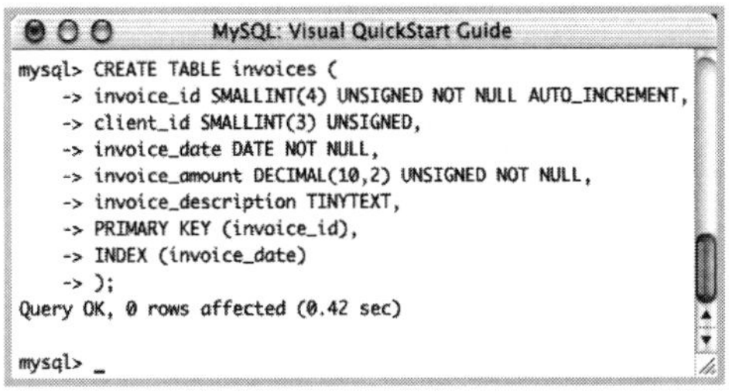

Figure 4.3 The mysql monitor allows you to enter commands over multiple lines, making long SQL statements more readable.

This first line, as you've already seen, creates the database (assuming that you are logged into mysql as a user with permission to create new databases). The second line tells MySQL that you want to work within this database from here on out. Remember that within the mysql monitor, you must terminate every SQL command with a semicolon.

Also, although SQL is case insensitive, I will make it a habit to capitalize the SQL words, helping to separate them from the database, table, and column names. If you would rather not capitalize these terms, you have that option.

3. Create the *invoices* table (**Figure 4.3**).

```
CREATE TABLE invoices (
invoice_id SMALLINT(4) UNSIGNED NOT
→ NULL AUTO_INCREMENT,
client_id SMALLINT(3) UNSIGNED,
invoice_date DATE NOT NULL,
invoice_amount DECIMAL(10,2) UNSIGNED
→ NOT NULL,
invoice_description TINYTEXT,
PRIMARY KEY (invoice_id),
INDEX (invoice_date)
);
```

This step takes the information about the *invoices* table I established in the previous chapter and integrates that within the CREATE table syntax. The order in which you enter the columns here will dictate the order the columns appear in the table. You'll also need to specify any indexes last so they are enacted after the column itself has been created.

Because the mysql monitor will not run a query until it encounters a semicolon, you can enter statements over multiple lines like I do in Figure 4.3.

continues on next page

When creating a table, you have the option of specifying a type, with MyISAM, BDB, InnoDB, temporary, and HEAP being the most common. If you do not specify a table type, MySQL will automatically create the table using the default type, most likely MyISAM (which is an upgrade from the older ISAM). In Chapter 11, "Advanced MySQL," you'll learn more about InnoDB tables.

4. Create the remaining three tables (**Figure 4.4**).

```
CREATE TABLE clients (
client_id SMALLINT(3) UNSIGNED NOT NULL
→ AUTO_INCREMENT,
client_name VARCHAR(40) NOT NULL,
client_street VARCHAR(80),
client_city VARCHAR(30),
client_state CHAR(2),
client_zip MEDIUMINT(5) UNSIGNED,
client_phone VARCHAR(14),
contact_name VARCHAR(40),
contact_email VARCHAR(60),
PRIMARY KEY (client_id),
INDEX (client_name)
);
CREATE TABLE expenses (
expense_id SMALLINT(4) UNSIGNED NOT
→ NULL AUTO_INCREMENT,
expense_category_id TINYINT(3)
→ UNSIGNED,
expense_amount DECIMAL(10,2) UNSIGNED,
expense_description TINYTEXT,
expense_date DATE,
PRIMARY KEY (expense_id)
);
CREATE TABLE expense_categories (
expense_category_id TINYINT(3)
→ UNSIGNED NOT NULL AUTO_INCREMENT,
expense_category VARCHAR(30),
PRIMARY KEY (expense_category_id)
);
```

```
mysql> CREATE TABLE clients (
    -> client_id SMALLINT(3) UNSIGNED NOT NULL AUTO_INCREMENT,
    -> client_name VARCHAR(40) NOT NULL,
    -> client_street VARCHAR(80),
    -> client_city VARCHAR(30),
    -> client_state CHAR(2),
    -> client_zip MEDIUMINT(5) UNSIGNED,
    -> client_phone VARCHAR(14),
    -> contact_name VARCHAR(40),
    -> contact_email VARCHAR(60),
    -> PRIMARY KEY (client_id),
    -> INDEX (client_name)
    -> );
Query OK, 0 rows affected (0.01 sec)
mysql> CREATE TABLE expenses (
    -> expense_id SMALLINT(4) UNSIGNED NOT NULL AUTO_INCREMENT,
    -> expense_category_id TINYINT(3) UNSIGNED,
    -> expense_amount DECIMAL(10,2) UNSIGNED,
    -> expense_description TINYTEXT,
    -> expense_date DATE,
    -> PRIMARY KEY (expense_id)
    -> );
Query OK, 0 rows affected (0.35 sec)
mysql> CREATE TABLE expense_categories (
    -> expense_category_id TINYINT(3) UNSIGNED NOT NULL AUTO_INCREMENT,
    -> expense_category VARCHAR(30),
    -> PRIMARY KEY (expense_category_id)
    -> );
Query OK, 0 rows affected (0.09 sec)
mysql> _
```

Figure 4.4 MySQL will report if a command worked, using the Query OK statement as indicated three times here.

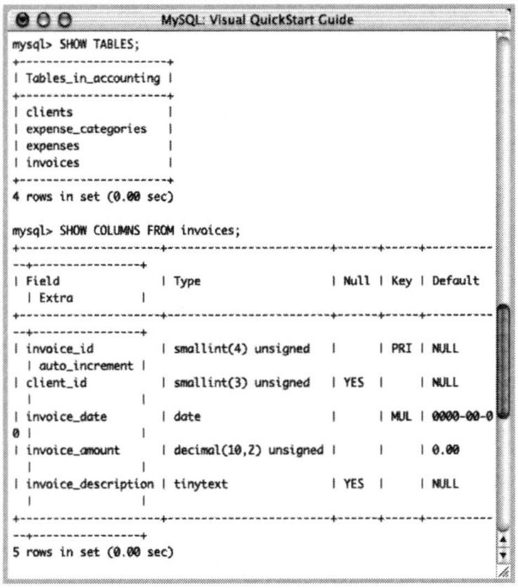

```
000           MySQL: Visual QuickStart Guide
mysql> SHOW TABLES;
+---------------------+
| Tables_in_accounting |
+---------------------+
| clients             |
| expense_categories  |
| expenses            |
| invoices            |
+---------------------+
4 rows in set (0.00 sec)

mysql> SHOW COLUMNS FROM invoices;
+--------------------+--------------------+------+-----+----------+
| Field              | Type               | Null | Key | Default  |
| Extra              |                    |      |     |          |
+--------------------+--------------------+------+-----+----------+
| invoice_id         | smallint(4) unsigned |      | PRI | NULL     |
| auto_increment     |                    |      |     |          |
| client_id          | smallint(3) unsigned | YES |     | NULL     |
|                    |                    |      |     |          |
| invoice_date       | date               |      | MUL | 0000-00-0 |
0 |                  |                    |      |     |          |
| invoice_amount     | decimal(10,2) unsigned |    |     | 0.00     |
|                    |                    |      |     |          |
| invoice_description | tinytext          | YES |     | NULL     |
|                    |                    |      |     |          |
+--------------------+--------------------+------+-----+----------+
5 rows in set (0.00 sec)
```

Figure 4.5 You can confirm the existence and structure of databases and tables using the SHOW command.

The other three tables of the *accounting* database use similar syntax to the *invoices* table, adjusting the column names and descriptions as necessary.

5. Confirm the existence of the tables (**Figure 4.5**).

   SHOW TABLES;

   SHOW COLUMNS FROM invoices;

   The SHOW command, which does not need to be discussed in detail, reveals the tables in a database or the column names and types in a table.

✔ Tips

■ Remember that you can also create databases, but not tables, using the mysqladmin application.

   mysqladmin –u root –p create databasename

■ Throughout the rest of this chapter, I will assume that you are using the mysql client and have already selected the *accounting* database with USE.

■ You can specify the database to use when you immediately run the mysql monitor, saving yourself the USE step, by typing:

   mysql -u root -p databasename

■ DESCRIBE tablename, which you might see in other resources, is the same statement as SHOW COLUMNS FROM tablename.

Inserting Data

After your database and tables have been created, you can start populating them with data using the INSERT command. There are two formats for inserting data. With the first, you specify the columns to be used.

```
INSERT INTO tablename (column1, column2 …)
→ VALUES ('value1', 'value2', …)
```

```
INSERT INTO tablename (column4, column8)
→ VALUES ('valueX', 'valueY')
```

Using this structure, you can add rows of records, populating only the columns that matter. The result will be that any columns not given a value will be treated as NULL (or given a default value, if that was established). Note that if a column cannot have a NULL value (it was defined as NOT NULL), not specifying a value will cause an error.

The second format for inserting records is not to specify any columns but to include every value.

```
INSERT INTO tablename VALUES ('value1',
→ NULL, 'value3', …)
```

If you use this second method, you must specify a value, even a NULL value, for every column, so if there are six columns in the table, you must list six values. Failure to match the values or number of values to the columns (or number of columns) will also cause an error. For this reason, the first format of inserting records is generally preferable.

MySQL also allows you to insert multiple rows at one time, separating each record by a comma.

```
INSERT INTO tablename (column1, column4)
→ VALUES ('valueA', 'valueB'), ('valueC',
→ 'valueD'), ('valueE', 'valueF')
```

While you can do this with MySQL, it is not acceptable within the ANSI SQL2 standard.

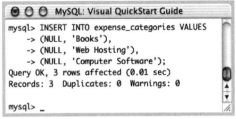

Figure 4.6 Here are the two ways you can insert data into a table.

```
MySQL: Visual QuickStart Guide
mysql> INSERT INTO expense_categories VALUES
    -> (NULL, 'Books'),
    -> (NULL, 'Web Hosting'),
    -> (NULL, 'Computer Software');
Query OK, 3 rows affected (0.01 sec)
Records: 3  Duplicates: 0  Warnings: 0

mysql> _
```

Figure 4.7 With MySQL, I can enter as many values into a table as I want in one command.

To insert data into a table:

1. Insert a new row of data into the *expense_categories* table (**Figure 4.6**). Your syntax would be one of the following:

   ▲ INSERT INTO expense_categories
      → (expense_category) VALUES
      → ('Travel-Hotel');

   ▲ INSERT INTO expense_categories
      → VALUES (NULL, 'Travel-Airfare');

   Since this table contains only two columns, one of which is automatically incremented, there's little difference between the two methods. You will notice from Figure 4.6 that MySQL performed the second query faster than it did the first, for what that's worth.

2. Insert several values into the *expense_categories* table (**Figure 4.7**).

   INSERT INTO expense_categories VALUES

   (NULL, 'Books'),

   (NULL, 'Web Hosting'),

   (NULL, 'Computer Software');

   Since MySQL allows you to insert multiple values at once, you can take advantage of this and fill up the table with records.

3. Continue steps 1 and 2 until you've thoroughly populated the *expense_categories* and *clients* tables.

   At this point, because of the more complicated nature of a relational database, I am not going to add records to either the *invoices* or *expenses* tables, as these rely on information in the *clients* and *expense_categories* tables. You'll see later in the chapter how to insert records into them.

   continues on next page

✔ Tips

- If you need to insert a value containing a single quotation mark, escape it with a backslash like this:

```
INSERT INTO users (last_name,
→ first_name) VALUES ('O\'Malley',
→ 'Juan')
```

- Spaces at the end of a value that has been inserted into a VARCHAR column will be automatically truncated by MySQL, which is another difference from the ANSI SQL2 standard.

- The term INTO in INSERT statements is optional in current versions of MySQL.

- As a rule of thumb, strings should be enclosed with single quotation marks and numbers should be entered without any quotation marks (the same applies to the word NULL).

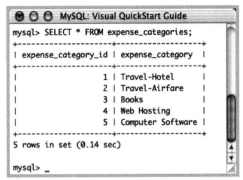

Figure 4.8 This is a simple SELECT query, returning all of the table's records and columns.

```
● ○ ○       MySQL: Visual QuickStart Guide
mysql> SELECT client_id, client_name FROM clients;
+-----------+------------------+
| client_id | client_name      |
+-----------+------------------+
|         1 | Acme Industries  |
|         2 | Winesburg Press  |
|         3 | Galt on the Hill |
|         4 | ABC Noun         |
+-----------+------------------+
4 rows in set (0.00 sec)

mysql> _
```

Figure 4.9 You can limit the information returned by a SELECT query by specifying the columns to include.

Selecting Data

Now that the database has some records in it, you can begin to retrieve the information with the most used of all SQL terms, SELECT. This term is used to return rows of records based upon certain criteria.

The simplest query is

SELECT * FROM tablename

The asterisk means that you want to view every column. Your other choice would be to specify the columns to be returned, with each separated by a comma.

SELECT user_id, first_name, last_name
→ FROM users

There are a few benefits to being explicit about which columns are selected. The first is performance: There's no reason to fetch columns that you will not be using. The second is order: You can return columns in an order other than their layout in the table. Third—and you'll see this in Chapter 5, "MySQL Functions," it allows you to manipulate the values in those columns.

To select data from a table:

1. Retrieve all the data from the *expense_categories* table (**Figure 4.8**).

   SELECT * FROM expense_categories;

   This very basic SQL command will retrieve every column of every row stored within that table and present them.

2. Retrieve just the *client_id* and *client_name* fields from *clients* (**Figure 4.9**).

   SELECT client_id, client_name FROM
   → clients;

   Instead of showing the data from every field in the *clients* table, you can use the SELECT statement to limit yourself to only the pertinent information.

continues on next page

SELECTING DATA

3. Using the information retrieved in steps 1 and 2, populate the *expenses* and *invoices* tables (**Figure 4.10**).

```
INSERT INTO expenses VALUES
(NULL, 3, 19.99, 'Larry Ullman\'s
→ "MySQL: Visual QuickStart Guide"',
→ '2002-04-20'),
(NULL, 1, 104.50, 'Palmer House Hotel,
→ Chicago', '2002-1-26'),
(NULL, 2, 689.00, 'Flight to Chicago',
→ '2002-01-26'),
(NULL, 5, 99.99, 'Mmmm...software',
→ NULL);
```

Now that you can view the primary keys from the *expense_categories* and *clients* tables (*expense_category_id* and *client_id*, respectively), it's possible to insert data into the other two tables. Because the database is relational, it's important to align records, matching up primary keys in one table with foreign keys in another. Thus, to indicate that an expense is a *Book*, you enter the expense using *3* as the *expense_category_id*. Maintaining these relationships is at the heart of a normalized database and requires use of both SELECT and INSERT commands.

You should notice that because the date column types are fairly flexible, you can enter dates as *2002-04-07, 20020407,* or *2002-4-7* (although not the American *4-7-2002*).

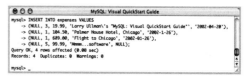

Figure 4.10 Now that my *expense_category_id* foreign keys have been established, I can populate the *expenses* table.

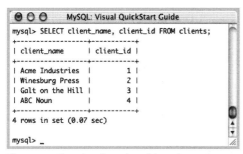

Figure 4.11 Changing the order of the columns in your SELECT query alters the order of the retrieved data.

4. Continue with this process until the database has oodles of information in it, in every table.

Throughout the rest of this chapter I will be performing queries based upon the records I enter into my database. Should your database not have the same specific records (clients, expense categories, etc.) as mine, change the particulars accordingly. That being said, the fundamental thinking behind the following queries should still apply regardless of the data since the *accounting* database has a set column and table structure.

✔ Tips

- Strange as it may sound, you can actually use SELECT without naming tables or columns. You'll see this in action in the next chapter.

- The order in which you list columns in your SELECT statement (assuming you are not retrieving everything) dictates the order in which the values are returned. Compare Figure 4.9 with **Figure 4.11**.

- With SELECT, you can even retrieve the same column multiple times, allowing you to manipulate the column in many different ways.

- In the next four chapters, you will learn easier ways to insert relational records rather than inserting one record, selecting it, and inserting another, as you have done here.

Using Conditionals

The problem with the SELECT statement as I have used it to date is that it will automatically retrieve every record. While this isn't a problem when dealing with a few rows of information, it will greatly hinder the performance of your database as the number of records grows. To improve the efficiency of your SELECT statements, there are different conditionals you can use in an almost limitless number of combinations. These conditionals utilize the SQL term WHERE and are written much like you'd write a conditional in any programming language.

```
SELECT * FROM tablename WHERE column =
→ 'value'
```

```
SELECT expense_amount FROM expenses WHERE
→ expense_amount >= 10.00
```

```
SELECT client_id FROM clients WHERE
→ client_name = 'Acme Industries'
```

Table 4.1 lists the most common operators you would use within a WHERE conditional. Next in this chapter I'll demonstrate LIKE and NOT LIKE, and finally, in Chapter 11, "Advanced MySQL," you'll see REGEX and how to perform full-text searching. These operators can be used together, along with parentheses, to create more complex conditionals.

```
SELECT expense_amount FROM expenses WHERE
→ (expense_amount >= 10.00) AND
→ (expense_amount <= 20.00)
```

```
SELECT * FROM expenses WHERE
→ (expense_category_id = 1) OR
→ (expense_category_id = 2)
```

To demonstrate using conditionals, I'll retrieve more specific data from the *accounting* database. The examples below will be just a few of the possibilities. Over the course of this chapter and the entire book you will see any number of variants on SELECT conditionals.

MySQL Operators

Operator	Meaning
=	equals
<	less than
>	greater than
<=	less than or equal to
>=	greater than or equal to
!=	not equal to
IS NOT NULL	has a value
IS NULL	does not have a value
BETWEEN	within a range
NOT BETWEEN	outside of a range
OR (also ||)	where one of two conditionals is true
AND (also &&)	where both conditionals are true
NOT (also !)	where the condition is not true

Table 4.1 These are the most common MySQL operators. Appendix B, "SQL & MySQL References," will contain the exhaustive list.

Figure 4.12 The conditional in this query uses the *expenses* table's *expense_category_id* foreign key to select a particular record.

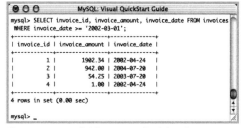

Figure 4.13 Date fields are very flexible in how you access the information, including being able to show dates relatively.

To select particular data from a table:

1. Select the *expense_description* for every *Books* expense type (**Figure 4.12**).

SELECT expense_description FROM
→ expenses WHERE expense_category_id = 3;

Since I know that *Books* in the *expense_categories* table has an *expense_category_id* of 3, I can create the SQL query above. This will return the *expense_description* for each record that has an *expense_category_id* foreign key of 3. Note that numbers should not be within quotation marks in your conditionals (or anywhere else in your query).

If you did not enter a *Books* expense type, change your query accordingly.

2. Select the invoice ID, amount, and date of every invoice entered since March 1, 2002 (**Figure 4.13**).

SELECT invoice_id, invoice_amount,
→ invoice_date FROM invoices WHERE
→ invoice_date >= '2002-03-01';

You can perform greater than and less than (or greater than or equals to, less than or equals to) calculations using dates, as I've done here.

continues on next page

USING CONDITIONALS

3. Select everything from every record in the *expenses* table that does not have a date (**Figure 4.14**).

SELECT * FROM expenses WHERE
→ expense_date IS NULL;

The IS NULL conditional is the same as saying "does not have a value." Keep in mind that an empty string is the same thing as a value, in NULL terms, and therefore would not match this condition. Such a case would match

SELECT * FROM expenses WHERE
→ expense_date = '';

Figure 4.14 Because NULL is a special value in databases, the IS NULL and IS NOT NULL operators are used for these cases.

✔ Tips

■ Strange as it may seem, you do not have to select a column on which you are performing a WHERE.

SELECT invoice_id FROM invoices WHERE
→ client_id = 4

The reason for this is that the columns listed after SELECT only indicate what values to return.

■ You can also use the IN and NOT IN operators to determine if a column's value is or is not one of a listed set of values.

SELECT * FROM invoices WHERE
→ invoice_date IN ('2002-04-24',
→ '2002-04-26', '2002-04-28')

■ There is an option to make conditionals using HAVING instead of WHERE, although you should always try to use WHERE first. See the MySQL documentation for more information on HAVING.

■ You can perform mathematical calculations within your queries using the numeric addition (+), subtraction (-), multiplication (*), and division (/) characters.

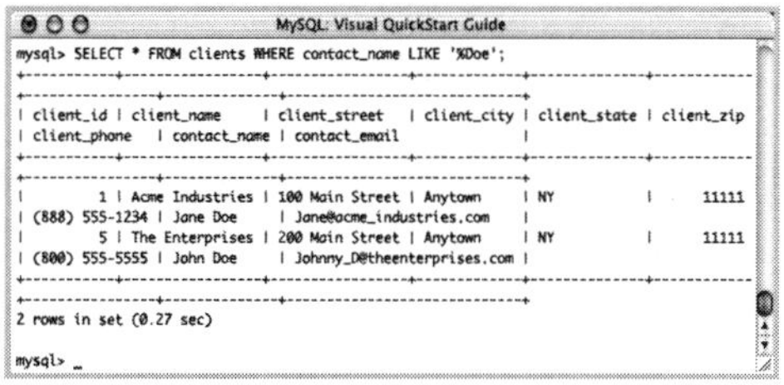

Figure 4.15 Using LIKE and a wildcard allow me to perform less exacting searches through fields.

Using LIKE and NOT LIKE

Using numbers, dates, and NULLs in conditionals is a straightforward process, but strings can be trickier. You can check for string equality with a query such as

SELECT * FROM users WHERE user_name =
→ 'trout';

However, comparing strings in a more liberal manner requires extra operators and characters. If, for example, you wanted to match a person's last name that could be *Smith* or *Smiths* or *Smithson*, you would need a more flexible query. This is where the LIKE and NOT LIKE conditionals come in. These are used—primarily with strings—in conjunction with two wildcard characters: the underscore (_), which matches a single character, and the percentage sign (%), which matches zero or more characters. In my last name example, the query I would write would be

SELECT * FROM users WHERE last_name LIKE
→ 'Smith%';

This query will perform a search on all columns whose *last_name* value begins with *Smith*. Because it's a case-insensitive search by default, it would also apply to names that begin with *smith*.

To use LIKE:

1. Select all of the client information in which the client's contact has a last name of *Doe* (**Figure 4.15**).

   SELECT * FROM clients WHERE
   → contact_name LIKE '%Doe';

   Because this table is not thoroughly normalized (in which case the contact name might be separated into first and last name fields), I'll have to use the wildcard to look for a last name of *Doe*.

   continues on next page

2. Select the client and contact names for
every record whose contact name is not
John, Joe, Joey, etc. (**Figure 4.16**).

SELECT client_name, contact_name FROM
→ clients WHERE contact_name NOT LIKE
→ 'Jo%';

If I want to rule out certain possibilities,
I can use NOT LIKE with the wildcard.

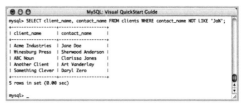

Figure 4.16 The NOT LIKE operator allows you to
eliminate certain records based upon loose
definitions (such as *Jo%*).

✔ Tips

■ Queries with a LIKE conditional are generally very slow because they won't take
advantage of indexes, so use this format
sparingly.

■ The wildcard characters can be used at
the front and/or the back of a string in
your queries.

SELECT * FROM users WHERE user_name =
→ '_Smith%';

■ Although LIKE and NOT LIKE are normally
used with strings, they can also be
applied to numeric columns, should the
need arise.

■ To use either the underscore or the percentage sign in a LIKE or NOT LIKE query,
you will need to escape them (by preceding the character with a backslash) so
they are not confused as wildcards.

■ The underscore can be used in combination with itself, so, as an example,
LIKE '__' would find any two-letter
combination.

Performing Joins

Because relational databases are more complexly structured, they sometimes require special query statements to retrieve the information you need most. Joins—SQL queries performed by cross-referencing tables—are used to extract more usable data from relational databases.

There are several types of joins conceivable according to SQL, although MySQL is slightly restricted in this one area. Beginning to intermediate users will find that the two most basic joins (which I'll teach in this chapter) will suffice for almost every application. The most used join is called an *inner* join (also called a *cross* join).

```
SELECT * FROM invoices, clients WHERE
→ invoices.client_id = clients.client_id
```

The benefit of this join in the example above is that it will retrieve all of the information from both the *invoices* and *clients* tables wherever an *invoices.client_id* is the same as the *clients.client_id*. In other words, the query will replace the *client_id* foreign key in the *invoices* table with all of the information for that client in the *clients* table. An inner join like this will only return records wherein a match is made (so if there was a client record that did not match an existing invoice, this information would not be displayed).

When selecting from multiple tables and columns, you must use the dot syntax (*table.column*) if there are columns with the same name. This is normally the case when dealing with relational databases because a primary key from one table will have the same name as a foreign key from another.

The second type of join I'll discuss—an *outer* or *left* join—differs from an inner join in that it could return records not matched by a conditional. The syntax of a left join is

SELECT * FROM clients LEFT JOIN invoices ON
→ invoices.client_id = clients.client_id

Note that the comma from the cross join is replaced by the words LEFT JOIN and the word WHERE is replaced with ON. The most important consideration with left joins is which table gets named first. In this example, all of the *clients* records will be returned along with all of the *invoices* information, if a match is made. You'll see this in action shortly, where it will make more sense.

If both tables in a left join have the same column name, you can simplify your query with

SELECT * FROM invoices LEFT JOIN clients
→ USING (client_id)

To use joins:

1. Retrieve the invoice amount, the invoice date, and the client names for every invoice (**Figure 4.17**).

    SELECT invoice_amount, invoice_date,
    → client_name FROM invoices, clients
    → WHERE invoices.client_id =
    → clients.client_id;

    This query, which includes an inner join, will effectively replace the *client_id* value from the *invoices* table with the corresponding *client_name* value from the *clients* table.

2. Retrieve the expense category, expense date, and expense amount for every expense (**Figure 4.18**).

    SELECT expense_category,
    expense_amount, expense_date
    → FROM expense_categories, expenses
    → WHERE expense_categories.
    → expense_category_id = expenses.
    → expense_category_id;

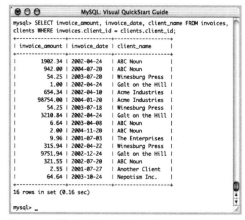

Figure 4.17 The basic inner join, albeit wordy, returns more usable information from your database than would a standard query.

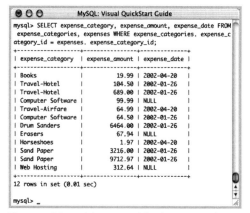

Figure 4.18 Inner joins are usable wherever you have a primary key-foreign key relationship, as I do here between *expenses* and *expense_categories*.

This query is another application of the same principle as that in step 1. Because I am again performing an inner join, the order of the tables will not matter (the end result will be the same if you reversed the table listings).

3. Retrieve all of the client names and all of the invoices for those clients (**Figure 4.19**).

```
SELECT client_name, invoice_id,
→ invoice_amount, invoice_date,
→ invoice_description FROM clients
→ LEFT JOIN invoices USING (client_id);
```

This query—an outer join—will retrieve every client name and then associate the appropriate invoices with each. Even if a client has no invoices (see "Something Clever" at bottom), the client will be listed. If I had used an inner join, Something Clever would be omitted from the returned results.

continues on next page

```
⊙ ⊙ ⊙                        MySQL: Visual QuickStart Guide
mysql> SELECT client_name, invoice_id, invoice_amount, invoice_date, invoice_description FROM clients LEFT JOIN
invoices USING (client_id);
+-------------------+------------+----------------+--------------+-----------------------------------------+
| client_name       | invoice_id | invoice_amount | invoice_date | invoice_description                     |
+-------------------+------------+----------------+--------------+-----------------------------------------+
| Acme Industries   |         5  |         654.34 | 2002-04-10   | Work, work, work.                       |
| Acme Industries   |         6  |       98754.00 | 2004-01-20   | Technical writing.                      |
| Winesburg Press   |         3  |          54.25 | 2003-07-20   | Hand wringing                           |
| Winesburg Press   |         7  |          54.25 | 2003-07-18   | Pacing.                                 |
| Winesburg Press   |        12  |         315.94 | 2002-04-22   | Miscellaneous Services                  |
| Galt on the Hill  |         4  |           1.00 | 2002-04-24   | Miscellaneous Services                  |
| Galt on the Hill  |         8  |        3210.84 | 2002-04-24   | Pondering                               |
| Galt on the Hill  |        13  |        9751.94 | 2002-12-24   | Reading.                                |
| ABC Noun          |         1  |        1902.34 | 2002-04-24   | Conjugation: verbs, nouns, adjectives.  |
| ABC Noun          |         2  |         942.00 | 2004-07-20   | Technical writing.                      |
| ABC Noun          |         9  |           6.64 | 2003-04-08   | Shady dealings.                         |
| ABC Noun          |        10  |           2.00 | 2004-11-20   | Brilliance.                             |
| ABC Noun          |        14  |         321.55 | 2002-07-20   | HTML, PHP, MySQL Web development.       |
| The Enterprises   |        11  |           9.96 | 2001-07-03   | Don't ask.                              |
| Another Client    |        15  |           2.55 | 2001-07-27   | Hand wringing                           |
| Nepotism Inc.     |        16  |          64.64 | 2003-10-24   | Miscellaneous Services                  |
| Something Clever  |      NULL  |           NULL | NULL         | NULL                                    |
+-------------------+------------+----------------+--------------+-----------------------------------------+
17 rows in set (0.00 sec)

mysql> _
```

Figure 4.19 Left joins are more particular in their wording than inner joins and do not require matches to return records. Compare this result with that in Figure 4.20.

4. Retrieve all of the invoice IDs, amounts, dates, and descriptions, along with the corresponding client name (**Figure 4.20**).

SELECT client_name, invoice_id,
→ invoice_amount, invoice_date,
→ invoice_description FROM invoices
→ LEFT JOIN clients USING (client_id);

This query only differs from that in step 3 in that here I am left joining *clients* to *invoices* rather than the other way around. The end result is that one fewer record is returned, namely the *Something Clever* client, as it has no invoice record.

✔ Tips

■ You can perform joins on more than two tables. You can even join a table with itself!

■ Joins can be created using conditionals involving any columns, not just the primary and foreign keys, as I have here.

■ You can perform joins across multiple databases using the *database.table.column* syntax, as long as every database is on the same server (you cannot do this across a network).

■ Joins that do not include a WHERE clause (e.g., SELECT * FROM invoices, clients) are called *full* joins and will return every record from both tables. This construct can have unwieldy results with larger tables.

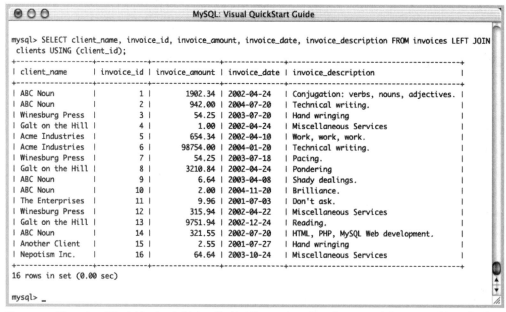

```
mysql> SELECT client_name, invoice_id, invoice_amount, invoice_date, invoice_description FROM invoices LEFT JOIN
    clients USING (client_id);
+------------------+------------+----------------+--------------+-------------------------------------+
| client_name      | invoice_id | invoice_amount | invoice_date | invoice_description                 |
+------------------+------------+----------------+--------------+-------------------------------------+
| ABC Noun         |          1 |        1902.34 | 2002-04-24   | Conjugation: verbs, nouns, adjectives. |
| ABC Noun         |          2 |         942.00 | 2004-07-20   | Technical writing.                  |
| Winesburg Press  |          3 |          54.25 | 2003-07-20   | Hand wringing                       |
| Galt on the Hill |          4 |           1.00 | 2002-04-24   | Miscellaneous Services              |
| Acme Industries  |          5 |         654.34 | 2002-04-10   | Work, work, work.                   |
| Acme Industries  |          6 |       98754.00 | 2004-01-20   | Technical writing.                  |
| Winesburg Press  |          7 |          54.25 | 2003-07-18   | Pacing.                             |
| Galt on the Hill |          8 |        3210.84 | 2002-04-24   | Pondering                           |
| ABC Noun         |          9 |           6.64 | 2003-04-08   | Shady dealings.                     |
| ABC Noun         |         10 |           2.00 | 2004-11-20   | Brilliance.                         |
| The Enterprises  |         11 |           9.96 | 2001-07-03   | Don't ask.                          |
| Winesburg Press  |         12 |         315.94 | 2002-04-22   | Miscellaneous Services              |
| Galt on the Hill |         13 |        9751.94 | 2002-12-24   | Reading.                            |
| ABC Noun         |         14 |         321.55 | 2002-07-20   | HTML, PHP, MySQL Web development.   |
| Another Client   |         15 |           2.55 | 2001-07-27   | Hand wringing                       |
| Nepotism Inc.    |         16 |          64.64 | 2003-10-24   | Miscellaneous Services              |
+------------------+------------+----------------+--------------+-------------------------------------+
16 rows in set (0.00 sec)

mysql> _
```

Figure 4.20 The order of the tables in a left join will affect the number of results returned. Every record from the first table will always be retrieved, regardless of the conditional.

PERFORMING JOINS

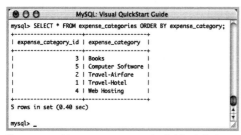

Figure 4.21 This ORDER BY returns the fields alphabetically by *expense_category*.

Sorting Query Results

Whereas the WHERE conditional places restrictions on what data is returned, the ORDER BY clause will affect how that data is returned. Much like listing the columns of a table arranges the returned order (compare Figures 4.9 and 4.11), ORDER BY structures the entire list. You use this phrase like so:

SELECT * FROM tablename ORDER BY column

SELECT invoice_amount, invoice_date FROM
→ invoices ORDER BY invoice_date

The default order when using ORDER BY is ascending, meaning that numbers increase from small to large and dates go from older to most recent. You can reverse this order by specifying DESC.

SELECT expense_description, expense_date
→ FROM expenses ORDER BY expense_date DESC

You can even order the returned values by multiple columns, as I'll demonstrate. It is important to understand that you cannot perform an ORDER BY on a column that is not selected. When you do not dictate the order of the returned data, it will be presented to you in somewhat unpredictable ways (although probably on the primary key ascending), so it's normally best to use this clause.

To sort data:

1. Show all of the expense categories in alphabetical order (**Figure 4.21**).

   SELECT * FROM expense_categories ORDER
   → BY expense_category;

   Since the *expenses* table has two columns, there are four ways of viewing the records in it: sorted by each column descending and ascending. This query will give an alphabetical presentation of the *expenses* table, based upon the *expense_category*.

continues on next page

2. Order the invoices by both client and invoice date (**Figure 4.22**).

SELECT client_id, invoice_date,
→ invoice_amount FROM invoices ORDER BY
→ client_id ASC, invoice_date DESC;

In this query, the effect would be that every column and row is returned, first ordered by the *client_id*, then by the *invoice_date* within the *client_id*s.

✔ Tips

■ Because MySQL works naturally with any number of languages, the ORDER BY will be based upon the language being used by the database (English as a default).

■ If the column that you chose to sort on contained NULL values, those will appear first, in both ascending and descending order.

■ You can, and frequently will, use ORDER BY in conjunction with WHERE, joins, or other clauses. When doing so, place the ORDER BY after the other conditions.

SELECT invoice_id, invoice_amount,
→ invoice_date FROM invoices WHERE
→ invoice_date >= '2002-03-01' ORDER BY
→ invoice_date DESC

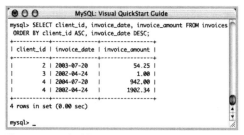

Figure 4.22 A double ORDER BY will sort the list by the first clause and then re-sort within that listing by the second clause.

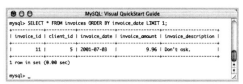

Figure 4.23 The LIMIT 1 clause will ensure that only one record is ever returned, saving me the hassle of viewing unnecessary rows of information.

Limiting Query Results

Another SQL term you can add to your SELECT statement is LIMIT. Unlike WHERE, which affects which records to return, or ORDER BY, which decides how those records are sorted, LIMIT states how many records to return. It is used like so:

SELECT * FROM tablename LIMIT 10

SELECT * FROM tablename LIMIT 10, 20

In the first example, only the initial 10 records from the query will be returned. In the second, 20 records will be returned, starting with the tenth.

You can use LIMIT with WHERE and/or ORDER BY, appending it to the end of your query.

SELECT * FROM invoices WHERE invoice_amount
→ > 100.00 ORDER BY invoice_amount ASC
→ LIMIT 10

Even though LIMIT does not reduce the strain of a query on the database (since it has to assemble every record, then cut down the list), it will minimize overhead when it comes to the client or programming interface. As a rule, when writing queries, there is never any reason to return columns or rows that you will not need.

To limit the amount of data returned:

1. Select the earliest invoice (**Figure 4.23**).

   SELECT * FROM invoices ORDER BY
   → invoice_date LIMIT 1;

   To return the earliest anything, I must sort the data by a date, in ascending order. Then, to see just one invoice, I apply a LIMIT 1 to the query.

   continues on next page

2. Select the two most expensive sand paper expenditures (**Figure 4.24**).

SELECT expense_amount,
→ expense_description FROM expenses,
→ expense_categories WHERE expenses.
→ expense_category_id = expense_
→ categories.expense_category_id AND
→ expense_category = 'Sand Paper' ORDER
→ BY expense_amount DESC LIMIT 2;

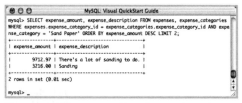

Figure 4.24 The very complicated query shown here distills the information stored in the *accounting* database into a supremely usable form.

This may look like a complex query, but it's just a good application of the information learned so far. First, I determine what columns to return, specifically naming the *expense_amount* and *expense_description* columns. Second, I list both tables to be used, since I'll be performing a join. Third, I establish my conditionals, which establish the join (expenses.expense_category_id = expense_categories.expense_category_id) and identify which category I want to use (expense_category = 'Sand Paper'). Finally, I sort the qualifying records so that the most expensive expenditures are listed first and then I limit it down to two records. If your database does not contain a sand paper expense category, alter this query using another example.

✔ Tips

- In Chapter 9, "Database Programming Techniques," you'll learn how to use LIMIT to create multiple pages of results from a query, like you would with a search engine.

- The LIMIT x, y clause is most frequently used when displaying multiple pages of query results where you would want to show the first 20 results, then the second 20, and so forth.

- In the next chapter, "MySQL Functions," you'll learn one last clause, GROUP BY, to use with your SELECT statements.

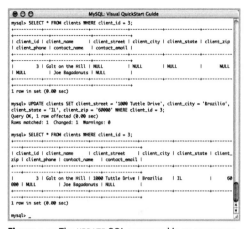

Figure 4.25 The UPDATE SQL command is an easy way to alter existing data in your tables.

Updating Data

Once your tables contain some data, you have the option of changing existing records. The most frequent reason for doing this would be if information were entered incorrectly. Or, in the case of user information, if data gets changed (such as a last name or email address) and that needs to be reflected in the database.

The syntax for updating columns is

UPDATE tablename SET column=value

You can adjust multiple columns at one time, separating each by a comma.

UPDATE tablename SET column1='value',
→ column2='value2'…

Normally you will want to use a WHERE clause to specify what rows to affect; otherwise, the change would be applied to every row.

UPDATE tablename SET column1='value' WHERE
→ column2='value2'

Updates, along with deletions, are one of the most important reasons to use a primary key. This number, which should never change, can be a reference point in WHERE clauses, even if every other field needs to be altered.

To update records:

◆ Add the client's address information for *Galt on the Hill* (**Figure 4.25**).

UPDATE clients SET client_street =
→ '1000 Tuttle Drive', client_city =
→ 'Brazilia', client_state = 'IL',
→ client_zip = '60000' WHERE client_id
→ = 3;

When I originally entered this client, I did not include this information. Using UPDATE, I can always go back in and retrieve this value later.

✔ Tips

■ Be extra certain to use a WHERE conditional whenever you use UPDATE unless you want the changes to affect every row.

■ You should never have to perform an UPDATE on the primary key column because this value should never change. Altering a primary key in one table could destroy the integrity of a relationship with another table.

Deleting Data

Another step you can easily take on existing data is to entirely remove it from the database. To do this, you use the DELETE command.

DELETE FROM tablename WHERE column=value

Note that once you have deleted a record, there is no way of retrieving it, so you may want to back up your database before performing any deletes. Also, you should get in the habit of using WHERE when deleting data or else you will delete all of the data in a table. The query

DELETE FROM tablename

will empty out a table, while still retaining its structure. Similarly, the command TRUNCATE TABLE tablename will delete an entire table (both the records and the structure) and recreate the structure. The end result is the same, but this method, which stems from Oracle, is faster and safer.

Another issue with deleting records has to do with the integrity of a relational database. In the *accounting* example, since the *invoices* table has a *client_id* field, if a client is deleted you might create phantom records because certain invoices, which kept that *client_id* reference, are now linked to a nonexistent client. Until MySQL formally supports foreign key relationships, this will be an issue to watch out for. In short, do not delete any records without altering the corresponding related records.

I'll go through an example of this by explaining the steps I would take if I decided to combine all of the *Travel* expense categories into one.

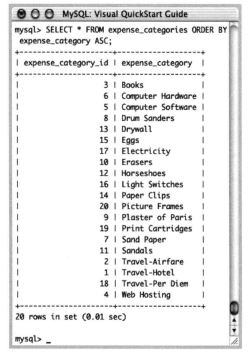

Figure 4.26 To delete all of the travel expense categories, I'll list them in alphabetical order first.

DELETING DATA

Figure 4.27 After deleting the records, I can view the table again to confirm the changes (compare with Figure 4.26).

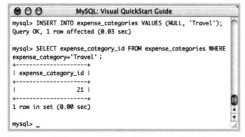

Figure 4.28 The next step in the process is to insert and select a new category.

To delete data:

1. View the current expense categories (**Figure 4.26**).

   SELECT * FROM expense_categories ORDER
   → BY expense_category ASC:

   To determine which fields I am combining, I'll look at the contents of the table one last time. I should also make note of what *expense_category_id*s are represented by travel categories, which are 1, 2, and 18.

2. Delete the three records from the table (**Figure 4.27**).

   DELETE FROM expense_categories WHERE
   → expense_category_id = 1 OR expense_
   → category_id = 2 OR expense_category_
   → id = 18;

   To be sure that I am deleting the right rows, I make use of the primary keys. I could have also used a query like DELETE FROM expense_categories WHERE
   → expense_category LIKE 'Travel-%' although that would have been less precise.

3. Create a new Travel category.

   INSERT INTO expense_categories VALUES
   → (NULL, 'Travel');

4. Retrieve the Travel category's *expense_category_id* (**Figure 4.28**).

   SELECT expense_category_id FROM
   → expense_categories WHERE
   → expense_category='Travel';

   You'll notice that deleting records from tables leaves gaps in your primary keys (in terms of auto-incrementation). Although *expense_categories* is currently missing numbers 1, 2, and 18, the next record is inserted at 21.

   continues on next page

5. Update the *expenses* table to reflect these changes (**Figure 4.29**).

UPDATE expenses SET
→ expense_category_id = 21 WHERE
→ expense_category_id = 1 OR
→ expense_category_id = 2 OR
→ expense_category_id = 18;

Because the *expense_categories* table relates to the *expenses* table, I must apply the changes made to the one to the other.

✔ Tips

■ To delete all of the data in a table, as well as the table itself, use DROP (**Figure 4.30**).

DROP TABLE tablename

■ To delete an entire database, including every table therein and all of its data, use

DROP DATABASE databasename

■ Remember that if you log into the mysql monitor with the --i-am-a-dummy parameter, mysql will not allow you to run UPDATE or DELETE queries without a WHERE conditional.

■ Beginning with MySQL version 4.0, you can run a DELETE query across multiple tables at the same time.

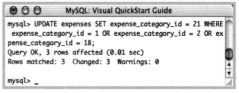

Figure 4.29 Finally, I should update the related *expenses* table to incorporate the new changes.

Figure 4.30 To delete an entire database or table (including both the structure and contents), use DROP.

Modifying Tables

The ALTER SQL keyword is primarily used to modify the structure of a table in your database. Commonly this refers to adding, deleting, or changing the columns therein. It also applies to renaming the table as a whole and altering the keys and indexes. While proper database design should give you the structure you need, in the real world, making alterations is commonplace. The basic syntax of ALTER is:

ALTER TABLE tablename CLAUSE

Because there are so many possible clauses, I've listed the common ones in **Table 4.2**. A more complete listing is included in Appendix B, "SQL and MySQL References."

ALTER TABLE Clauses

CLAUSE	USAGE	MEANING
ADD COLUMN	ALTER TABLE tablename ADD COLUMN column_name VARCHAR(40)	Adds a new column to the end of the table.
CHANGE COLUMN	ALTER TABLE tablename CHANGE COLUMN column_name column_name VARCHAR(60)	Allows you to change the data type and properties of a column.
DROP COLUMN	ALTER TABLE tablename DROP COLUMN column_name	Removes a column from a table, including all of its data.
ADD INDEX	ALTER TABLE tablename ADD INDEX indexname (column_name)	Adds a new index on column_name.
DROP INDEX	ALTER TABLE tablename DROP INDEX indexname	Removes an existing index.
RENAME AS	ALTER TABLE tablename RENAME AS new_tablename	Changes the name of a table.

Table 4.2 The ALTER SQL command can be used to modify tables in numerous ways.

To demonstrate using the ALTER command, I'll modify clients to separate the *contact_name* field into the more normalized *contact_first_name* and *contact_last_name* columns.

To alter a table's structure:

1. Rename the contact_name field (**Figure 4.31**).

   ALTER TABLE clients CHANGE COLUMN
   → contact_name contact_first_name
   → VARCHAR(15);

   This command merely changes the name and data type definition of the *contact_name* column. Instead of being a VARCHAR(40), the column is now called *contact_first_name* and is a VARCHAR(15). All of the data in the column has remained but will be truncated to 15 characters long.

2. Create a new contact_last_name column (**Figure 4.32**).

   ALTER TABLE clients ADD COLUMN contact_
   → last_name VARCHAR(25);

   Now the table contains a new column, although there are currently no values in it.

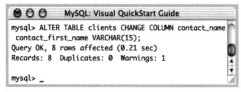

Figure 4.31 To rename or redefine a column, use the ALTER TABLE tablename CHANGE COLUMN syntax.

Figure 4.32 To add a new column to a table, use ALTER TABLE tablename ADD COLUMN.

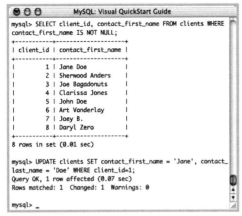

Figure 4.33 Once I've altered the table's structure, I'll need to update the records to include the new columns.

3. Update the contact name information (**Figure 4.33**).

```
SELECT client_id, contact_first_name
→ FROM clients WHERE contact_first_
→ name IS NOT NULL;
```

```
UPDATE clients SET contact_first_name =
→ 'Jane', contact_last_name = 'Doe'
→ WHERE client_id=1;
```

The last step in changing the table is to alter the data accordingly. To do so, I first view all of the current information and then perform an UPDATE for each row. The tediousness of this step is another reason to hopefully not make alterations once a database is up and running.

✔ Tips

- Because an ALTER command could have serious repercussions on a table, you should always back up the table before execution.

- The word COLUMN in most ALTER statements is optional.

- When adding a new column to a table, you can use the AFTER columnname description to indicate where in the table the new column should be placed.
  ```
  ALTER TABLE clients ADD COLUMN contact_
  → last_name VARCHAR(25) AFTER contact_
  → first_name;
  ```

MySQL Functions

MySQL has dozens of built-in functions that are designed to simplify common tasks. I'll cover the most useful ones here. If you are comfortable programming with C and C++, you can even write your own (although such a task is beyond the scope of this book).

Most of the functions you'll learn in this chapter are used in conjunction with SQL queries to format and alter the returned data. As with the previous chapter, every example will be demonstrated from within the mysql monitor. Each example will be based upon the existing *accounting* database and be used to illustrate common database techniques.

Text Functions

The first group of functions I will demonstrate are those meant for manipulating the various text and character columns. Most of the functions in this category are listed in **Table 5.1**.

To use any function, you need to modify your query so that you specify to which column or columns the function should be applied.

SELECT FUNCTION(column) FROM tablename

To specify multiple columns, you can write a query like either of these:

◆ SELECT *, FUNCTION(column) FROM
  → tablename

◆ SELECT column1, FUNCTION(column2),
  → column3 FROM tablename

Text Functions

FUNCTION	USAGE	PURPOSE
LENGTH()	LENGTH(column)	Returns the length of the string stored in the column.
LEFT()	LEFT(column, x)	Returns the leftmost x characters from a column.
RIGHT()	RIGHT(column, x)	Returns the rightmost x characters from a column.
TRIM()	TRIM(column)	Trims excess spaces from the beginning and end of the stored string.
UPPER()	UPPER(column)	Capitalizes the entire stored string.
LOWER()	LOWER(column)	Turns the stored string into an all-lowercase format.
SUBSTRING()	SUBSTRING(column, start, length)	Returns *length* characters from *column* beginning with *start* (indexed from 0).

Table 5.1 These are some, but not all, of the functions you can use on text columns in MySQL.

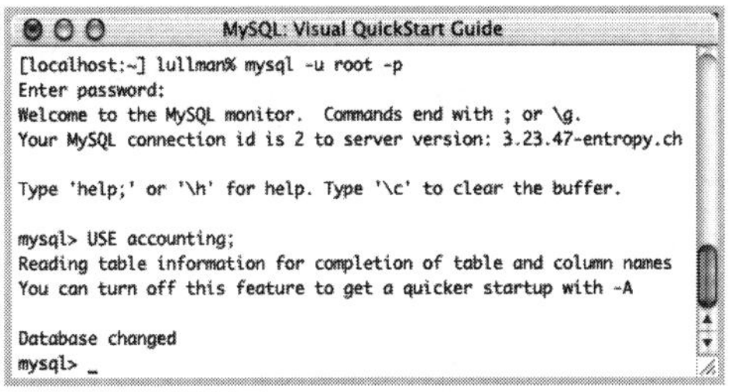

Figure 5.1 Once again, the mysql monitor and the *accounting* database will be the basis of all examples in this chapter.

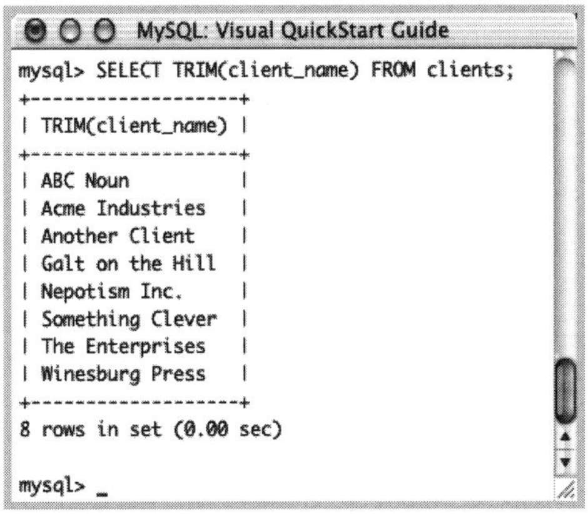

Figure 5.2 The TRIM() function eliminates superfluous spaces from the beginning and ends of returned values.

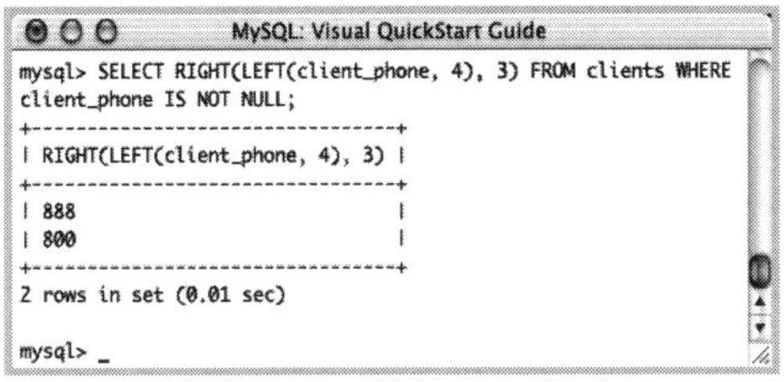

Figure 5.3 This application of the RIGHT() and LEFT() functions—which duplicates what you can do with SUBSTRING()—helps to return only the most important part of a stored value.

While the function names themselves are case-insensitive, I will continue to write them in an all-capitalized format, to help distinguish them from table and column names (as I do with SQL terms). One important rule with functions is that you cannot have spaces between the function name and the opening parentheses, although spaces within the parentheses are acceptable.

To format text:

1. Open the mysql monitor and select the accounting database (**Figure 5.1**).

   mysql -u username -p
   USE accounting;

   As with the previous chapter, from here on I will assume you are already using the *accounting* database within the mysql monitor.

2. Remove all extraneous white spaces from the client names (**Figure 5.2**).

   SELECT TRIM(client_name) FROM clients;

   The TRIM() function will automatically strip white spaces (spaces, tabs, and returns) from both the beginning and end of a string.

3. View all of the area codes of client phone numbers (**Figure 5.3**).

   SELECT RIGHT(LEFT(client_phone, 4), 3)
   → FROM clients WHERE client_phone IS
   → NOT NULL;

   continues on next page

While this query may look very complicated, it's really just a simple adaptation of two functions. The first step is to select every client phone number that is not null. Since phone numbers are stored as, for example, *(123) 456-7890*, I know that the area code is the second through fifth characters. To retrieve this value, I could either use the SUBSTRING() function or use a combination of LEFT() and RIGHT() (as I have to demonstrate how to combine functions). This query will first return the four leftmost characters and then strip that down to the three rightmost characters.

4. Find the longest expense category name (**Figure 5.4**).

SELECT LENGTH(expense_category),
→ expense_category FROM expense_
→ categories ORDER BY LENGTH(expense_
→ category) DESC;

This query returns all of the expense categories, along with their length, but it sorts this data from the longest category on down.

✔ Tips

■ A query like that in step 4 (also Figure 5.4) may be useful for helping to fine-tune your column lengths once your database has some records in it.

■ You can use most of the MySQL functions while running queries other than SELECT. Most frequently you might use a function while formatting data used with an INSERT.

■ Functions can be equally applied to both columns and manually entered strings. For example, the following is perfectly acceptable:

SELECT UPPER('makemebig')

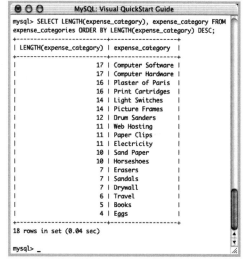

Figure 5.4 You can even use a function within an ORDER BY clause.

TEXT FUNCTIONS

Concatenation and Aliases

CONCAT(), perhaps the most useful of the text functions, deserves its own discussion, along with its frequent SQL companion, aliases. The CONCAT() function accomplishes concatenation, a programming concept for appending multiple values together. The syntax for concatenation requires you to place, within parentheses, the various values you want assembled, in order and separated by commas:

```
CONCAT(column1, column2)
```

While you can—and normally will—apply CONCAT() to columns, you can also incorporate strings, entered within single quotation marks. To format a person's name as *Surname, First* from two columns, you would use

```
CONCAT(last_name, ', ', first_name)
```

Because concatenation is used to create a new value, you'll need a new way to refer to the returned result. This is where the SQL concept of *aliases* comes in. An alias is merely a symbolic renaming and works using the term AS:

```
SELECT CONCAT(last_name, ', ', first_name)
→ AS name FROM users
```

The result of this query would be that all users in the table would have their name formatted as you might want it displayed, and the returned column would be called *name*. This alias is also what you would use within your programming language to refer to the returned values. The general syntax of AS

```
SELECT column AS alias_name FROM table
```

can be applied to any column or columns within a query, as needed, whether or not you alter the values of them.

To use concatenation and aliases:

1. Display all of the client address information as one value (**Figure 5.5**).

   SELECT client_name, CONCAT
   → (client_street, ', ', client_city,
   → ', ', client_state, ' ', client_zip)
   → AS address FROM clients;

   This first use of the CONCAT() function assembles all of the address information into one neat column, renamed address.

2. Select every expense, along with its description and category (**Figure 5.6**).

   SELECT expense_amount, expense_date,
   → CONCAT(expense_category, ': ',
   → expense_description) FROM expenses,
   → expense_categories WHERE expenses.
   → expense_category_id = expense_
   → categories.expense_category_id;

   In this query, I have performed a join so that I can display both expense and expense category information at the same time. The concatenation takes place over two columns from two different tables.

3. Show the ten most-expensive invoices, along with the client name and identification number (**Figure 5.7**).

   SELECT invoices.*, CONCAT(client_name,
   → ' - ', clients.client_id) AS
   → client_info FROM invoices LEFT JOIN
   → clients USING (client_id) ORDER BY
   → invoice_amount DESC LIMIT 10;

   To perform this query, I use a left join, order the results by the *invoice_amount*, and limit the results to just ten records. The CONCAT() function is applied to the client's name and ID.

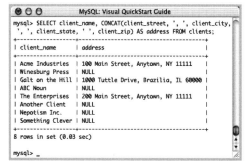

Figure 5.5 The CONCAT() function is one of the most useful tools for refining your query results.

Figure 5.6 Functions can be applied in different ways, including across multiple tables.

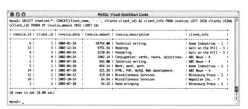

Figure 5.7 The CONCAT() and alias techniques can be applied to any query, including joins.

4. Simplify the query from step 2 using aliases for table names (**Figure 5.8**).

```
SELECT expense_amount, expense_date,
→ CONCAT(expense_category, ': ',
→ expense_description) FROM expenses
→ AS e, expense_categories AS e_c
→ WHERE e.expense_category_id =
→ e_c.expense_category_id;
```

The query itself is the same as it was in step 2 except that I have simplified typing it by using aliases for the table names.

✔ Tips

■ An alias can be up to 255 characters long and is always case-sensitive.

■ The AS term used to create an alias is optional. You could write a query more simply as

```
SELECT column alias_name FROM table
```

■ CONCAT() has a corollary function called CONCAT_WS(), which stands for *with separator*. The syntax is CONCAT_WS(separator, column1, column2, ...). The separator will be inserted between each of the columns listed.

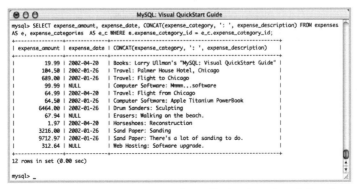

```
mysql> SELECT expense_amount, expense_date, CONCAT(expense_category, ': ', expense_description) FROM expenses
AS e, expense_categories  AS e_c WHERE e.expense_category_id = e_c.expense_category_id;
+----------------+--------------+-------------------------------------------------------------+
| expense_amount | expense_date | CONCAT(expense_category, ': ', expense_description)          |
+----------------+--------------+-------------------------------------------------------------+
|          19.99 | 2002-04-20   | Books: Larry Ullman's "MySQL: Visual QuickStart Guide"       |
|         104.50 | 2002-01-26   | Travel: Palmer House Hotel, Chicago                          |
|         689.00 | 2002-01-26   | Travel: Flight to Chicago                                    |
|          99.99 | NULL         | Computer Software: Mmmm...software                           |
|          64.99 | 2002-04-20   | Travel: Flight from Chicago                                  |
|          64.50 | 2002-01-26   | Computer Software: Apple Titanium PowerBook                  |
|        6464.00 | 2002-01-26   | Drum Sanders: Sculpting                                      |
|          67.94 | NULL         | Erasers: Walking on the beach.                               |
|           1.97 | 2002-04-20   | Horseshoes: Reconstruction                                   |
|        3216.00 | 2002-01-26   | Sand Paper: Sanding                                          |
|        9712.97 | 2002-01-26   | Sand Paper: There's a lot of sanding to do.                 |
|         312.64 | NULL         | Web Hosting: Software upgrade.                               |
+----------------+--------------+-------------------------------------------------------------+
12 rows in set (0.00 sec)

mysql>
```

Figure 5.8 I've simplified my queries, without affecting the end result, by using aliases for my table names (compare with Figure 5.6).

Numeric Functions

Besides the standard math operators that
MySQL uses (for addition, subtraction, multiplication, and division), there are about two
dozen functions dedicated to formatting and
performing calculations on number columns.
Table 5.2 lists the most common of these,
some of which I will demonstrate shortly.

I want to specifically mention three of these
functions: FORMAT(), ROUND(), and RAND().
The first—which is not technically number-
specific—turns any number into a more
conventionally formatted layout. For example,
if you stored the cost of a car as *20198.20,*
FORMAT(car_cost, 2) would turn that number into the more common *20,198.20.*

Numeric Functions

FUNCTION	USAGE	PURPOSE
ABS()	ABS(column)	Returns the absolute value of *column.*
CEILING()	CEILING(column)	Returns the next-highest integer based upon the value of *column.*
FLOOR()	FLOOR(column)	Returns the integer value of *column.*
FORMAT()	FORMAT(column, y)	Returns *column* formatted as a number with *y* decimal places and commas inserted every three spaces.
MOD()	MOD(x, y)	Returns the remainder of dividing *x* by *y* (either or both can be a column).
RAND()	RAND()	Returns a random number between 0 and 1.0.
ROUND()	ROUND(x,y)	Returns the number *x* rounded to *y* decimal places.
SIGN()	SIGN(column)	Returns a value indicating whether a number is negative (-1), zero (0), or positive (+1).
SQRT()	SQRT(column)	Calculates the square root of the column.

Table 5.2 Here are the most-used number functions, omitting the various trigonometry and exponential ones.

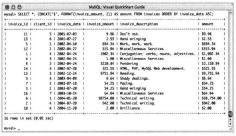

Figure 5.9 Applying two functions and the right formatting to the *invoice_amount* column generates the better *amount* values.

```
●○○          MySQL: Visual QuickStart Guide
mysql> SELECT ROUND(expense_amount), expense_amount
    FROM expenses;
+-----------------------+-----------------+
| ROUND(expense_amount) | expense_amount  |
+-----------------------+-----------------+
|                    20 |           19.99 |
|                   104 |          104.50 |
|                   689 |          689.00 |
|                   100 |           99.99 |
|                    65 |           64.99 |
|                    64 |           64.50 |
|                  6464 |         6464.00 |
|                    68 |           67.94 |
|                     2 |            1.97 |
|                  3216 |         3216.00 |
|                  9713 |         9712.97 |
|                   313 |          312.64 |
+-----------------------+-----------------+
12 rows in set (0.02 sec)

mysql> _
```

Figure 5.10 The ROUND() function is good in cases where decimals may not matter.

ROUND() will take one value, presumably from a column, and round that to a specified number of decimal places. If no decimal places are indicated, it will round the number to the nearest integer. If more decimal places are indicated than exist in the original number, the remaining spaces are padded with zeros (to the right of the decimal point).

The RAND() function, as you might infer, is used for returning random numbers between 0 and 1.0.

SELECT RAND()

A further benefit to the RAND() function is that it can be used with your queries to return the result in a random order.

SELECT * FROM table ORDER BY RAND()

To use numeric functions:

1. Display the invoices by date, formatting the amounts as dollars (**Figure 5.9**).

   SELECT *, CONCAT('$', FORMAT
   → (invoice_amount, 2)) AS amount FROM
   → invoices ORDER BY invoice_date ASC;

   Using the FORMAT() function, as described above, in conjunction with CONCAT(), you can turn any number into a currency format as you might display it in a Web page or application.

2. Round each expense amount to the nearest dollar (**Figure 5.10**).

   SELECT ROUND(expense_amount),
   → expense_amount FROM expenses;

   The ROUND() function, when you do not specify a decimal argument, simply rounds every value to the nearest integer.

continues on next page

NUMERIC FUNCTIONS

3. Retrieve all of the client names in a random order twice (**Figures 5.11** and **5.12**).

SELECT client_id, client_name FROM
→ clients ORDER BY RAND();

Although this may not be the most practical use of the ORDER BY RAND() clause, it does give you an idea of how it works. While the RAND() function is not absolutely random, it is effective enough for most cases. Notice that you do not specify to which column the RAND() is applied.

✔ Tips

■ Along with the mathematical functions listed here, there are a number trigonometry, exponential, and other types of functions available.

■ The MOD() function is the same as using the percentage sign:

SELECT MOD(9,2);

SELECT 9%2;

■ One good use of the ORDER BY RAND() technique are advertising banners in a Web page that could be retrieved from a table randomly.

■ Once again, remember that functions can be applied to columns or to hardcoded values. The following queries are perfectly acceptable:

SELECT ROUND(34.089, 1)

SELECT SQRT(81)

SELECT ABS(-8)

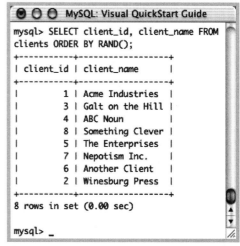

Figure 5.11 Running the same query twice with the ORDER BY RAND() clause...

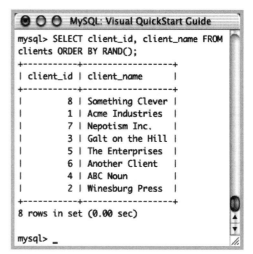

Figure 5.12 ...returns the same results but in different order.

Date and Time Functions

The date and time column types in MySQL are particularly flexible and utilitarian. But because many database users are not familiar with all of the available date and time functions, these options are frequently underused.

Whether you want to make calculations based upon a date or return only the month name from a stored value, MySQL has a function for that purpose. **Table 5.3** lists most of these.

Date and Time Functions

FUNCTION	USAGE	PURPOSE
HOUR()	HOUR(column)	Returns just the hour value of a stored date.
MINUTE()	MINUTE(column)	Returns just the minute value of a stored date.
SECOND()	SECOND(column)	Returns just the second value of a stored date.
DAYNAME()	DAYNAME(column)	Returns the name of the day for a date value.
DAYOFMONTH()	DAYOFMONTH(column)	Returns just the numerical day value of a stored date.
MONTHNAME()	MONTHNAME(column)	Returns the name of the month in a date value.
MONTH()	MONTH(column)	Returns just the numerical month value of a stored date.
YEAR()	YEAR(column)	Returns just the year value of a stored date.
ADDDATE()	ADDDATE(column, INTERVAL x type)	Returns the value of x units added to *column* (see the sidebar).
SUBDATE()	SUBDATE(column, INTERVAL x type)	Returns the value of x units subtracted from *column* (see the sidebar).
CURDATE()	CURDATE()	Returns the current date.
CURTIME()	CURTIME()	Returns the current time.
NOW()	NOW()	Returns the current date and time.
UNIX_TIMESTAMP()	UNIX_TIMESTAMP(date)	Returns the number of seconds since the epoch or since the date specified.

Table 5.3 MySQL uses several different functions for working with dates and times in your databases.

As you can tell, the many date and time functions range from those returning portions of a date column to those that return the current date or time. These are all best taught by example.

To use date and time functions:

1. Display every invoice billed in April (**Figure 5.13**).

   SELECT * FROM invoices WHERE MONTH
   → (invoice_date) = 4;

   Because April is the fourth month, this query will return only those invoices billed then. Another way of writing it would be to use WHERE MONTHNAME (invoice_date) = 'April' (although it's best to use numbers instead of strings wherever possible).

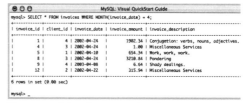

Figure 5.13 Using the MONTH() function, I can narrow down my search results using a date column.

DATE AND TIME FUNCTIONS

ADDDATE() and SUBDATE()

The ADDDATE() and SUBDATE() functions, which are synonyms for DATE_ADD() and DATE_SUB(), perform calculations upon date values. The syntax for using them is

ADDDATE(date, INTERVAL x type)

In the example, *date* can be either an entered date or a value retrieved from a column. The *x* value differs based upon which *type* you specify. The available types are SECOND, MINUTE, HOUR, DAY, MONTH, and YEAR. There are even combinations of these: MINUTE_SECOND, HOUR_MINUTE, DAY_HOUR, and YEARS_MONTH.

To add 2 hours to a date, you would write

ADDATE(date, INTERVAL 2 HOUR)

To add two weeks from December 31, 2002:

ADDDATE('2002-12-31', INTERVAL 14 DAY)

To subtract 15 months from a date:

SUBDATE(date, INTERVAL '1-3' YEAR_MONTH)

This last query tells MySQL that you want to add 1 year and 3 months to the value stored in the *date* column.

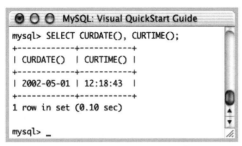

Figure 5.14 The CURDATE() and CURTIME() functions return the current date and time. The same can be accomplished with NOW().

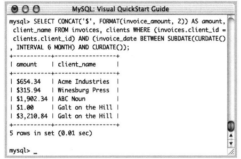

Figure 5.15 Here I've used the CURDATE() function again (see Figure 5.14) to set a range of acceptable dates for selecting invoices.

✔ Tips

- Because MySQL is such a fast and powerful application, you should try to let it handle most of the formatting of values. Beginning programmers will commonly retrieve values from MySQL and then use the programming language to format the data, which is less efficient.

- Be careful when using the ADDDATE() function to include all three *D*'s. It's all too easy to write ADDATE() instead, causing an error. If you continue to make this mistake use DATE_ADD() instead.

2. Show the current date and time, according to MySQL (**Figure 5.14**).

```
SELECT CURDATE(), CURTIME();
```

To show what date and time MySQL currently thinks it is, you can select the CURDATE() and CURTIME() functions, which return these values. This is an example of a query that can be run without referring to a particular table name.

3. Display every invoice amount and client name billed in the past six months (**Figure 5.15**).

```
SELECT CONCAT('$', FORMAT
→ (invoice_amount, 2)) AS amount,
→ client_name FROM invoices, clients
→ WHERE (invoices.client_id =
→ clients.client_id) AND (invoice_date
→ BETWEEN SUBDATE(CURDATE(), INTERVAL
→ 6 MONTH) AND CURDATE());
```

This query uses a lot of different techniques covered to this point. For starters, it's a simple join to incorporate the client's name along with the invoice amount. Second, I've converted the invoice amount into a more readable format. Third, there are two conditions set in the WHERE clause: one for the join and another limiting results to the previous six months. The BETWEEN term is used to specify a range from six months ago SUBDATE(CURDATE(), INTERVAL 6 MONTH) and today CURDATE(), which rules out invoices that may have been pre-billed (i.e., are in the future).

Formatting the Date and Time

There are two additional date and time functions that you might find yourself using more than all of the others combined. These are DATE_FORMAT() and TIME_FORMAT(). There is some overlap between the two in that DATE_FORMAT() can be used to alter both the date and time at the same instance, whereas TIME_FORMAT() can alter only the time value and must be used only if the time value is being altered. The syntax is

```
SELECT DATE_FORMAT(date_column,
→ 'formatting') AS the_date FROM tablename
```

The *formatting* relies upon combinations of key codes and the percentage sign to indicate what values you want returned. **Table 5.4** lists the available date and time formatting parameters. You can use these in any combination, along with textual additions such as punctuation to return a date and time in a more presentable form.

Assuming that a column called *the_date* has the date and time of *2002-04-30 23:07:45* stored in it, common formatting tasks and results would be

◆ Time (11:07:02 PM)

   DATE_FORMAT(the_date, '%r')

◆ Time without seconds (11:07 PM)

   DATE_FORMAT(the_date, '%l:%i %p')

◆ Date (April 30th, 2002)

   DATE_FORMAT(the_date, '%M %D, %Y')

DATE_FORMAT() and TIME_FORMAT() Parameters

TERM	USAGE	EXAMPLE
%e	Day of the month	1-31
%d	Day of the month, two digit	01-31
%D	Day with suffix	1st-31st
%W	Weekday name	Sunday-Saturday
%a	Abbreviated weekday name	Sun-Sat
%c	Month number	1-12
%m	Month number, two digit	01-12
%M	Month name	January-December
%b	Month name, abbreviated	Jan-Dec
%Y	Year	2002
%y	Year	02
%l	Hour	1-12
%h	Hour, two digit	01-12
%k	Hour, 24-hour clock	0-23
%H	Hour, 24-hour clock, two digit	00-23
%i	Minutes	00-59
%S	Seconds	00-59
%r	Time	8:17:02 PM
%T	Time, 24-hour clock	20:17:02
%p	AM or PM	AM or PM

Table 5.4 The terms for date and time formatting are not obvious, but this table lists the most important ones.

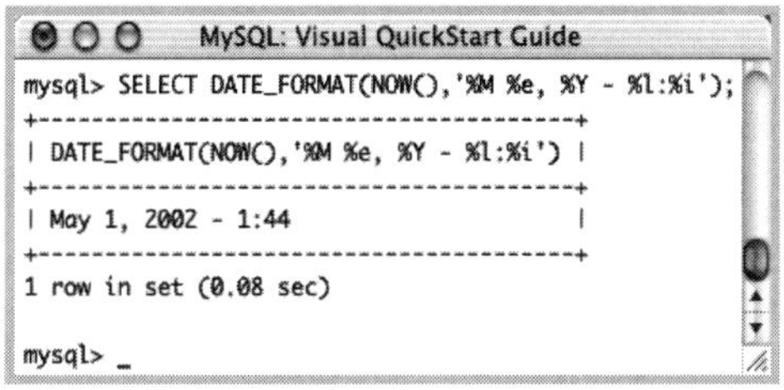

Figure 5.16 The DATE_FORMAT() function uses combinations of parameters to return a formatted date.

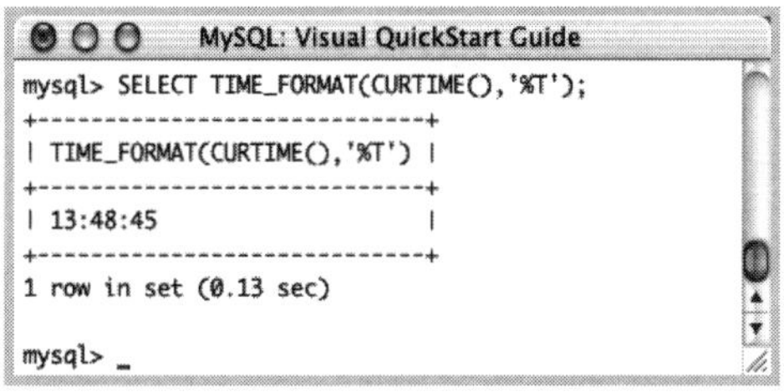

Figure 5.17 If you are formatting the time, you must use the TIME_FORMAT() function.

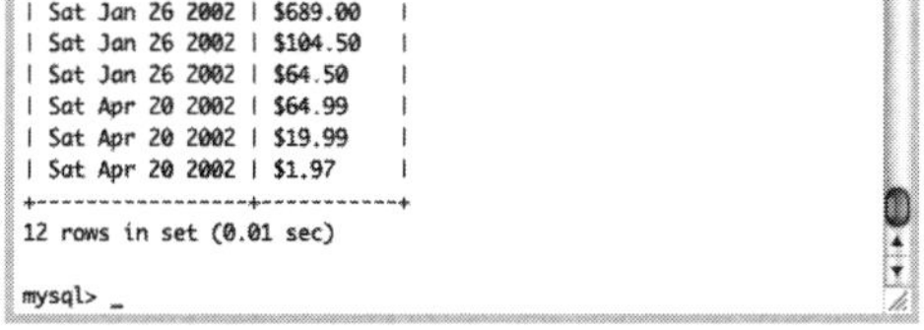

Figure 5.18 DATE_FORMAT() will apply only to stored date values; NULL values will not be affected.

To format the date and time:

1. Return the current date and time as *Month DD, YYYY - HH:MM* (**Figure 5.16**).

   ```
   SELECT DATE_FORMAT(NOW(),'%M %e,
   → %Y - %l:%i');
   ```

   Using the NOW() function, which returns the current date and time, I can practice my formatting to see what results are returned.

2. Display the current time, using 24-hour notation (**Figure 5.17**).

   ```
   SELECT TIME_FORMAT(CURTIME(),'%T');
   ```

   Although the DATE_FORMAT() can be used to format both the date and the time (or just the date), if you want to format just the time, you must use the TIME_FORMAT() function. This can be applied to a time value (like CURTIME() returns) or a date-time value (from NOW()).

3. Select every expense, ordered by date and amount, formatting the date as *Weekday (abbreviated) Day Month (abbreviated) Year* (**Figure 5.18**).

   ```
   SELECT DATE_FORMAT(expense_date,
   → '%a %b %e %Y') AS the_date, CONCAT
   → ('$', FORMAT(expense_amount, 2))
   → AS amount FROM expenses ORDER BY
   → expense_date ASC, expense_amount DESC;
   ```

   This is just one more example of how you can use these formatting functions to alter the output of a SQL query.

FORMATTING THE DATE AND TIME

Encryption Functions

MySQL has several different encryption functions and one decryption function built into the software. You've already seen one of these, PASSWORD(), since it's used to encrypt the various user passwords for MySQL access.

```
INSERT INTO users (user_id, username,
→ user_pass) VALUES (NULL, 'trout',
→ PASSWORD('password'))
```

Another function, ENCRYPT(), is like PASSWORD() in that it returns an encrypted string but differs in that you can add a *salt* parameter to help randomize the encryption process.

```
INSERT INTO users (user_id, username,
→ user_pass) VALUES (NULL, 'trout',
→ ENCRYPT('password', 'salt'))
```

ENCRYPT() uses the Unix crypt() software, so it may not be available on your particular system. MySQL has another encryption function called DES_ENCRYPT(), usable with an SSL connection.

Both the PASSWORD() and ENCRYPT() functions create an encrypted string that cannot be decrypted. This is a great safety feature because it means that stored passwords can never be retrieved in readable form. If you require information be stored in an encrypted form that can be decrypted, you'll need to use ENCODE() and DECODE(). These functions also take a *salt* argument, which helps to randomize the encryption.

```
INSERT INTO users (user_id, username,
→ user_ssn) VALUES (NULL, 'trout',
→ ENCODE('123-45-6789', 'salt'))
SELECT username, DECODE(user_ssn, 'salt')
→ FROM users WHERE user_id=8
```

ENCRYPTION FUNCTIONS

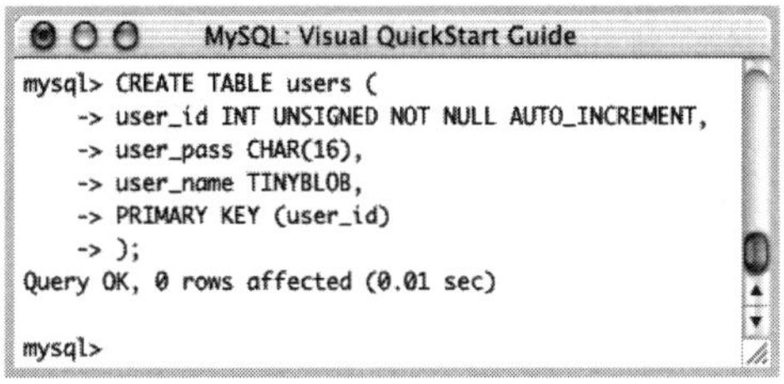

Figure 5.19 The *users* table, while not necessarily part of the *accounting* database, will be used to demonstrate encryption and decryption.

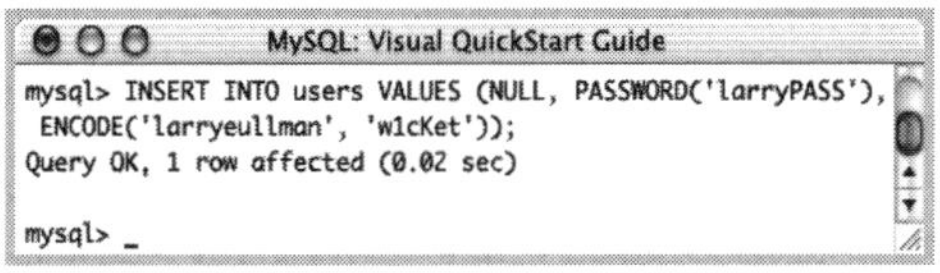

Figure 5.20 I encrypt values when storing them...

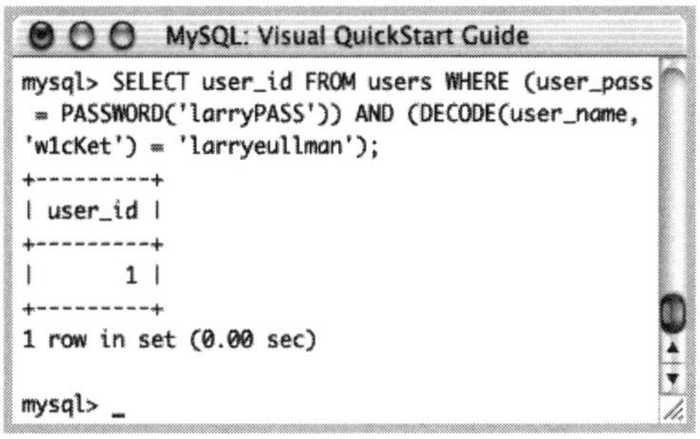

Figure 5.21 ...and decrypt them for retrieval.

To encrypt and decrypt data:

1. Create a new *users* table (**Figure 5.19**).

```
CREATE TABLE users (
user_id INT UNSIGNED NOT NULL
→ AUTO_INCREMENT,
user_pass CHAR(16),
user_name TINYBLOB,
PRIMARY KEY (user_id)
);
```

Because none of the current tables would logically use encryption, I'm creating an arbitrary new one. This table, *users*, will contain a *user_id*, a *user_pass*, and a *user_name*. The *user_pass* field will store a PASSWORD() encrypted string. Since PASSWORD() always returns a string 16 characters long, I'll set this column to be CHAR(16). The *user_name* will be encrypted using ENCODE() so that it can be decoded. ENCODE() returns a binary value that ought to be stored in a BLOB column type.

2. Insert a new user (**Figure 5.20**).

```
INSERT INTO users VALUES (NULL,
→ PASSWORD('larryPASS'), ENCODE
→ ('larryeullman', 'w1cKet'));
```

Here I am adding a new user to the table, using the PASSWORD() function to encrypt the password (*larrypass*) and ENCODE() with a salt of *w1cKet* to encrypt the user name (*larryeullman*).

3. Retrieve the user's information (**Figure 5.21**).

```
SELECT user_id FROM users WHERE
→ (user_pass = PASSWORD('larryPASS'))
→ AND (DECODE(user_name, 'w1cKet') =
→ 'larryeullman');
```

continues on next page

ENCRYPTION FUNCTIONS

Whenever you store a PASSWORD() encrypted string, to make a comparison match, you simply use PASSWORD() again. So, for user registration and log in, you would store passwords this way, then compare it with an encrypted version of the password the user submitted upon log in. If these match, the right password was entered; otherwise, no value will be returned (**Figure 5.22**).

Any value stored using ENCODE() can be retrieved (and matched) using DECODE(), as long as the same salt is used (here, *w1cKet*).

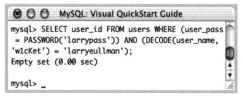

Figure 5.22 These functions are case-sensitive, so entering a password incorrectly will return no results.

✔ Tips

- When using ENCRYPT(), ENCODE(), or DECODE() from a programming language, be sure to store the salt in a secure place.

- The MySQL manual reference page for these functions can be found at www.mysql.com/doc/M/i/Miscellaneous _functions.html.

- As a rule of thumb, use PASSWORD() for information that will never need to be viewable, such as passwords and perhaps user names. Use ENCODE() for information that needs to be protected but may need to be viewable at a later date, such as credit card information, Social Security numbers, addresses (perhaps), and so forth.

ENCRYPTION FUNCTIONS

Grouping Functions

The theory of grouping query results is similar to ordering and limiting query results in that it uses a GROUP BY clause. However, this is significantly different from the other clauses because it functions by grouping the returned data into similar blocks of information. For example, to group all of the invoices by client, you would use

```
SELECT * FROM invoices GROUP BY client_id
```

The returned data is altered in that you've now aggregated the information instead of returned just the specific itemized records. So where you might have seven invoices for one client, the GROUP BY would return all seven of those records as one. I did not discuss the idea in the previous chapter because you will normally use one of several grouping (or aggregate) functions in conjunction with GROUP BY. **Table 5.5** lists these.

Grouping Functions

FUNCTION	USAGE	PURPOSE
MIN()	MIN(column)	Returns the smallest value from the column.
MAX()	MAX(column)	Returns the largest value from the column.
SUM()	SUM(column)	Returns the sum of all of the values in the column.
COUNT()	COUNT(column)	Counts the number of rows.

Table 5.5 The grouping, aka or aggregate, functions are normally used with the GROUP BY clause in a SQL query.

You can apply combinations of WHERE, ORDER BY, and LIMIT conditions to a GROUP BY, normally structuring your query like this:

SELECT columns FROM table WHERE clause
→ GROUP BY column ORDER BY column LIMIT x

To group data:

1. Find the largest invoice amount (**Figure 5.23**).

   SELECT MAX(invoice_amount) FROM
   → invoices;

   Since the MAX() function returns the largest value for a column, this is the easiest way to return the desired result. Another option would be to write SELECT invoice_amount FROM invoices ORDER BY invoice_amount DESC LIMIT 1.

2. Determine how much has been spent under each expense category (**Figure 5.24**).

   SELECT SUM(expense_amount),
   → expense_category FROM expenses LEFT
   → JOIN expense_categories USING
   → (expense_category_id) GROUP BY
   → (expenses.expense_category_id);

   To accomplish this task I first use a left join to incorporate the name of the expense category into the results. Then I simply group all of the expenses together by category ID, and summarize their respective amounts. MySQL will return a table of two columns: the total and the category.

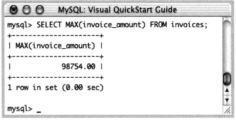

Figure 5.23 The MAX() function performs a type of grouping, even if the GROUP BY clause is not formally stated.

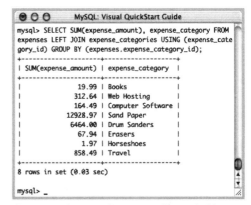

Figure 5.24 The SUM() function can be used with GROUP BY to total up fields with similar *expense_category_id*s.

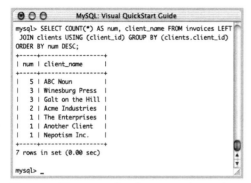

Figure 5.25 The COUNT() function returns the number of records that apply to the GROUP BY criteria (here, *client_id*).

```
● ○ ○        MySQL: Visual QuickStart Guide
mysql> SELECT COUNT(*), SUM(expense_amount), expense_category
FROM expenses LEFT JOIN expense_categories USING (expense_cate
gory_id) GROUP BY (expenses.expense_category_id);
+----------+---------------------+-------------------+
| COUNT(*) | SUM(expense_amount) | expense_category  |
+----------+---------------------+-------------------+
|        1 |               19.99 | Books             |
|        1 |              312.64 | Web Hosting       |
|        2 |              164.49 | Computer Software |
|        2 |            12928.97 | Sand Paper        |
|        1 |             6464.00 | Drum Sanders      |
|        1 |               67.94 | Erasers           |
|        1 |                1.97 | Horseshoes        |
|        3 |              858.49 | Travel            |
+----------+---------------------+-------------------+
8 rows in set (0.01 sec)

mysql> _
```

Figure 5.26 By adding COUNT() to the query in Figure 5.24, I can also show how many invoices are included in each SUM() column.

3. See how many invoices have been billed to each client (**Figure 5.25**).

   SELECT COUNT(*) AS num, client_name
   → FROM invoices LEFT JOIN clients
   → USING (client_id) GROUP BY
   → (clients.client_id) ORDER BY num DESC;

   Whenever you need to determine how many records fall into a certain category, a combination of COUNT() and GROUP BY will get the desired result. I've applied the COUNT() to every column (*) but could use *invoice_id* just the same. With grouping, you can order the results as you would with any other query.

4. Alter the query in step 2 so that it reflects how many invoices are tied into each total amount (**Figure 5.26**).

   SELECT COUNT(*), SUM(expense_amount),
   → expense_category FROM expenses LEFT
   → JOIN expense_categories USING
   → (expense_category_id) GROUP BY
   → (expenses.expense_category_id);

   Here I've used the COUNT() function again, along with an alias, to count each record in each grouping. You can apply multiple aggregate functions within the same query.

✔ Tips

- NULL is a peculiar value, as you've seen, and it's interesting to know that GROUP BY will group NULL values together, since they have the same nonvalue.

- The COUNT() function will count only non-null values.

- The GROUP BY clause, and the functions listed here, take some time to figure out, and MySQL will report an error whenever your syntax is inapplicable. Experiment within the mysql monitor to determine the exact wording of any query you might want to run in an application.

Other Functions

To conclude this chapter, I'll discuss two final functions that do not fit neatly into any of the earlier categories. The first, LAST_INSERT_ID(), is critical for working within a relational database. The second, DISTINCT(), assists you in adjusting what results to return from a table.

LAST_INSERT_ID() is a function that returns the value set by the last INSERT statement for a column that's automatically incremented. For example, in the *accounting* database example, the *expense_categories* table uses an *expense_category_id* column that was defined as a not null, unsigned, integer that was the primary key and would be auto-incremented. This meant that every time a NULL value was entered for that column, MySQL would automatically use the next logical value. LAST_INSERT_ID() will return that value. This, then, can be used as the foreign key in a related table.

SELECT LAST_INSERT_ID()

The DISTINCT() function is used to weed out duplicate values and is normally applied to a column.

SELECT DISTINCT(column) FROM tablename

This is frequently used in conjunction with GROUP BY so that the number of unique records, based upon a category, can be retrieved and possibly counted.

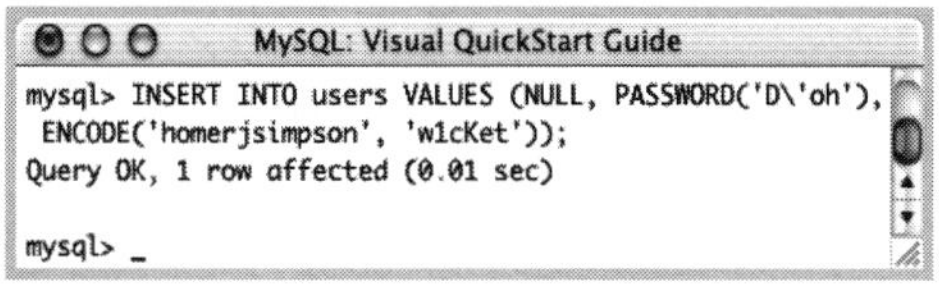

Figure 5.27 To test LAST_INSERT_ID() (Figure 5.28), I'll add another record to the *users* table.

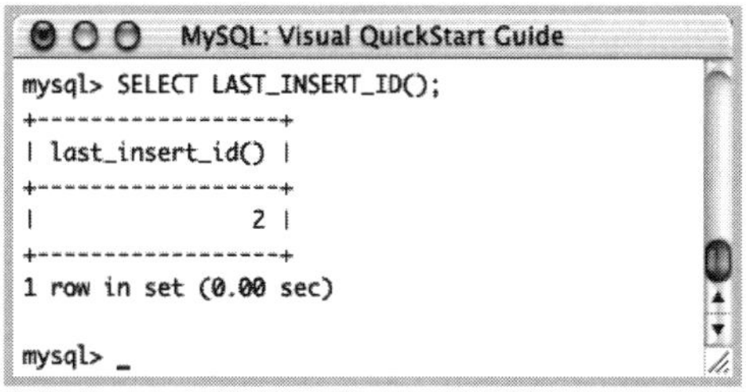

Figure 5.28 LAST_INSERT_ID() is a specific function that returns only the number corresponding to the previous insert.

To use LAST_INSERT_ID():

1. Insert another user into the *users* table (**Figure 5.27**).

```
INSERT INTO users VALUES (NULL,
→ PASSWORD('D\'oh'), ENCODE
→ ('homerjsimpson', 'w1cKet'));
```

Make sure when working with encryption that you use the same encryption function and salt for every record in the table, or else you will have difficulty accurately retrieving data later.

2. Retrieve that user's *user_id* (**Figure 5.28**).

```
SELECT LAST_INSERT_ID();
```

This command returns just one value in one column, which reflects the primary key inserted in place of the NULL in step 1. When using relational databases, use LAST_INSERT_ID() to ensure proper primary key to foreign key integrity.

LAST_INSERT_ID() Confusion

A common misunderstanding about LAST_INSERT_ID() is that it will return the last inserted value into the table, regardless of where it comes from. This is not true. The function will return only the last inserted ID for a query made by the same connection as LAST_INSERT_ID() is called. Therefore, if ten scripts and three mysql monitors are all connected to a database at the same time, and each inserts a value into a table and then recalls this value, each script or monitor will return only the ID correlating to that session's previous insert.

To use DISTINCT():

1. List the different clients that have been billed (**Figure 5.29**).

    SELECT DISTINCT(invoices.client_id),
    → client_name FROM invoices, clients
    → WHERE invoices.client_id =
    → clients.client_id;

    Instead of listing every client for every invoice, this query will list only each unique client.

2. Count how many different clients have been billed (**Figure 5.30**).

    SELECT COUNT(DISTINCT(client_id))
    → FROM invoices;

    The combination of the COUNT() and DISTINCT() functions returns just the one number, rather than every applicable record.

✔ Tips

■ The LAST_INSERT_ID() function is the same as PHP's mysql_insert_id().

■ The LAST_INSERT_ID() function will return the first ID created if you insert several records at one time.

■ There are other miscellaneous MySQL functions, such as DATABASE(), used in SELECT DATABASE(), will tell you which database is currently being used.

■ The USER() function, used like SELECT USER(), will tell you which user is currently being used.

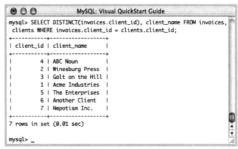

Figure 5.29 DISTINCT() is somewhat like the aggregate functions in that it helps to group the returned records.

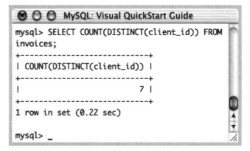

Figure 5.30 Using DISTINCT() along with COUNT() returns the number of unique values in a table.

MySQL and PHP

Of the available APIs that you can use with MySQL, including Perl, Java, C, C++, and Python, PHP may be the most common. An open-source tool, PHP has a sizeable and growing community of users, and its strong integration with MySQL is just one reason so many programmers have embraced it.

Support for the MySQL database, which must be built into the PHP configuration, has been included by default since the advent of PHP version 4. The current version of PHP at the time of this writing (4.2) includes a number of MySQL-specific fixes and upgrades and has support for the forthcoming MySQL 4.0. (I will assume in this chapter that you will be working with version 4.0 or higher of PHP.)

This chapter is for several different types of users: the PHP user who has not yet worked with MySQL; the PHP user who has worked with MySQL but wants a quick refresher on the basics; and non-PHP developers who would like to see how readily PHP interacts with MySQL.

In this chapter I will use the existing *accounting* database, creating a PHP interface for managing the expenses side of the application. Using the knowledge taught here, it would be easy to make the corresponding scripts for the invoices half of the database.

Connecting to MySQL and Selecting a Database

The first step when dealing with MySQL—connecting to the server—requires the appropriately named mysql_connect() function:

$db_connection = mysql_connect (host,
⇢ user,password);

These values are determined based upon the users and privileges set up within the *mysql* database (see Chapter 2, "Running MySQL," for more information). Commonly, the host will be *localhost*, but not necessarily.

The $db_connection variable is a reference point that PHP will use to the newly created connection. Most of the PHP functions for working with MySQL can take this as an optional argument or, if omitted, will automatically use an open connection.

Once you have connected to MySQL, you will need to choose which database you want to work with. This is the equivalent of saying USE databasename within the mysql monitor and is accomplished with the mysql_select _db() function:

mysql_select_db(database_name);

I'll start the demonstration of connecting to MySQL by creating a special file just for that purpose. Every other PHP script that requires a MySQL connection can include this file.

To connect to and select a database:

1. Create a new PHP document in your text editor (**Script 6.1**).

    <?php

2. Add the appropriate comments.

    // ***** mysql_connect.inc *****

    // ***** Script 6.1 *****

    // Developed by Larry E. Ullman

    // MySQL: Visual QuickStart Guide

    // Contact: mysql@DMCinsights.com

Script 6.1 The mysql_connect.inc script will be used by every other script in this application to establish a connection to the database.

```
script
1    <?php
2
3    // ***** mysql_connect.inc *****
4    // ***** Script 6.1 *****
5    // Developed by Larry E. Ullman
6    // MySQL: Visual QuickStart Guide
7    // Contact: mysql@DMCinsights.com
8    // Created: May 7, 2002
9    // Last modified: May 7, 2002
10   // This file contains the database access
     information for the accounting database.
11   // This file also establishes a connection
     to MySQL and selects the accounting
     database.
12
13   // Database-specific information:
14   DEFINE (DB_USER, "username");
15   DEFINE (DB_PASSWORD, "password");
16   DEFINE (DB_HOST, "localhost");
17   DEFINE (DB_NAME, "accounting");
18
19   // Connect to MySQL:
20   $db_connection = mysql_connect (DB_HOST,
     DB_USER, DB_PASSWORD);
21
22   // Select the database:
23   mysql_select_db (DB_NAME);
24   ?>
```

```
// Created: May 7, 2002
// Last modified: May 7, 2002
// This file contains the database
→ access information for the accounting
→ database.
// This file also establishes a
→ connection to MySQL and selects the
→ accounting database.
```

For the most part, I will refrain from including comments within the steps, but I did want to pinpoint these lines to give you a sense of how I might document a configuration file. Also, as a matter of convenience, I'll include the filename and script name as a comment in every script in this book (for easier reference).

3. Set the database host, user name, password, and database name as constants.

```
DEFINE (DB_USER, "username");
DEFINE (DB_PASSWORD, "password");
DEFINE (DB_HOST, "localhost");
DEFINE (DB_NAME, "accounting");
```

I prefer to establish these variables as constants for security reasons (they cannot be changed this way), but that isn't required. Setting these values as some sort of variable makes sense so that you can separate the configuration parameters from the functions that use them, but, again, this is not required.

4. Connect to MySQL.

```
$db_connection = mysql_connect
→ (DB_HOST, DB_USER, DB_PASSWORD);
```

The mysql_connect() function, if it successfully connects to MySQL, will return a resource link that corresponds to the open connection. This link will be assigned to the $db_connection variable, even though I will not directly use this variable in any of the PHP scripts.

continues on next page

5. Select the database to be used.

`mysql_select_db (DB_NAME);`

This final step tells MySQL to which database every query should be applied. Failure to select the database will create problems in later scripts, although if an application uses multiple databases, you might not want to globally select one here.

6. Close the PHP and save the file as

`mysql_connect.inc.`

`?>`

I chose to name the file with a `.inc` extension, which is fine as long as the file is safely stored outside of the Web directory (see step 7). You can also save this file as `.php`, if you prefer.

7. Upload the file to your server, below the Web document root (**Figure 6.1**).

Because the file contains sensitive MySQL access information, it ought to be stored securely. If you can, place it in the directory immediately before or otherwise outside of the Web directory. This way the file will not be accessible from a Web browser. Otherwise, use the `.php` extension and place the file within a password-protected directory.

✔ Tips

■ If you receive an error that claims `mysql_connect()` is an undefined function, it means that PHP has not been compiled with MySQL support.

■ PHP also has a `mysql_pconnect()` function that establishes a permanent connection to MySQL. Using it requires that you rethink your applications because how the database connections are used will differ greatly.

■ Once you've written one `mysql_connect.inc` file, you can easily make changes to the `DEFINE()` lines to use the script for other projects.

Figure 6.1 Assuming that `html` is the root directory of my Web documents (e.g., www.dmcinsights.com would lead there), the configuration files should be stored outside of it.

CONNECTING TO MYSQL AND SELECTING A DATABASE

Executing Simple Queries

Once you have successfully connected to and selected a database, you can start performing queries. These queries can be as simple as inserts, updates, and deletions—as I'll demonstrate here—or as involved as complex joins returning numerous rows, as you'll see later in the chapter. In any case, the PHP function for executing a query is

`mysql_query()`:

```
$query_result = mysql_query($query);
```

The `$query_result` variable will, in layman's terms, contain reference information for the result of a query. In other words, `$query_result` will be a pointer to the data being returned by MySQL and can be used to determine the successful execution of a query.

Two final, albeit optional, steps in your script would be to free up the query result resources and to close the existing MySQL connection:

```
mysql_free_result ($query_result);
mysql_close();
```

The first line removes the overhead (memory) represented by `$query_result`. The second closes the database connection established by the `mysql_connect()` function. Neither of these functions is required because PHP and MySQL will automatically free up the resources and close the connection at the end of a script, but it does make for good programming form.

To demonstrate this process, I'll make a PHP page that displays and handles a form, expressly for the purpose of adding different expense categories to the database.

To execute simple queries:

1. Create a new PHP document in your text editor (**Script 6.2**).

2. Begin with the standard HTML code.

   ```
   <!DOCTYPE html PUBLIC "-//W3C//DTD
   → XHTML 1.0 Transitional//EN"
   "http://www.w3.org/TR/2000/REC-xhtml1-
   → 20000126/DTD/xhtml1-transitional.
   → dtd">
   <html xmlns="http://www.w3.org/1999/
   → xhtml">
   <head>
   <title>Add An Expense Category</title>
   </head>
   <body>
   ```

Script 6.2 This PHP page makes it possible to add records to the database via your Web browser.

```
1    <!DOCTYPE html PUBLIC "-//W3C//DTD XHTML 1.0 Transitional//EN"
2            "http://www.w3.org/TR/2000/REC-xhtml1-20000126/DTD/xhtml1-transitional.dtd">
3    <html xmlns="http://www.w3.org/1999/xhtml">
4    <head>
5        <title>Add An Expense Category</title>
6    </head>
7    <body>
8    <?php
9
10   // ***** add_expense_category.php *****
11   // ***** Script 6.2 *****
12   // This page displays and handles a form for inserting records into the expense_categories table.
13
14   if (isset($HTTP_POST_VARS['submit'])) { // If the form has been submitted, handle it.
15
16       // Check the required form fields.
17       if (strlen($HTTP_POST_VARS['expense_category']) > 0) {
18
19           // Include the MySQL information:
20           require_once ("../mysql_connect.inc");
21
22           // Create the query:
23           $query = "INSERT INTO expense_categories VALUES (NULL, '{$HTTP_POST_VARS['expense_
             category']}')";
24
25           // Execute the query:
26           $query_result = mysql_query ($query);
27
```

Script continues on next page

In this book I will be following XHTML guidelines, so my HTML may look slightly different from what you are accustomed to. This is a minor point and immaterial to the topic at hand.

3. Start the PHP section of the page.

`<?php`

4. Write a conditional that checks if the form has been submitted.

```
if (isset($HTTP_POST_VARS['submit']))
{
```

continues on next page

Script 6.2 *continued*

```
28        // Print a message indicating success or not:
29        if ($query_result) {
30            echo '<b><font color="green">The category has been added!</font></b>';
31        } else {
32            echo '<b><font color="red">The category could not be added!</font></b>';
33        }
34
35        // Free up the resources and close the database connection:
36        mysql_close();
37
38    } else { // Print a message if they failed to enter a category.
39        echo '<b><font color="red">You forgot to enter the category!</font></b>';
40    }
41
42 } else { // If the form has not been submitted, display it.
43
44 // Close out of the PHP for ease of coding.
45 ?>
46        Add a new category to the expense_categories table:<br />
47        <form action="add_expense_category.php" method="post">
48        <input type="text" name="expense_category" size="30" maxlength="30" /><p />
49        <input type="submit" name="submit" value="Submit!" />
50        </form>
51 <?php
52 } // Finish the main "submit" conditional.
53 ?>
54 </body>
55 </html>
```

This page will both display an HTML form and handle its submission. Therefore I'll create one large conditional that determines which step to take (display or handle) based upon whether or not the submit variable has a value. You'll see this pattern repeated in other scripts in this chapter.

5. Verify that all of the required fields were filled out.

```
if (strlen ($HTTP_POST_VARS['expense_
→ category']) > 0) {
```

Because I do not want the script inserting blank expense categories into the table, I first make sure that text was entered into this field before proceeding. As a rule, any field that cannot be NULL in the database, aside from primary keys, ought to be checked by your scripts for values. Validating form-submitted data is critical for the security of your databases!

6. Include the MySQL connection page.

```
require_once ("../mysql_connect.inc");
```

This one line of code will insert the contents of mysql_connect.inc into this script, thereby creating a connection to MySQL and selecting the database. You may need to change the reference to the location of the file as it is on your server.

7. Write and run the query.

```
$query = "INSERT INTO expense_categories
→ VALUES (NULL, '{$HTTP_POST_VARS
→ ['expense_category']}')";
$query_result = mysql_query ($query);
```

This query itself is similar to those demonstrated in Chapter 4, "SQL." After assigning the query to a variable, it is run through the mysql_query() function, which sends the SQL to MySQL.

8. Print out the appropriate messages.

```
if ($query_result) {
echo '<b><font color="green">The
→ category has been added!</font></b>';
} else {
echo '<b><font color="red">The category
→ could not be added!</font></b>';
}
```

The `$query_result` variable, which is assigned the value returned by `mysql_query()`, can be used in a conditional to indicate the successful operation of the query. In this example, you could also save yourself a line of code by writing the conditional as

```
if (mysql_query ($query)) {
```

9. Close the database connection.

```
mysql_close();
```

While closing the database connection is not required, it's always a good idea (assuming the connection is no longer required). In a simple query like this one, there's no need to use the `mysql_free_result()` function because the result of the query is essentially nothing (since no rows of data are returned).

10. Finish up the first part of the conditional and display the second part.

```
} else {
echo '<b><font color="red">You forgot
→ to enter the category!</font></b>';
}
} else {
```

This completes the "handle" part of the script. The rest of this page will be used for displaying the form.

continues on next page

11. Create the HTML form.

```
?>

Add a new category to the expense_
→ categories table:<br />
<form action="add_expense_category.
→ php" method="post">
<input type="text" name="expense_
→ category" size="30" maxlength="30"/>
→ <p />
<input type="submit" name="submit"
→ value="Submit!" />
</form>
```

I've kept the form and HTML as simple as possible. Here you should notice that I use an HTML input name (`expense_category`) that corresponds exactly to what the MySQL column name is. This is not required but makes for fewer mistakes. Also, since this page both displays and handles the form, the `action` attribute refers to this script.

One change you could make would be to offer up multiple text boxes for inserting expense categories. Then you could change your query on the handle side to perform multiple inserts.

12. Complete the script.

```
<?php
}
?>
</body>
</html>
```

13. Save the file as `add_expense_category.php`.

I prefer longer, more descriptive filenames, but if you would like to use something different, be sure to also change the initial `<form>` tag accordingly.

14. Test the file by running the script in your Web browser (**Figures 6.2**, **6.3**, and **6.4**).

After running the script, you can always ensure that it worked by using the mysql monitor to view the values in the table.

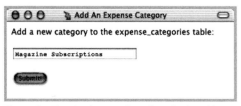

Figure 6.2 The simple HTML form first displayed by `add_expense_category.php` allows you to add records to the *expense_categories* table.

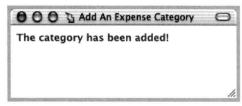

Figure 6.3 The script will display a message indicating successful insertion of a new category...

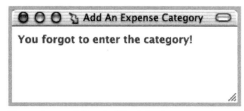

Figure 6.4 ...or failure to fill out the form properly.

✔ Tips

■ You should not end your queries with a semicolon in PHP, as you did when using the mysql monitor. This is a common, albeit harmless, mistake to make.

■ If, in the form, you submit text that contains a single quotation mark, the character will need to be escaped (preceded by a backslash) before the string is inserted into the database. Otherwise, the quotation mark will interfere with those delineating column values. For more information, see the "Magic Quotes" sidebar under "Security" later in this chapter.

■ You are not always obligated to create a $query variable as I tend to do (you could directly insert your query text into mysql_query()). However, as the construction of your queries becomes more complex, using a variable will be the only option.

$HTTP_POST_VARS

For security purposes, I'm making use of PHP's $HTTP_POST_VARS array instead of referring to form variables directly as globals. The difference is that I use, for example, $HTTP_POST_VARS ['expense_category'] instead of $expense_category, which means that when I create my query, I must code {$HTTP_POST_VARS['expense_category']} for PHP to insert the value properly. You can use the $HTTP_POST_VARS array whenever you have a form with a POST method (use $HTTP_GET_VARS with the GET method).

Since PHP has been moving toward limiting usage of global variables, PHP coders should embrace this new technique as well. If you are using version 4.1 of PHP or higher, you can take this one step further and use the superglobal arrays $_POST and $_GET, which are like $HTTP_POST_VARS and $HTTP_GET_VARS but are global in scope.

Retrieving Query Results

In the previous section of this chapter I discussed and demonstrated how to execute simple queries on a MySQL database. A simple query, as I'm calling it, could be defined as one that begins with INSERT, UPDATE, DELETE, or ALTER. What all four of these have in common is that they return no data, just an indication of their success. Conversely, a SELECT query generates information (i.e., it will return rows of records) that has to be handled by other PHP functions.

The primary tool for handling SELECT query results is mysql_fetch_array() which returns one row of data at a time, in an array format. You'll want to use this function within a loop that will continue to access every returned row as long as there are more to be read. The basic construction for reading every record from a query is

```
while ($row = mysql_fetch_array($query_
→ result)) {
// Do something with $row.

}
```

This function takes an optional parameter dictating what type of array is returned: associative, indexed, or both. An associative array allows you to refer to column values by name, whereas an indexed array requires you to use only numbers (starting at 0 for the first column). Each parameter is defined by a constant listed in **Table 6.1**.

To demonstrate how to handle results returned by a query, I will create a script for adding an expense to the database. In the script, a pull-down menu will be created based upon the values in the *expense_categories* table. The overall structure of the script will be very similar to add_expense_category.php.

mysql_fetch_array() Constants

Constant	Example
MYSQL_ASSOC	$row['column']
MSYQL_NUM	$row[0]
MYSQL_BOTH	$row[0] or $row['column']

Table 6.1 Adding one of these constants as an optional parameter to the mysql_fetch_array() function dictates how you can access the values returned.

To retrieve query results:

1. Create a new PHP document in your text editor (**Script 6.3**).

2. Begin with the standard HTML code.

   ```
   <!DOCTYPE html PUBLIC "-//W3C//DTD
   → XHTML 1.0 Transitional//EN"
   "http://www.w3.org/TR/2000/REC-xhtml1-
   → 20000126/DTD/xhtml1-transitional.
   → dtd">
   <html xmlns="http://www.w3.org/1999/
   → xhtml">
   <head>
   <title>Enter An Expense</title>
   </head>
   <body>
   ```

   continues on next page

Script 6.3 The add_expense.php script retrieves the values from the *expense_categories* table to create a pull-down menu.

```
script

1   <!DOCTYPE html PUBLIC "-//W3C//DTD XHTML 1.0 Transitional//EN"
2           "http://www.w3.org/TR/2000/REC-xhtml1-20000126/DTD/xhtml1-transitional.dtd">
3   <html xmlns="http://www.w3.org/1999/xhtml">
4   <head>
5       <title>Enter An Expense</title>
6   </head>
7   <body>
8   <?php
9
10  // ***** add_expense.php *****
11  // ***** Script 6.3 *****
12  // This page displays and handles a form for inserting records into the expenses table.
13
14  // Include the MySQL information:
15  require_once ("../mysql_connect.inc");
16
17  if (isset($HTTP_POST_VARS['submit'])) { // If the form has been submitted, handle it.
18
19      // Check the required form fields:
20      if (isset($HTTP_POST_VARS['expense_category_id']) AND (strlen($HTTP_POST_VARS['expense_
        amount']) > 0) AND (strlen($HTTP_POST_VARS['expense_description']) > 0) ) {
21
22          // Create the query:
23          $query = "INSERT INTO expenses VALUES (NULL, {$HTTP_POST_VARS['expense_category_id']},
            '" . addslashes($HTTP_POST_VARS['expense_amount']) . "', '" .
            addslashes($HTTP_POST_VARS['expense_description']) . "', NOW())";
24
```

Script continues on next page

3. Begin the PHP section and include the MySQL connection script.

```
<?php
require_once ("../mysql_connect.inc");
```

Because both steps of this script (displaying and handling the form) require database access, I'll need to include this file immediately within the PHP, rather than within the conditional, as I had done previously.

Script 6.3 *continued*

```
                                    script
25          // Execute the query and print a message indicating success or not:
26          if (mysql_query ($query)) {
27              echo '<b><font color="green">The expense has been added!</font></b>';
28          } else {
29              echo '<b><font color="red">The expense was not entered into the table!</font></b>';
30          }
31      } else { // Print a message if they failed to enter a required field:
32          echo '<b><font color="red">You missed a required field!</font></b>';
33      }
34
35  } else { // If the form has not been submitted, display it.
36
37      echo 'Enter an expense:<br />
38      <form action="add_expense.php" method="post">
39      Expense Category: <select name="expense_category_id">';
40
41      // Display the expense categories:
42      $query_result = mysql_query ('SELECT * FROM expense_categories ORDER BY expense_category');
43      while ($row = mysql_fetch_array ($query_result, MYSQL_NUM)) {
44          echo "<option value=\"$row[0]\">$row[1]</option>\n";
45      }
46
47      mysql_free_result($query_result);
48      mysql_close();
49
50      // Finish the form:
51      echo '</select><p />
52      Expense Amount: <input type="text" name="expense_amount" size="10" maxlength="10" /><p />
53      Expense Description: <textarea name="expense_description" rows="5" cols="40"></textarea><p />
54      <input type="submit" name="submit" value="Submit!" />
55      </form>';
56
57  } // Finish the main "submit" conditional.
58
59  ?>
60  </body>
61  </html>
```

4. Create the main conditional.

```
if (isset($HTTP_POST_VARS['submit'])) {
```

Once again, this conditional will determine which role (handle or display the form) the script will be playing.

5. Check all of the required form fields.

```
if (isset ($HTTP_POST_VARS['expense_
→ category_id']) AND (strlen ($HTTP_
→ POST_VARS['expense_amount']) > 0)
→ AND (strlen ($HTTP_POST_VARS
→ ['expense_description']) > 0) ) {
```

For this script, I'm checking three fields: the *expense_category_id*, the *expense_amount*, and the *expense_description*. Because the last two inputs are text boxes, which can pass the isset ($HTTP_POST_VARS['expense_amount']) test even if nothing was entered, I instead check to make sure they have a positive string length.

6. Create the appropriate MySQL query.

```
$query = "INSERT INTO expenses VALUES
→ (NULL, {$HTTP_POST_VARS['expense_
→ category_id']}, '" . addslashes
→ ($HTTP_POST_VARS['expense_amount'])
→ . "', '" . addslashes($HTTP_POST_
→ VARS['expense_description']) . "',
→ NOW())";
```

This query differs slightly from that in Script 6.2 because I have incorporated the addslashes() function. This function will automatically escape any problem characters. You will learn more about this issue later in the chapter, but I'm going to start using this technique from here on.

continues on next page

RETRIEVING QUERY RESULTS

7. Run the query.

```
if (mysql_query ($query)) {
echo '<b><font color="green">The
→ expense has been added!</font></b>';
} else {
echo '<b><font color="red">The expense
→ was not entered into the table!</font>
→ </b>';
}
```

As I stated in the previous section, for simple queries, you can make the execution of the query itself a condition, saving yourself a line of code.

8. Complete the first part of the main conditional.

```
} else
{echo '<b><font color="red">You
→ missed a required field!</font></b>';
}
} else {
```

If you wanted to make the script more professional, you could add conditionals here to specify which field or fields in particular were omitted.

9. Start the HTML form.

```
echo 'Enter an expense:<br />
<form action="add_expense.php" method=
→ "post">
Expense Category: <select name=
→ "expense_category_id">';
```

The *expense_category_id* pull-down menu will be created by PHP using the stored values in the database. The first step in making this happen is to create the initial SELECT tag in the HTML form.

10. Generate a pull-down menu based upon the *expense_categories* table.

```
$query_result = mysql_query ('SELECT
→ * FROM expense_categories ORDER BY
→ expense_category');
while ($row = mysql_fetch_array ($query_
→ result, MYSQL_NUM)) {
```

```
echo "<option value=\"$row[0]\">$row[1]
→ </option>\n";

}
```

Turning a table into a pull-down menu is a three-step process:

▲ Create the query and run it.

▲ Retrieve the results using `mysql_fetch_array()` within a loop.

▲ Print out the `<option>` HTML values for each returned row.

For my query—which I directly run in the `mysql_query()` function without the use of a `$query` variable—I have decided to select everything from the table, ordering it by the *expense_category*. The `ORDER BY` aspect of the query will dictate the order of the pull-down menu. The `mysql_fetch_array()` function is fed the `MYSQL_NUM` parameter so that I can only refer to the returned values using indexes (which is not a taxing endeavor since there are only two columns).

11. Free up the MySQL resources and close the database connection.

```
mysql_free_result($query_result);

mysql_close();
```

Since this query returned several rows of data, I'm going to run the `mysql_free_result()` function before formally closing the connection.

12. Complete the HTML form.

```
echo '</select><p />

Expense Amount: <input type="text"
→ name="expense_amount" size="10"
→ maxlength="10" /><p />

Expense Description: <textarea name=
→ "expense_description" rows="5"
→ cols="40"></textarea><p />

<input type="submit" name="submit"
→ value="Submit!" />

</form>';
```

continues on next page

The form finishes the HTML for the pull-down menu and displays the last two input boxes. Make sure that the name of your submit button is the same (capitalization included) as it is in the script's main conditional.

13. Finish the script.

```
}
?>
</body>
</html>
```

14. Save the file as add_expense.php, upload it to your Web server, and test in your browser (**Figures 6.5** and **6.6**).

To see the result of the mysql_fetch_array() function, in conjunction with a *while* loop, also check out the HTML source (**Figure 6.7**).

✔ Tips

■ This book's companion Web site—www.dmcinsights.com/mysql—contains extras that did not make it into the printed book. One such example is a user-defined function for easily creating pull-down menus from database tables.

■ The function mysql_fetch_row() (which you might run across) is the equivalent of mysql_fetch_array($query_link, MYSQL_NUM);

■ The function mysql_fetch_assoc() is the equivalent of mysql_fetch_array($query_link, MYSQL_ASSOC);

■ PHP also has a mysql_fetch_object() function for retrieving query results. It returns a row as an object.

Figure 6.5 This script brings in the values of the *expense_categories* table as a pull-down menu when the user adds an expense.

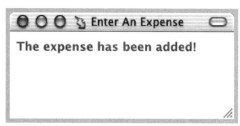

Figure 6.6 If there were no problems adding the expense to the database, a basic message is displayed.

Figure 6.7 Viewing the HTML source of the page (Figure 6.5) reveals the pull-down menu code created by PHP.

Using mysql_insert_id()

Relational databases can be tricky when it comes to using primary and foreign keys. To maintain the integrity of this relationship, a primary key must be created in one table (e.g., *expense_categories*) before being used as a foreign key in another (*expenses*). As you witnessed in Chapter 5, "MySQL Functions," the LAST_INSERT_ID() function works within the mysql monitor to return the previously created primary key (auto-incremented number). In PHP, there is the similar mysql_insert_id() function.

$id = mysql_insert_id();

When making an application based upon a relational database, you'll frequently create scripts like add_expense.php, which ties in the primary key of one table (*expense_categories*) as a foreign key in another (*expenses*). However, if, when adding an expense, you'd like to choose an expense category that has not yet been created, you'll need to establish a new primary key (i.e., a new *expense_category_id*) before using it as a foreign key (in the new expense record). Such situations can be a challenge when using relational databases.

To demonstrate the mysql_insert_id() function, I'll modify the PHP page that displays and handles a form for entering expenses. A pull-down menu of existing expense categories will still be created, but the user will have the option of adding a new expense category on the spot. If a new expense category is entered, it will be added and its primary key will be used as the foreign key within the *expenses* table.

USING MYSQL_INSERT_ID()

To use mysql_insert_id():

1. Open add_expense.php (Script 6.3) in your text editor.

2. Within the first part of the conditional (Script 6.3, line 23), rewrite the query (**Script 6.4**).

   $query = "INSERT INTO expenses VALUES
   → (NULL, ";

   The query in this script will, in the end, be similar to that in Script 6.3, but it will be built differently to take into account the possibility of a new expense category being entered. On this line I have begun the query.

Script 6.4 The more complex add_expense2.php script (as I've called it) can use either a pull-down menu or a new entry for determining the expense category.

```
                                        script
1    <!DOCTYPE html PUBLIC "-//W3C//DTD XHTML 1.0 Transitional//EN"
2            "http://www.w3.org/TR/2000/REC-xhtml1-20000126/DTD/xhtml1-transitional.dtd">
3    <html xmlns="http://www.w3.org/1999/xhtml">
4    <head>
5        <title>Enter An Expense</title>
6    </head>
7    <body>
8    <?php
9
10   // ***** add_expense2.php *****
11   // ***** Script 6.4 *****
12   // This page displays and handles a form for inserting records into the expenses table.
13
14   // Include the MySQL information:
15   require_once ("../mysql_connect.inc");
16
17   if (isset($HTTP_POST_VARS['submit'])) { // If the form has been submitted, handle it.
18
19       // Check the required form fields:
20       if (isset($HTTP_POST_VARS['expense_category_id']) AND (strlen($HTTP_POST_VARS['expense_
         amount']) > 0) AND (strlen($HTTP_POST_VARS['expense_description']) > 0) ) {
21
22           // Start the query:
23           $query = "INSERT INTO expenses VALUES (NULL, ";
24
25           // Determine if a new expense category was entered:
26           if (strlen($HTTP_POST_VARS['expense_category']) > 0) {
27
28               // Create a second query:
```

Script continues on next page

3. Add a new expense category if one was entered.

```
if (strlen ($HTTP_POST_VARS['expense_
→ category']) > 0) {
$query2 = "INSERT INTO expense_categories
→ VALUES (NULL, '" . addslashes($HTTP_
→ POST_VARS['expense_category']) . "')";
if (mysql_query ($query2)) {
echo '<b><font color="green">The expense
→ category has been added!</font></b>
→ <br />';
$query .= mysql_insert_id() . ", ";
} else {
echo '<b><font color="red">The expense
→ category was not entered into the
→ table!</font></b><br />';
$problem = TRUE;
}
} else {
$query .= "{$HTTP_POST_VARS['expense_
→ category_id']}, ";
}
```

continues on next page

Script 6.4 *continued*

```
                                    script
29          $query2 = "INSERT INTO expense_categories VALUES (NULL, '" .
            addslashes($HTTP_POST_VARS['expense_category']) . "')";
30
31          // Execute the second query and react accordingly:
32          if (mysql_query ($query2)) {
33              echo '<b><font color="green">The expense category has been added!</font></b><br />';
34              $query .= mysql_insert_id() . ", ";
35          } else {
36              echo '<b><font color="red">The expense category was not entered into the table!
                </font></b><br />';
37              $problem = TRUE;
38          }
39
40      } else { // Finish the expense_category conditional.
41          $query .= "{$HTTP_POST_VARS['expense_category_id']}, ";
42      }
43
44      // Finish the query:
```

Script continues on next page

This code is an application of that in add_expense_category.php (Script 6.2). First it checks if an expense category was entered. If so, it will add that record to the *expense_categories* table and use the mysql_insert_id() function to add that expense category's primary key value to the main query. Messages are printed indicating the successful running of the query.

If no expense category was entered, the main query will be appended with the *expense_category_id* value, which is set by the pull-down menu based upon existing categories.

Script 6.4 *continued*

```
45        $query .= "'" . addslashes($HTTP_POST_VARS['expense_amount']) . "', '" . addslashes
          ($HTTP_POST_VARS['expense_description']) . "', NOW())";
46
47        // Check to see if there was a problem:
48        if (!$problem) {
49
50            // Print a message indicating success or not:
51            if (mysql_query ($query)) {
52                echo '<b><font color="green">The expense has been added!</font></b>';
53            } else {
54                echo '<b><font color="red">The expense was not entered into the table!</font></b>';
55            }
56        } else { // If there was a problem:
57            echo '<b><font color="red">The expense was not entered into the table because the
                 expense_category could not be added!</font></b>';
58        }
59
60    } else { // Print a message if they failed to enter a required field:
61        echo '<b><font color="red">You missed a required field!</font></b>';
62    }
63
64 } else { // If the form has not been submitted, display it.
65
66    echo 'Enter an expense:<br />
67    <form action="add_expense2.php" method="post">
68    <ul>
69    <li>Expense Category: <select name="expense_category_id">';
70
71    // Display the expense categories:
72    $query_result = mysql_query ('SELECT * FROM expense_categories ORDER BY expense_category');
73    while ($row = mysql_fetch_array ($query_result, MYSQL_NUM)) {
```

Script continues on next page

4. Complete the main query.

```
$query .= "'" . addslashes($HTTP_
→ POST_VARS['expense_amount']) . "',
→ '" . addslashes($HTTP_POST_VARS
→ ['expense_description']) . "',
→ NOW())";
```

5. Check for problems and run the query.

```
if (!$problem) {
if (mysql_query ($query)) {
echo '<b><font color="green">The
→ expense has been added!</font></b>';
} else {
echo '<b><font color="red">The
→ expense was not entered into the
→ table!</font></b>';
}
} else {
echo '<b><font color="red">The
→ expense was not entered into the
→ table because the expense_category
→ could not be added!</font></b>';
```

continues on next page

Script 6.4 *continued*

```
74          echo "<option value=\"$row[0]\">$row[1]</option>\n";
75      }
76
77      mysql_free_result($query_result);
78      mysql_close();
79
80      // Finish the form:
81      echo '</select></li>
82      or<br />
83      <li>Enter a new expense category: <input type="text" name="expense_category" size="30"
        maxlength="30" /></li>
84      </ul>
85      Expense Amount: <input type="text" name="expense_amount" size="10" maxlength="10" /><p />
86      Expense Description: <textarea name="expense_description" rows="5" cols="40"></textarea><p />
87      <input type="submit" name="submit" value="Submit!" />
88      </form>';
89
90  } // Finish the main "submit" conditional.
91
92  ?>
93  </body>
94  </html>
```

The $problem variable, set in Step 3, is TRUE if the script was not able to add the new expense category (in which case, the expense itself should not entered). Otherwise, this part of the script behaves as it previously had.

6. Add an expense_category input to the form.

```
<li>Enter a new expense category:
→ <input type="text" name="expense_
→ category" size="30" maxlength="30"
→ /></li>
```

In addition to adding this field, I've changed the HTML slightly by adding a bullet list so the user sees the two possible options as selecting an expense category or adding a new one.

7. Save the file, upload it to your Web server, and test in a Web browser (**Figures 6.8**, **6.9**, **6.10**, and **6.11**).

For ease of demonstration, I've chosen to rename this script add_expense2.php to distinguish it from its predecessor. With that in mind, I also changed the form's action attribute. This is an optional change.

Figure 6.8 The form is more user-friendly now because it no longer requires the user to create an expense category before entering an expense.

Figure 6.9 Dual messages reveal how the script successfully completed each database insertion.

Figure 6.10 If no new expense category is entered...

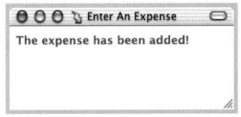

Figure 6.11 ...the script will function as it had before.

✔ Tips

- You must call `mysql_insert_id()` immediately after an `INSERT` query and before running any other queries.

- The `mysql_insert_id()` function will return `0` if no `AUTO_INCREMENT` value was created.

- Remember that when you are dealing with numbers in SQL, they need not be enclosed by quotation marks (in fact, they really shouldn't). For this reason, the *expense_category_id* values are not enclosed. I do enclose the *expense_amount* values, though, because they are coming from a text field and could possibly not be numeric, due to user error.

Error Handling

Error handling, which is important in any script, is even more of an issue when dealing with databases since the probability for errors will increase dramatically. Common errors you will encounter are

◆ Failure in connecting to a database

◆ Failure in selecting a database

◆ Inability to run a query

◆ No results being returned by a query

Experience will teach you why these errors normally occur, but immediately seeing what the problem is in your scripts can save you much debugging time. To have your scripts give informative reports about errors that occur, you make use of the `mysql_error()` and `mysql_errno()` functions. The former will print a textual version of the error that MySQL returned and the latter will return the corresponding number.

Along with these functions are two PHP terms you can use for error handling: @ and `die()`. The @, when used preceding a function name, will suppress any error messages or warnings the function might invoke, while `die()` will terminate the execution of a script and send any message within the parentheses to the Web browser. Normal usage of these would be

```
$db_connection = mysql_connect (DB_HOST,
→ DB_USER, DB_PASSWORD) or die (mysql_
→ error());
$query_result = @mysql_query ($query);
```

As a rule of thumb, use `die()` with any function whose successful execution is mandated by the remainder of the script (such as connecting to MySQL and selecting the database). Use @ with functions that might be problematic but would not necessitate stopping the script.

Script 6.5 In the new version of `mysql_connect.inc`, I've added different error-handling techniques for a more professional result.

```
script
1   <?php
2
3   // ***** mysql_connect2.inc *****
4   // ***** Script 6.5 *****
5   // Developed by Larry E. Ullman
6   // MySQL: Visual QuickStart Guide
7   // Contact: mysql@DMCinsights.com
8   // Created: May 7, 2002
9   // Last modified: May 7, 2002
10  // This file contains the database access
    information for the accounting database.
11  // This file also establishes a connection
    to MySQL and selects the accounting
    database.
12
13  // Database-specific information:
14  DEFINE (DB_USER, "username");
15  DEFINE (DB_PASSWORD, "password");
16  DEFINE (DB_HOST, "localhost");
17  DEFINE (DB_NAME, "accounting");
18
19  // Connect to MySQL:
20  $db_connection = mysql_connect (DB_HOST,
    DB_USER, DB_PASSWORD) or die ('Could not
    connect to MySQL: ' . mysql_error());
21
22  // Select the database:
23  mysql_select_db (DB_NAME) or die ('Could
    not select the database: ' .
    mysql_error());
24  ?>
```

To use error handling:

1. Open `mysql_connect.inc` (Script 6.1) in your text editor.

2. Change the connection code (line 20) to include `die()` and `mysql_error()` (**Script 6.5**).

   ```
   $db_connection = mysql_connect (DB_HOST,
   → DB_USER, DB_PASSWORD) or die
   → ('Could not connect to MySQL: ' .
   → mysql_error());
   ```

   Since the `die()` function can take any string within its parentheses, you can make your error messages as descriptive or customized as you'd like. Here I'm using `mysql_error()` along with a text string, but I could also add HTML formatting to the code.

3. Change the selection code (line 23) to also use these new ideas.

   ```
   mysql_select_db (DB_NAME) or die
   → ('Could not select the database: ' .
   → mysql_error());
   ```

4. Save the file and upload it to your Web server.

   Once again, for ease of reference, I'll be renaming my script as `mysql_connect2.inc`.

continues on next page

5. Test how these changes affect the execution of your scripts by altering the
DB_USER, DB_PASSWORD, DB_HOST, or
DB_NAME values to purposefully create
errors (**Figures 6.12**, **6.13**, and **6.14**).

✔ Tips

■ Appendix A, "Troubleshooting," covers
common MySQL errors in more detail,
along with common causes.

■ Perhaps the best method of debugging
PHP scripts that interact with MySQL is
to use the mysql monitor to confirm
what results you should be seeing.

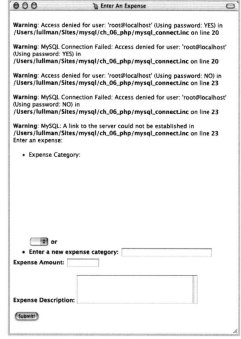

Figure 6.12 Without including error management in
your scripts, a simple mistake can result in multiple
error messages and an ugly page.

Figure 6.13 The or die() construct helps turn the
messages from Figure 6.12 into a less intimidating
and more informative display.

Figure 6.14 If the script could not select the proper
database, a plain message is stated and the script's
execution is halted.

Security

Database security with respect to PHP comes down to two broad issues:

◆ Protecting the database access information

◆ Inspecting the information being stored in the database

You can accomplish the first objective by securing the MySQL connection script. I discussed some of the options for safeguarding the `mysql_connect.inc` file earlier in this chapter. The best, although not always possible, method is to store the file outside of the Web document root (Figure 6.1) so that it is never viewable from a Web browser.

For the second objective, there are numerous options. One, as I've been doing in this chapter, is to use the `$HTTP_POST_VARS` array (or `$HTTP_GET_VARS`, `$_POST`, or `$_GET`) instead of global variables. Second, and this is beyond the scope of this book, is to use regular expressions to make sure that submitted data matches what you would expect it to be. A third option, as I've already incorporated, is to use the `addslashes()` function on submitted data to escape problematic characters. (The same benefit could be achieved by using PHP's Magic Quotes feature, as mentioned in the sidebar.) Finally, as of PHP 4.0.3, you could use the specific `mysql_escape_string()` function:

`$data = mysql_escape_string ($data);`

This function acts like `addslashes()`—and should be used with any form text fields—but is more database-specific.

To demonstrate this function, and also to show one last PHP/MySQL technique, I will write a script that allows a user to edit an expense record.

Magic Quotes

Magic Quotes—PHP's ability to automatically escape problem characters —has changed significantly over PHP's development. As a convenience, Magic Quotes handles single and double quotation marks submitted by an HTML form, retrieved from a database, and so forth. But, to encourage more security-conscious programming, PHP now comes with Magic Quotes disabled. If this is the case with your server, you must use either the `addslashes()` or `mysql_escape_string()` functions instead.

You can easily determine what you need to do by running some of the scripts in this chapter using strings with single quotation marks in them as examples. If the queries are not being entered, Magic Quotes is turned off and you must escape these characters. If data is being entered with multiple backslashes, this means that you have Magic Quotes turned on and are also using `addslashes()` or `mysql_escape_string()` and you should therefore eliminate one of these features.

To use mysql_escape_string():

1. Create a new PHP document in your
text editor, beginning with the HTML
(**Script 6.6**).

```
<!DOCTYPE html PUBLIC "-//W3C//DTD
→ XHTML 1.0 Transitional//EN"
"http://www.w3.org/TR/2000/REC-xhtml1
→ -20000126/DTD/xhtml1-transitional.
→ dtd">
<html xmlns="http://www.w3.org/1999/
→ xhtml">
<head>
    <title>Edit An Expense</title>
</head>
<body>
```

Script 6.6 The final script in this chapter incorporates better security by way of the mysql_escape_string()
function. It also demonstrates how to run an UPDATE query.

```
1   <!DOCTYPE html PUBLIC "-//W3C//DTD XHTML 1.0 Transitional//EN"
2          "http://www.w3.org/TR/2000/REC-xhtml1-20000126/DTD/xhtml1-transitional.dtd">
3   <html xmlns="http://www.w3.org/1999/xhtml">
4   <head>
5       <title>Edit An Expense</title>
6   </head>
7   <body>
8   <?php
9
10  // ***** edit_expense.php *****
11  // ***** Script 6.6 *****
12  // This page displays and handles a form for editing records in the expenses table.
13  // This page requires receipt of an eid (expense_id).
14
15  // Include the MySQL information:
16  require_once ("../mysql_connect.inc");
17
18  if (isset($HTTP_POST_VARS['submit'])) { // If the form has been submitted, handle it.
19
20      // Check the required form fields:
21      if ( (isset($HTTP_POST_VARS['expense_category_id']) OR (strlen($HTTP_POST_VARS['expense_
        category']) > 0)) AND (strlen($HTTP_POST_VARS['expense_amount']) > 0) AND (strlen($HTTP_
        POST_VARS['expense_description']) > 0) ) {
22
23          // Start the query:
24          $query = "UPDATE expenses SET ";
25
26          // Determine if a new expense category was entered:
```

Script continues on next page

2. Start the PHP section, including the MySQL information.

```php
<?php

require_once ("../mysql_connect.inc");
```

If you renamed the mysql_connect.inc script in the previous section, be sure to use the correct script name here.

3. Create the conditional for displaying or handling the form.

```php
if (isset($HTTP_POST_VARS['submit'])) {
```

4. Check the required form fields.

```php
if ( (isset($HTTP_POST_VARS['expense_
→ category_id']) OR (strlen($HTTP_POST_
→ VARS['expense_category']) > 0)) AND
→ (strlen($HTTP_POST_VARS['expense_
→ amount'])> 0) AND (strlen($HTTP_POST_
→ VARS['expense_description']) > 0) ) {
```

continues on next page

Script 6.6 *continued*

```
┌──────────────────────────── script ────────────────────────────┐
27        if (strlen($HTTP_POST_VARS['expense_category']) > 0) {
28
29            // Create a second query:
30            $query2 = "INSERT INTO expense_categories VALUES (NULL, '{$HTTP_POST_VARS['expense_
              category']}')";
31
32            // Execute the second query and react accordingly:
33            if (mysql_query ($query2)) {
34                echo '<b><font color="green">The expense category has been added!</font></b><br />';
35                $query .= "expense_category_id=" . mysql_insert_id() . ", ";
36            } else {
37                echo '<b><font color="red">The expense category was not entered into the table!
                  </font></b><br />';
38                $problem = TRUE;
39            }
40
41        } else { // Finish the expense_category conditional.
42            $query .= "expense_category_id={$HTTP_POST_VARS['expense_category_id']}, ";
43        }
44
45        // Finish the query:
46        $query .= "expense_amount='" . mysql_escape_string($HTTP_POST_VARS['expense_amount']) . "',
          expense_description='" . mysql_escape_string($HTTP_POST_VARS['expense_description']) . "',
          expense_date='" . mysql_escape_string($HTTP_POST_VARS['expense_date']) . "' WHERE
          expense_id={$HTTP_POST_VARS['expense_id']}";
47
```

Script continues on next page

SECURITY

This code is similar to that in
add_expense.php except that I've made a
change by allowing either isset($HTTP_
POST_VARS['expense_category_id'])
or strlen($HTTP_POST_VARS['expense_
category']) > 0). If a choice from the
pull-down menu is selected, the first
condition will be true; if a new category
is entered, the second will be.

5. Begin the query.

```
$query = "UPDATE expenses SET ";
```

Since this form will be for editing existing records, the query will be an UPDATE
rather than an INSERT. Otherwise, this
section (and the next) of the script is
familiar territory.

Script 6.6 *continued*

```
48          // Check to see if there was a problem:
49          if (!$problem) {
50
51              // Execute the query:
52              $query_result = mysql_query ($query);
53
54              // Print a message indicating success or not:
55              if (mysql_affected_rows() == 1) {
56                  echo '<b><font color="green">The expense has been edited!</font></b>';
57              } else {
58                  echo '<b><font color="red">The expense was not edited!</font></b>';
59              }
60          } else { // If there was a problem:
61              echo '<b><font color="red">The expense was not eduted because the expense category
                 could not be added!</font></b>';
62          }
63
64      } else { // Print a message if they failed to enter a required field:
65          echo '<b><font color="red">You missed a required field!</font></b>';
66      }
67
68  } else { // If the form has not been submitted, display it.
69
70      // Create the query:
71      $query = "SELECT * FROM expenses WHERE expense_id = {$HTTP_GET_VARS['eid']} LIMIT 1";
72
73      // Execute the query:
74      $query_result = @mysql_query ($query);
75
```

Script continues on next page

6. Check for a new expense category and handle it accordingly.

```
if (strlen($HTTP_POST_VARS['expense_
→ category'])) > 0) {
$query2 = "INSERT INTO expense_
→ categories VALUES (NULL, '{$HTTP_
→ POST_VARS['expense_category']}')";
if (mysql_query ($query2)) {
echo '<b><font color="green">The
→ expense category has been added!
→ </font></b><br />';
$query .= "expense_category_id=" .
→ mysql_insert_id() . ", ";
} else {
```

continues on next page

Script 6.6 *continued*

```
script
76    // Retrieve and print the results:
77    $row = @mysql_fetch_array ($query_result, MYSQL_ASSOC);
78    @mysql_free_result($query_result);
79
80    echo 'Edit this expense:<br />
81    <form action="edit_expense.php" method="post">
82    <ul>
83    <li>Expense Category: <select name="expense_category_id">';
84
85    // Display the expense categories:
86    $query_result2 = mysql_query ('SELECT * FROM expense_categories ORDER BY expense_category');
87    while ($row2 = mysql_fetch_array ($query_result2, MYSQL_NUM)) {
88        if ($row2[0] == $row['expense_category_id']) {
89            echo "<option value=\"$row2[0]\" selected=\"selected\">$row2[1]</option>\n";
90        } else {
91            echo "<option value=\"$row2[0]\">$row2[1]</option>\n";
92        }
93    }
94
95    @mysql_free_result($query_result2);
96    mysql_close();
97
98    // Finish the form:
99    echo '</select></li>
100   or<br />
101   <li>Enter a new expense category: <input type="text" name="expense_category" size="30"
      maxlength="30" /></li>
102   </ul>
```

Script continues on next page

SECURITY

```
echo '<b><font color="red">The
→ expense category was not entered
→ into the table!</font></b><br />';
$problem = TRUE;
}
} else {
$query .= "expense_category_id={$HTTP_
→ POST_VARS['expense_category_id']}, ";
}
```

One change you'll need to make when using an UPDATE is that instead of a query being of the form INSERT INTO tablename VALUES ('value', 'value2'...), it will now be UPDATE tablename SET column='value', column2='value2', ... In this part of the script, if the *expense_category_id* is changed, it will be updated by the query.

7. Complete the query.

```
$query .= "expense_amount='" . mysql_
→ escape_string($HTTP_POST_VARS
→ ['expense_amount']) . "', expense_
→ description='" . mysql_escape_($HTTP_
→ POST_VARS['expense_description']) .
→ "', expense_date='" . mysql_escape_
→ string($HTTP_POST_VARS['expense_
→ date']) . "' WHERE expense_id={$HTTP_
→ POST_VARS['expense_id']}";
```

Script 6.6 *continued*

```
                                              script
103    Expense Amount: <input type="text" name="expense_amount" value="' . $row['expense_amount'] . '"
       size="10" maxlength="10" /><p />
104    Expense Date: <input type="text" name="expense_date" value="' . $row['expense_date'] . '"
       size="10" maxlength="10" /><p />
105    Expense Description: <textarea name="expense_description" rows="5" cols="40">' . stripslashes
       ($row['expense_description']) . '</textarea>      <p />
106    <input type="submit" name="submit" value="Submit!" />
107    <input type="hidden" name="expense_id" value="' . $HTTP_GET_VARS['eid'] . '" />
108    </form>';
109
110  } // Finish the main "submit" conditional.
111
112  ?>
113  </body>
114  </html>
```

8. Execute the query.

```
if (!$problem) {
$query_result = mysql_query ($query);
if (mysql_affected_rows() == 1) {
echo '<b><font color="green">The
→ expense has been edited!</font>
→ </b>';
} else {
echo '<b><font color="red">The
→ expense was not edited!</font></b>';
}
```

In this example, I've decided to use the `mysql_affected_rows()` function, which returns the number of rows affected by the previous query. It's usable whenever you run an `UPDATE`, `ALTER`, `DELETE`, or `INSERT`.

9. Complete the conditionals.

```
} else {
echo '<b><font color="red">The
→ expense was not eduted because the
→ expense category could not be
→ added!</font></b>';
}
} else {
echo '<b><font color="red">You missed
→ a required field!</font></b>';
}
} else {
```

This completes the "handling" section of the form, which updates the record. The rest of the form will display the record, within an HTML form, for editing purposes.

continues on next page

10. Select the current record from the database.

```
$query = "SELECT * FROM expenses WHERE
→ expense_id = {$HTTP_GET_VARS['eid']}
→ LIMIT 1";
$query_result = @mysql_query ($query);
$row = @mysql_fetch_array ($query_
→ result, MYSQL_ASSOC);
@mysql_free_result($query_result);
```

To edit a record, I'll need to retrieve it from the database. The best way of doing so is to refer to the record's primary key (*expense_id*). This script assumes that it will receive the *expense_id* as a variable called *eid*. Since I am retrieving only one record, there's no need for a more elaborate *while* loop. At the end of this section of code, the $row associative array will contain all of the information related to one expense.

11. Display the HTML form.

```
echo 'Edit this expense:<br />
<form action="edit_expense.php" method=
→ "post">
<ul>
<li>Expense Category: <select name=
→ "expense_category_id">';
```

12. Create the pull-down menu.

```
$query_result2 = mysql_query ('SELECT
→ * FROM expense_categories ORDER BY
→ expense_category');
while ($row2 = mysql_fetch_array
→ ($query_result2, MYSQL_NUM)) {
if ($row2[0] == $row['expense_
→ category_id']) {
echo "<option value=\"$row2[0]\"
→ selected=\"selected\">$row2[1]
→ </option>\n";
} else {
echo "<option value=\"$row2[0]\">
→ $row2[1]</option>\n";
```

```
}
}
@mysql_free_result($query_result2);
mysql_close();
```

This pull-down menu is more involved than the similar one used in **add_expense.php** because I want to match up the current *expense_category_id* value with that in the pull-down menu so the current category is automatically displayed. This can be accomplished with a basic *if-else* conditional and the **selected** HTML code.

13. Finish the rest of the HTML form.

```
echo '</select></li>

or<br />

<li>Enter a new expense category:
→ <input type="text" name="expense_
→ category" size="30" maxlength="30"
→ /></li>

</ul>

Expense Amount: <input type="text"
→ name="expense_amount" value="' .
→ $row['expense_amount'] . '" size=
→ "10" maxlength="10" /><p />

Expense Date: <input type="text"
→ name="expense_date" value="' .
→ $row['expense_date'] . '" size=
→ "10" maxlength="10" /><p />

Expense Description: <textarea
→ name="expense_description" rows="5"
→ cols="40">' . stripslashes($row
→ ['expense_description']) . '
→ </textarea><p />

<input type="submit" name="submit"
→ value="Submit!" />

<input type="hidden" name="expense_id"
→ value="' . $HTTP_GET_VARS['eid'] . '"
→ />

</form>';
```

continues on next page

For standard text inputs and text areas, you can preset a value based upon stored information by using the value attribute for text boxes or simply entering the stored information between the text area tags. The record's primary key must be stored as a hidden variable so that the script knows on which record to run the UPDATE query.

14. Complete the PHP script and the HTML code.

```
}
?>
</body>
</html>
```

15. Save the file as edit_expense.php, upload it to your server, and test in your Web browser (**Figures 6.15**, **6.16**, and **6.17**).

As it stands, to test this script, you'll need to append the URL with code like ?eid=x where *x* refers to an *expense_id* of a record in the database.

✔ Tips

■ The mysql_real_escape_string() function escapes a string in accordance with the language being used, which is an added advantage over addslashes().

■ The information discussed in this and the previous section can easily be applied to the earlier scripts as well to improve their security and error management.

■ On the book's Web site, you can download a browse_expenses.php that links to this edit_expense.php script.

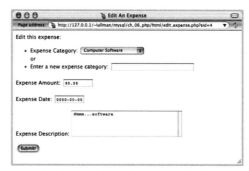

Figure 6.15 Since this record was entered without a date value, I can update that item using this form.

Figure 6.16 As with the other scripts in this chapter, a standard message indicates successful completion of the script.

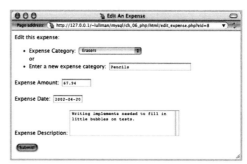

Figure 6.17 The edit_expense.php script, like add_expense.php, also allows you to enter a new category for an item.

7

MySQL and Perl

Long before PHP came along as a major player in Web development, programmers were using Perl (Practical Extraction and Report Language) for system management and Web applications alike. Perl was developed by Larry Wall nearly 20 years ago and since then has become a popular language for writing CGI (Common Gateway Interface) scripts for dynamic HTML creation.

This chapter is for several different types of users. The first would be the Perl user who has not yet worked with MySQL. The second is the Perl user who has worked with MySQL but wants a quick refresher on the basics. Finally, this chapter should be read by non-Perl developers who would like to see how readily Perl interacts with MySQL (especially compared with, say, PHP or Java).

Perl can be used on nearly any operating system, including Unix, Windows, and Macintosh. While you can create CGI scripts with Perl, all of the examples in the chapter will be run as simple Perl scripts on the server, without using a Web browser. I will demonstrate how to install the extra Perl modules to support MySQL, but it will be assumed that you have at least version 5.004 or higher of Perl already.

Installing Perl with MySQL Support on Windows

Although Perl was not created with Windows in mind, being able to program in Perl on your Windows computer is remarkably easy thanks to a product called ActivePerl. ActivePerl is freely distributed by ActiveState, which you can find at www.activestate.com (**Figure 7.1**). ActivePerl is a complete Perl package, easy to install and run on any Windows platform (including non-NT versions such as Me, 98, and 95).

Along with Perl, you will need the DBI and DBD modules to write scripts that interact with MySQL. On Windows, with ActivePerl, you can use the Programmer's Package Manager (PPM) to add the extra DBI and DBD modules. The Programmer's Package Manager (formerly called the Perl Package Manager) comes with ActivePerl and simplifies the task of installing CPAN modules. (CPAN, short for Comprehensive Perl Archive Network, is a library of shared code that simplifies common programming tasks.) Despite all of these different tools, the only requirement of the following installation instructions is that you are connected to the Internet as you proceed through them.

Figure 7.1 The good people at ActiveState (www.activestate.com) maintain ActivePerl, the default Perl distribution for Windows.

Figure 7.2 The ActivePerl Setup Wizard will take you through the installation of Perl on Windows.

Figure 7.3 If ActivePerl was installed correctly, you should see a message like this after running perl -v.

To install Perl with MySQL support on Windows:

1. Download the most current version of ActivePerl from www.activestate.com.

   If you are installing ActivePerl on Windows 2000 or XP, you need to download only the Windows Installer Package (an MSI file). Otherwise, you'll see the other requirements needed for installation when you go through the download steps. At the time of this writing the current version of ActivePerl was 5.6.1.

2. Run the downloaded executable by double-clicking on the file (**Figure 7.2**).

   The installer will take you through a few steps, giving you prompts at certain points to help customize the installation. Accepting the default settings will best ensure problem-free operation of ActivePerl.

   This concludes the installation of ActivePerl on your system. Now you'll need to install the database modules.

3. Access a DOS prompt.

   There are many ways of doing this, including clicking on the Start menu, selecting Run, and entering cmd in the box that appears (then pressing Return).

4. Test that Perl was successfully installed by entering the following and pressing Return (**Figure 7.3**).

   perl -v

   The command perl -v will report on the version of Perl currently installed and running on your system, along with any other pertinent information.

   continues on next page

5. At the prompt, enter ppm (**Figure 7.4**).

This command should start up the ActivePerl Programmer's Package Manager. You'll see a PPM> prompt once you are within the application.

6. Install the DBI module (**Figure 7.5**).

install DBI

After you confirm that you want to install the package, PPM will download and install all of the necessary files.

7. Install the MySQL module for Perl (**Figure 7.6**).

install DBD-MySQL

Once the DBI package has been installed, you'll need to install the database-specific modules, such as DBD-MySQL. The Perl scripts will use DBI and DBD-MySQL together to connect to the databases.

8. Exit out of PPM by entering quit and pressing Return.

✔ Tips

■ ActivePerl is also available in versions for Linux and Solaris, although it's most frequently referenced as a Windows solution.

■ To learn more about Perl and CPAN, see www.perl.com and www.cpan.org, respectively.

■ If you intend to use Perl to write CGI scripts, run install CGI within PPM.

■ Within PPM you can check what modules have been installed by entering query within the application (after step 4).

Figure 7.4 The Programmer's Package Manager simplifies the installation of extra Perl modules.

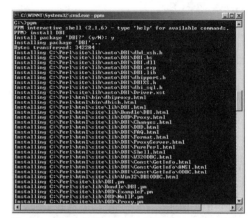

Figure 7.5 Using PPM, you should first install the DBI module for general database interactions.

Figure 7.6 To use Perl with the MySQL database in particular, you'll need to install the DBD-MySQL package.

Installing Perl Support for MySQL on Unix and Mac OS X

Like PHP, Perl is automatically installed on most Unix operating systems, including Mac OS X. Along with Perl you will need several modules to access MySQL, primarily DBI and DBD::mysql. Current versions of these—and a third called Data-Dumper—can be found at www.mysql.com/downloads/api-dbi.html.

You have two options for installation:

◆ Use CPAN

◆ Build and install each manually

The former is much easier than the latter and should be navigable territory for those familiar with Perl. In this section I will manually build and install each module to show how that should be done. These instructions rely upon your having the MySQL client libraries installed on your computer as well as Perl.

To install Perl support for MySQL:

1. Log in as the root user.

   `su root`

   You will need administrative-level access to complete these steps.

2. Download the three required modules from the aforementioned Web address: Data-Dumper, DBI, and Msql-Mysql.

   The MySQL Web site keeps the most current versions of these files, but they are also available through www.cpan.org.

   continues on next page

Perl on Mac OS X

Perl, like PHP, comes built into Mac OS X, but it does not require activation before use. Because manually building and installing different modules is a challenge—and requires extra tools from the Mac OS X Developer's CD-ROM, I recommend beginning OS X programmers use CPAN instead.

CPAN was created to provide a regulated system of code for performing certain tasks. CPAN itself is also able to install modules you might need (in other words, CPAN can upgrade its own capabilities).

To access CPAN, use the Terminal application and enter the following (pressing Return afterward):

`perl -MCPAN -e shell`

The first time you use CPAN, you'll need to answer a slew of questions, most of which will work with the default settings. Once you are in CPAN, you should install several packages, starting with Bundle:: libnet, followed by DBI and DBD::mysql. To install any package with CPAN, enter `install packagename`.

3. Move the downloaded files to the proper directory (**Figure 7.7**).

You can either use mv or drag and drop these three files into the proper directory (which depends upon your Perl installation). In my example, I will use /Library/Perl/darwin.

4. Unpack each file (**Figure 7.8**).

tar zxf Data-Dumper-2.101.tar.gz

tar zxf DBI-1.18.tar.gz

tar zxf Msql-Mysql-modules-1.2216.tar.gz

The tar command will turn each .tar.gz file into an uncompressed folder. You will need to change the particulars of each command so that it refers to the version of each module that you are using.

5. Enter the Data-Dumper directory.

cd Data-Dumper-2.101

6. Run the Makefile script (**Figure 7.9**).

perl Makefile.pl

make

To build each module you will use Perl to run the Makefile.pl script. Next, you run the make command.

7. Make test and make install (**Figure 7.10**).

make test

make install

Follow closely how the make test step works before proceeding to make install. If no or minor problems were reported, it is safe to install the software. Otherwise, you'll need to follow the error messages to see what changes you'll need to make.

One thing the beginning user should keep in mind is that the tests were developed to be run across many different platforms and therefore certain ones may fail on operating systems they were not made for. This is a normal result and not cause for alarm.

Figure 7.7 I will install the extra modules within the system's default Perl directory (which may be different depending upon your operating system).

Figure 7.8 Before building each module, you'll need to decompress them using tar.

Figure 7.9 The first two steps in building each module are to run the Makefile.pl script and then enter the make command.

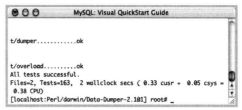

Figure 7.10 If the make test command was successful, you can run make install.

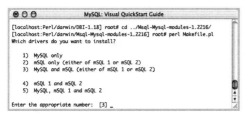

Figure 7.11 The Msql-Mysql `Makefile.pl` script will ask you a number of questions to help configure its installation.

8. Repeat the process to install DBI.

   After you have successfully built the Data-Dumper module, follow steps 5 through 7 for the DBI package.

9. Repeat the process again to install Msql-Mysql (**Figure 7.11**).

   You'll notice that the `Makefile.pl` script for this module is more complex, asking you a number of questions, including:

   ▲ Which driver to install (MySQL, mSQL, or both)

   ▲ Where the MySQL software is located (and/or the mSQL software)

   ▲ The name of a test database

   ▲ The proper host, user name, and password

   The script will provide default options for most of these, but you should make sure it has accurate answers for each prompt, especially if you have customized your MySQL installation. In the end, this script will attempt to connect to the database, verifying that you can use Perl with MySQL.

✔ Tips

- To see if your Perl system is already configured to interact with MySQL, enter `perldoc DBD::mysql` at the prompt.

- Red Hat Linux comes with the DBI Perl module already installed. You can install the MySQL-specific DBD module using an RPM or CPAN.

- MySQL has a discussion list dedicated solely to the Msql-Mysql-modules. You can go there for more information or for solutions to any problems you might encounter. Check the mailing list's archives before posting a new message, though.

Testing Perl and MySQL

Before I go into great detail on how to use Perl to connect to MySQL, I'll go through a quick exercise first. This script will demonstrate how I will be writing Perl scripts throughout the chapter. Further, it will test that MySQL support is available before you start writing the remaining Perl scripts.

While this chapter will in no way replace a solid Perl book or tutorial, I'll quickly go over the steps of a basic Perl script. Even those programmers coming from other languages (such as PHP) ought to be able to follow these guidelines to write basic Perl documents. Also, most of the steps will be explained in some detail here, but knowledge of them will be assumed (and therefore not explained) in later sections.

To write a simple Perl script:

1. Create a new document in your text editor (**Script 7.1**).

   Since Perl scripts are just text files, it will not matter what text editor you use.

2. Include the shebang line (unless you are using ActivePerl on Windows).

   `#!/usr/bin/perl`

   This line tells the server to use the Perl application to process this text file. You'll need to change this line based upon the location of the `perl` file on your system. Another common variant on this version would be `#!/usr/local/bin/perl`. On Windows with ActivePerl, you can omit this line entirely.

3. Enforce strict programming.

   `use strict;`

   The `use strict` command ensures a safer form of programming without adding too much overhead to your scripts. I'll be using it throughout this chapter with the main result being that I need to declare variables before using them (see step 5).

Script 7.1 This simple Perl script tests for the presence of the MySQL driver.

```
                          script
1    #!/usr/bin/perl
2
3    # Script 7.1, 'test.pl'
4
5    # Use what needs to be used.
6    use strict;
7    use DBI;
8
9    # Create the @drivers array.
10   my @drivers = DBI->available_drivers();
11
12   # Print each driver.
13   foreach (@drivers) {
14       print $_ . "\n";
15   }
```

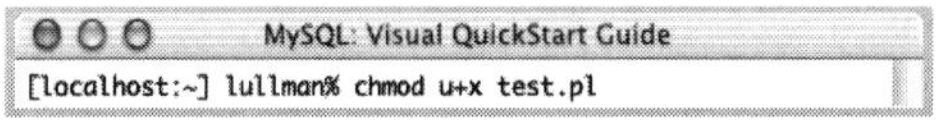

Figure 7.12 To make a file executable (which means it can be run by entering ./filename.pl), you need to change its permissions.

For non-Perl programmers, I'll also mention that every line in Perl, aside from the shebang and control structures, must end in a semicolon. Single-line comments can be preceded by a number (or pound) sign.

4. Include the DBI module.

```
use DBI;
```

This line will be required in all of the scripts throughout this chapter because it tells the script to make use of the DBI module that is used to interact with MySQL.

5. Declare and initialize the required variable.

```
my @drivers = DBI->available_drivers();
```

The @drivers array will contain all of the drivers that are available to the DBI in this particular installation of Perl. Those values are automatically determined by the available_drivers() method of the DBI class. The my statement is required when doing strict programming and you'll see an error if omitted.

6. Loop through and print each driver.

```
foreach (@drivers) {
print $_ . "\n";
}
```

The construct here will loop through the @drivers array, accessing each element one at a time. The elements, now referred to by the special $_ variable, will be printed, followed by a new line (\n).

7. Save the file as test.pl.

I'll be using the .pl extension throughout this chapter (which ActivePerl on Windows will recognize automatically).

8. Change the permissions of the file from the command line, if required (**Figure 7.12**).

```
chmod u+x test.pl
```

continues on next page

On Unix and Mac OS X operating systems, you need to tell the OS that this file should be executable. To do so you use the chmod command to add executable status (x) to the file for the file's user (u). Again, this step is not necessary for Windows users.

9. Run the file.

   On Windows systems, either

   ▲ Enter perl C:\path\to\test.pl at the command prompt and press Return.

   or

   ▲ Double-click on the test.pl file within Explorer (I would advise against this method, though).

   Unix and Mac OS X users can do one of two things:

   ▲ Enter ./test.pl at the command prompt and press Return (**Figure 7.13**).

   or

   ▲ Enter perl /path/to/test.pl at the command prompt and press Return.

   As a rule of thumb, if you use the ./test.pl method, you'll need to include the shebang line and change the file's permissions. When using the two other methods, you can skip those two steps.

   However you run the file, you should see the word *mysql* included in the list of drivers printed out (Figure 7.13). This confirms that you can connect to MySQL from a Perl script.

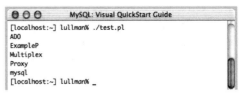

Figure 7.13 Running the script prints out a list of every DBI driver that your Perl installation can now use.

✔ Tips

■ To check a script for problems without executing it, use perl -c /path/to/filename.pl.

■ When specifically using Perl for Web development, you have the option of using the *mod_perl* Apache module, in which case you would use *Apache::DBI* rather than just *DBI*. You'll also need the CGI module.

Connecting to MySQL

Once you know that you can successfully get a Perl script to work and that the mysql DBI module is present, you can start writing scripts that interact with the database. The first step in doing so is to connect to the server.

```
$dbh = DBI-> connect('DBI:mysql:
→ database:host', 'user', 'password',
→ {RaiseError => 1})
```

The first argument in the line above, `DBI:mysql:database:host`, is referred to as the *data source name* and is sometimes assigned to a `$dsn` variable, then incorporated into this function (in which case you should use double quotation marks: `"$dsn"`). The *user* and *password* values are those you need to connect to MySQL, as determined by the *mysql* database. Finally, the `{RaiseError => 1}` part of the line dictates how Perl will manage errors (see the sidebar, "Error Management"). Because DBI includes strong error management, this is probably the best way to handle problems that might occur. The result of the `DBI->connect()` line is assigned to a `$dbh` (database handle) variable that the rest of the script will refer to. Notice that in Perl you specify a database to use when connecting to the MySQL server.

Whenever you use the `DBI->connect()` method, you also need to use `disconnect()` when the script has concluded using the database:

```
$dbh->disconnect();
```

For the first MySQL-Perl script, I'll use these techniques to simply connect to and disconnect from the database. Once you have this working, you can begin to execute queries.

Error Management

RaiseError uses the `die()` function to print an error message and stop the script whenever a MySQL error occurs. Conversely, PrintError prints the message but does not stop the script. To use PrintError, code

```
$dbh = DBI-> connect('DBI:mysql:
→ database:host', 'user', 'password',
→ {PrintError => 1})
```

Another option is to use the `or exit()` construct. This will stop the script if an error occurs, but it allows you to fine-tune your error management.

To reference a specific error, use `DBI->err()` for the error number and `DBI->errstr()` for a textual version. Both of these return errors should they occur in the most recent database interaction.

To connect to MySQL:

1. Create a new text document in your text editor.

2. Start with the shebang line, if necessary (**Script 7.2**).

   ```
   #!/usr/bin/perl
   ```

3. Incorporate the DBI module and enforce strict programming.

   ```
   use DBI;
   use strict;
   ```

4. Connect to MySQL.

   ```
   my $dbh = DBI->connect('DBI:mysql:
   → accounting', 'username', 'password',
   → {RaiseError => 1});
   ```

   For this example, I will be using the *accounting* database that has been discussed throughout the book. Change the *username* and *password* values to whatever has permission to access this database on your server.

5. Print a message indicating success.

   ```
   if ($dbh) {
       print "Successfully connected to the
       → database! \n";
   }
   ```

   The **$dbh** variable, which is a reference to the database connection, can be used to test whether or not the connection went through. Because I am using RaiseError, an inability to establish a connection will kill the script so a "Could not connect to the database!" message (the potential **else** part of this conditional) is unnecessary.

Script 7.2 The mysql_connect.pl script merely checks for a successful connection to the MySQL server.

```
script
1   #!/usr/bin/perl
2
3   # Script 7.2, 'mysql_connect.pl'
4
5   # Use what needs to be used.
6   use DBI;
7   use strict;
8
9   # Connect to the database.
10  my $dbh = DBI->connect('DBI:mysql:
    accounting', 'username', 'password',
    {RaiseError => 1});
11
12  # Report on the success of the connection
    attempt.
13  if ($dbh) {
14      print "Successfully connected to the
        database! \n";
15  }
16
17  # Disconnect.
18  $dbh->disconnect;
```

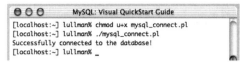

Figure 7.14 If you have the proper permissions to access the database, you'll see this message; otherwise...

Figure 7.15 ...you'll see an error message and the script will stop running.

6. Close the connection.

`$dbh->disconnect;`

This is an important step because it clears up resources used by both MySQL and Perl.

7. Save the file as `mysql_connect.pl`, change the permissions (if necessary), and run the script (**Figures 7.14** and **7.15**).

This script—assuming you have successfully run the `test.pl` script—should work or not work solely on the basis of the permissions of the user name and password you use. If you have problems connecting to the database, check those parameters first.

✔ Tips

- In Perl you cannot make persistent connections to MySQL, as you can with PHP, unless you use mod_perl.

- In the data source name (DSN), `mysql` must be lowercase, and the host can be omitted if it is `localhost`.

CONNECTING TO MySQL

Executing Simple Queries

Once you know how to connect to MySQL, you can start querying the database. There are two general types of queries: those that return records (i.e., SELECT queries) and those that do not (ALTER, CREATE, UPDATE, and DELETE). The first type of queries are more complicated and will be demonstrated next. In this section, I'll show how to execute simple queries using the do() method.

$query = $dbh->do("QUERY STATEMENT");

The do() function is run using the database handler created when connecting to the database (e.g., $dbh). It will normally return the number of rows affected by a query, if applicable.

To demonstrate this function, I'll write a Perl script that will add a new user to the accounting database. The *user* table was added to this database in Chapter 5, "MySQL Functions," and makes use of both the PASSWORD() and ENCODE() functions.

To execute simple queries:

1. Create a new Perl script in your text editor with the standard beginning lines of code (**Script 7.3**).

   ```
   #!/usr/bin/perl
   use DBI;
   use strict;
   ```

2. Prompt for a new user name.

   ```
   print "Enter the new username: ";
   my $username = <STDIN>;
   ```

   This script will prompt for a new user name and a password using <STDIN>. The value keyed in at the prompt will be assigned to the $username variable.

Script 7.3 This script add_user.pl takes inputted information to add records to the database.

```
1   #!/usr/bin/perl
2
3   # Script 7.3, 'add_user.pl'
4
5   # Use what needs to be used.
6   use DBI;
7   use strict;
8
9   # Get the information.
10  print "Enter the new username: ";
11  my $username = <STDIN>;
12  print "Enter the password: ";
13  my $pass1 = <STDIN>;
14  print "Confirm the password: ";
15  my $pass2 = <STDIN>;
16
17  # Make sure the passwords match.
18  while ($pass1 ne $pass2) {
19      print "The passwords you entered did
        not match! Try again!\n";
20      print "Enter the password: ";
21      $pass1 = <STDIN>;
22      print "Confirm the password: ";
23      $pass2 = <STDIN>;
24  }
25
26  # Connect to the database.
27  my $dbh = DBI->connect('DBI:mysql:
        accounting', 'username', 'password',
        {RaiseError => 1});
28
29  # Query the database.
30  my $sql = "INSERT INTO users (user_pass,
        user_name) VALUES (PASSWORD('$pass1'),
        ENCODE('$username', 'w1cKet'))";
31  my $query = $dbh->do ($sql);
32
33  # Report on the success of the query
    attempt.
34  if ($query == 1) {
35      print "The user has been added! \n";
36  } else {
37      print "The user could not be added!
        \n";
38  }
39
40  # Disconnect.
41  $dbh->disconnect;
```

3. Prompt for the password.

```
print "Enter the password: ";
my $pass1 = <STDIN>;
print "Confirm the password: ";
my $pass2 = <STDIN>;
```

To make sure there are no errors in the inputted password, it will be requested twice and then compared.

4. Confirm that the passwords match.

```
while ($pass1 ne $pass2) {
    print "The passwords you entered did
→ not match! Try again!\n";
    print "Enter the password: ";
    $pass1 = <STDIN>;
    print "Confirm the password: ";
    $pass2 = <STDIN>;
}
```

This loop checks to see if the first entered password matches the second, confirmed one. If it does not, it will print an error message and give another chance to re-enter both. This process will be repeated until the passwords match.

5. Establish a connection to the database.

```
my $dbh = DBI->connect('DBI:mysql:
→ accounting', 'username', 'password',
→ {RaiseError => 1});
```

6. Create the query and send it to the database.

```
my $sql = "INSERT INTO users (user_pass,
→ user_name) VALUES (PASSWORD('$pass1'),
→ ENCODE('$username', 'w1cKet'))";
my $query = $dbh->do ($sql);
```

This query is nearly identical to that from Chapter 5 except that it uses the values submitted by a user rather than hard-coded ones. Once the query has been created, it is run through the do() function.

continues on next page

7. Print a message indicating the success of the query.

```
if ($query == 1) {
    print "The user has been added! \n";
} else {
    print "The user could not be added!
    → \n";
}
```

The do() function in step 6 will return the number of affected rows for queries such as ALTER, UPDATE, and DELETE. The number of affected rows was assigned to the $query variable, so if it is equal to 1, the query worked.

8. Close the database connection.

```
$dbh->disconnect;
```

9. Save the file as add_user.pl, change the permissions (if necessary), and run the script (**Figures 7.16** and **7.17**).

✔ Tips

- Do not end your SQL queries with a semicolon as you would within the mysql monitor.

- To simplify the creation of your queries with respect to quotation marks, use qq{}, which will quote the entire phrase and handle single and double quotation marks appropriately.

  ```
  $query = qq{UPDATE table SET column=
  → 'value' where column='othervalue'}
  ```

- To increase the security of this script, you could use regular expressions to check the values entered by the script's user.

- The qq{} technique mentioned above will not escape single and double quotation marks submitted as <STDIN> values. To accomplish this, you can also use regular expressions.

Figure 7.16 When you run the script, you will be prompted three times for information, which will then be added to the database to make a new user.

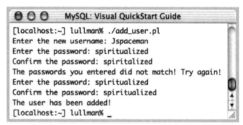

Figure 7.17 If the two passwords entered do not match, you'll be prompted to re-enter these values.

Retrieving Query Results

While executing simple queries with Perl and MySQL is straightforward, retrieving query results is slightly more complicated. First of all, it's a two-step process just to send the query to the database, using the prepare() and execute() methods.

```
$query = $dbh->prepare("SQL QUERY
→ STATEMENT");
```

The result returned by the prepare() call is assigned to a variable that I'll call $query (you'll also see it as $sth, for *statement handle*). Normally before you execute the query, you'll want to make sure that prepare() returned a good result. The easiest way to do so is to use the defined() function.

```
if (defined($query)) {
    $query->execute();
} else {
    print "Could not execute the query! \n";
}
```

After executing the query, you can retrieve all of the returned values using the fetchrow_array() function. It returns each record as an indexed array, beginning with 0. (See the sidebar, "Referring to Columns by Name," for other options.)

```
while (@row = $query->fetchrow_array()) {
    print "$row[1] \n";
}
```

Perl will return the value undef if the column's value is NULL, so it's a good idea to use defined() again to check the value of the column before using it. The defined() function will not catch empty strings, however.

Then, once you have finished retrieving the values, you conclude the query process.

```
$query->finish();
```

continues on next page

Referring to Columns by Name

The fetchrow_array() method is the most efficient and common way to retrieve values from the database, but it does have one significant drawback: You cannot refer to the columns by name to get their values. There are other, more complex, options, though.

The first and easiest is to use fetchrow_hashref(). It works like fetchrow_array() but allows you to name the columns to retrieve their values.

```
while ($row = $query->
→ fetchrow_hashref()) {
    print $row->{'column'};
}
```

Unfortunately, this method is significantly slower than fetchrow_array().

Second, if you know exactly how many columns will be returned, and in what order, you can assign these values to variables when you use fetchrow_array()

```
while ( ($column1, $column2, $column3) =
→ $query->fetchrow_array()) ) {...
```

The third option is to use the bind_col() method to preassign column numbers to variable names. This system requires significantly more programming so see the MySQL and Perl documentation for examples.

As a simple example of using this information, I'll write a Perl script that takes the name of a database as an argument and displays all of the tables in that database.

To retrieve query results:

1. Create a new Perl script (**Script 7.4**).

   ```
   #!/usr/bin/perl
   use DBI;
   use strict;
   ```

2. Determine which database to use and check that one was entered.

   ```
   my $database = $ARGV[0];
   if (defined($database)) {
   ```

   This script will take one argument, the database name. It will be accessed via the @ARGV array and assigned to the $database variable. If the variable has a value, it's safe to proceed with the script.

3. Connect to MySQL and prepare the query.

   ```
   my $dbh = DBI->connect("DBI:mysql:
   → $database", 'username', 'password',
   → {RaiseError => 1});
   my $sql = "SHOW TABLES";
   my $query = $dbh->prepare ($sql);
   ```

   The connection line in this script is slightly different from its predecessors in that it now uses a variable for the database name. To do this, I had to change the quotation marks from single to double, so that the script would insert the value of $database (*interpolate* the variable).

4. Execute the query.

   ```
   if (defined($query)) {
       $query->execute();
   ```

   If the prepare() statement worked, $query has a good value and the query can be executed.

Script 7.4 The browse_tables.pl script is a simple interface to show the table structure of a database.

```
1   #!/usr/bin/perl
2
3   # Script 7.4, 'show_tables.pl'
4
5   # Use what needs to be used.
6   use DBI;
7   use strict;
8
9   # This script takes one argument, the
    database name.
10  my $database = $ARGV[0];
11
12  if (defined($database)) {
13
14      # Connect to the database.
15      my $dbh = DBI->connect("DBI:mysql:
        $database", 'username', 'password',
        {RaiseError => 1});
16
17      # Query the database.
18      my $sql = "SHOW TABLES";
19
20      my $query = $dbh->prepare ($sql);
21
22      if (defined($query)) {
23          $query->execute();
24          my @row;
25          while (@row = $query->
            fetchrow_array()) {
26              foreach (@row) {
27                  print "$_ \n";
28              }
29          }
30      }
31      $query->finish();
32
33      # Disconnect.
34      $dbh->disconnect;
35
36  } else {
37      print "Please enter a database name
        when calling this script! \n";
38  }
```

RETRIEVING QUERY RESULTS

Figure 7.18 The show_tables.pl script will list every table in the database named, such as *accounting* here.

Figure 7.19 As long as the script has permission to access a database, it will list its tables without further modification.

✔ Tips

■ Because this particular query returns only one column per record, you could change the while loop to

```
while (@row = $query->fetchrow_array()) {
    print "$row[0] \n";
}
```

■ You cannot count the number of applicable records to a SELECT query within Perl, but you can mimic this functionality by using MySQL's COUNT() function and returning its result.

■ Assuming you are using a database type that supports transactions (for example, InnoDB), you can use transactions with DBD::mysql as of version 1.2216. See the MySQL manual for more information.

■ The term undef means NULL as well as no result returned.

5. Retrieve and print every record.

```
my @row;
while (@row = $query->fetchrow_array()) {
    foreach (@row) {
        print "$_ \n";
    }
}
```

The most foolproof method to access every column returned for every row is to use this construct here. It will print out each element, one line at a time. With the SHOW TABLES query, each element will be a single table name.

6. Finish the query and close the database connection.

```
}
$query->finish();
$dbh->disconnect;
```

7. Finish the main conditional.

```
} else {
    print "Please enter a database name
    → when calling this script! \n";
}
```

If the script's user failed to enter a database name, a message will be printed saying so.

8. Save the script as show_tables.pl, change the permissions (if necessary), and run the script using the syntax ./show_tables.pl databasename or perl show_tables.pl databasename (**Figures 7.18** and **7.19**).

Remember that your script will still need the proper permissions to access any database you enter here. With that in mind, you'll have the easiest time if you use the root user name and password to connect.

Retrieving the Insert ID

In Chapter 5, "MySQL Functions," I covered the LAST_INSERT_ID() function, which is a MySQL-specific tool for retrieving the value inserted into an auto-incremented field. In Chapter 6, "MySQL and PHP," I demonstrated PHP's mysql_insert_id() function, which serves the same purpose. With Perl, you would use a construct like this:

```
$query = $dbh->do ("INSERT INTO tablename
→ (table_id, column) VALUES (NULL,
→ 'value')");
$insert_id = $dbh->{'mysql_insertid'}
```

With this in mind, I'll modify the add_user.pl script to report back the user number just entered.

To retrieve an insert ID:

1. Open add_user.pl (Script 7.3) in your text editor.

2. After the query has been executed (line 31), add the following (**Script 7.5**):

   my $userid = $dbh->{'mysql_insertid'};

   When a new user is added to the table, a NULL value is given for the user ID. MySQL will then make this value for this record the next-highest integer, on account of its AUTO_INCREMENT attribute. The Perl script will return this value and store it in the $userid variable.

Script 7.5 This script add_user2.pl retrieves the last automatically incremented value from the *users* table.

```
1    #!/usr/bin/perl
2
3    # Script 7.5, 'add_user2.pl'
4
5    # Use what needs to be used.
6    use DBI;
7    use strict;
8
9    # Get the information.
10   print "Enter the new username: ";
11   my $username = <STDIN>;
12   print "Enter the password: ";
13   my $pass1 = <STDIN>;
14   print "Confirm the password: ";
15   my $pass2 = <STDIN>;
16
17   # Make sure the passwords match.
18   while ($pass1 ne $pass2) {
19       print "The passwords you entered did
         not match! Try again!\n";
20       print "Enter the password: ";
21       $pass1 = <STDIN>;
22       print "Confirm the password: ";
23       $pass2 = <STDIN>;
24   }
25
26   # Connect to the database.
27   my $dbh = DBI->connect('DBI:mysql:
     accounting', 'username', 'password',
     {RaiseError => 1});
28
29   # Query the database.
30   my $sql = "INSERT INTO users (user_pass,
     user_name) VALUES (PASSWORD('$pass1'),
     ENCODE('$username', 'w1cKet'))";
31   my $query = $dbh->do ($sql);
32
33   # Retrieve the user_id.
34   my $userid = $dbh->{'mysql_insertid'};
35
36   # Report on the success of the query
     attempt.
37   if ($query == 1) {
38       print "User number $userid has been
         added! \n";
39   } else {
40       print "The user could not be added! \n";
41   }
42
43   # Disconnect.
44   $dbh->disconnect;
```

[localhost:~] lullman% ./add_user2.pl
Enter the new username: air
Enter the password: moonsafari
Confirm the password: moonsafari
User number 19 has been added!
[localhost:~] lullman% _

Figure 7.20 The add_user.pl script (renamed add_user2.pl) will now return the new user's ID.

3. Alter the successful print statement (line 35 of the original script) so that it prints the user ID.

   print "User number $userid has been
   → added! \n";

   To use the retrieved insert ID, I'll just print out the new user's number.

4. Save the script as add_user2.pl, change its permissions, and run the file (**Figure 7.20**).

✔ Tip

- Another option for obtaining the last MySQL insert ID is to use the format $query->{'insertid'}.

Security

Ever since version 3.22 of MySQL, the software has had the extra feature of being able to store particular information in an external configuration file. This information can then be used by the different MySQL clients and APIs automatically. This process is not only easier than manually inputting values, but it can also be more secure.

With the Msql-Mysql-modules (since version 1.2009), you can use one of these configuration files to save yourself the hassle of hard-coding access information in your scripts. To do so, you add the following to the data source name part of the connection:

```
mysql_read_default_file=file_name
```

For example, a modified version of your connection line could be

```
$dbh = DBI->connect('DBI:mysql:
→ databasename;mysql_read_default_file=
→ /path/to/.my.cnf', $user, $password);
```

The script will take get the $user and $password values from the configuration file, which is hopefully stored in a secure location or manner.

MySQL uses a number of different configuration and option files for different purposes. See **Table 7.1** for the list. In short, any parameter that can be added when starting an application from the command line (e.g., --database or --host) can be stored in an option file. Note that MySQL will access these files in the order listed in the table, with later settings overruling those found earlier (in other words, a password in a user's .my.cnf file will overwrite a password stored in a global my.cnf file). Finally, options passed to the application from the command line will overrule any value stored in a file.

Script 7.6 The option file will be used by all MySQL clients so that I no longer have to enter in a user name and password.

```
1   # My configuration file
2   [client]
3   user=username
4   password=password
```

To use a configuration file:

1. Create a new document in your text editor (**Script 7.6**).

   # My configuration file

   Use the pound (or number) sign to create comments, as you would in Perl.

2. Establish the user name and password for accessing the MySQL client.

   [client]

   user=username

   password=password

   The [client] header tells MySQL that the following lines will apply to all client applications. This includes the mysql monitor and Perl scripts. Do not quote your user name or password values.

3. Save the file as

   ▲ ~/.my.cnf on Unix on Mac OS X systems (where ~ is your home directory).

   ▲ C:\my.cnf, C:\WINNT\my.ini, or C:\WINDOWS\my.ini on Windows, changing the drive and pathname accordingly.

continues on next page

SECURITY

Option Files		
FILENAME	**PLATFORM**	**USAGE**
/etc/my.cnf	Unix & Mac OS X	global settings
<DATADIR>/my.cnf	Unix & Mac OS X	server-specific settings (where <DATADIR> is the server's MySQL data directory)
~/.my.cnf	Unix & Mac OS X	user-specific settings (where ~ is the user's home directory)
windows-system-directory\my.ini	Windows	global settings
C:\my.cnf	Windows	global settings

Table 7.1 The MySQL server, its client applications, and even Perl scripts can use option files like these listed here to preset certain parameters.

When saving this file, be careful not to overwrite an existing MySQL configuration file, which is sometimes hidden. On Windows, for example, the WinMySQLAdmin application will have already created a my.ini file. Also, do not forget the initial period in the filename on Unix and Mac OS X platforms.

4. Change the file's permissions.

chmod 600 .my.cnf

This command (for Unix and Mac OS X only) will restrict access to the file so that others cannot view its contents.

Now that the configuration file has been written, I'll improve the security of the mysql_connect.pl script by removing the existing user name and password.

5. Open mysql_connect.pl (Script 7.2) in your text editor.

6. Define two new variables (**Script 7.7**).

my $user;

my $password;

Since I'm using strict programming, I'll need to establish these variables before referring to them. The script will take their values from the configuration file.

7. Alter the connection line to use the option file.

my $dbh = DBI->connect('DBI:mysql:
→ accounting;mysql_read_default_file=
→ ~/.my.cnf', $user, $password,
→ {RaiseError => 1});

You will need to change the syntax of this line so that it correctly refers to the configuration file you created on your server in step 3. You can either use an absolute (e.g., /Users/lullman/.my.cnf) or relative path name (e.g., ../.my.cnf). By using the tilde, I am stating that the configuration file to be used is located in the home directory of the user executing the script.

Script 7.7 The mysql_connect.pl script (renamed) is more secure and portable now because it no longer includes a hard-coded user name and password.

```
1    #!/usr/bin/perl
2
3    # Script 7.7, 'mysql_connect2.pl'
4
5    # Use what needs to be used.
6    use DBI;
7    use strict;
8
9    # Connect to the database.
10   my $user;
11   my $password;
12   my $dbh = DBI->connect('DBI:mysql:
     accounting;mysql_read_default_file=
     ~/.my.cnf', $user, $password,
     {RaiseError => 1}   );
13
14   # Report on the success of the connection
     attempt.
15   if ($dbh) {
16       print "Successfully connected to the
         database! \n";
17   }
18
19   # Disconnect.
20   $dbh->disconnect;
```

SECURITY

Figure 7.21 The connection script still works the same as it previously did, but it does so more securely now.

8. Save the file (I changed the name of mine to `mysql_connect2.pl`) and run it on your server (**Figure 7.21**).

9. If you want, follow steps 5 through 8 to improve the security of your other Perl scripts.

✔ Tips

■ Once you've created an option file, it will be usable by all MySQL applications, not just your Perl scripts.

■ To have a Perl script automatically use a configuration file stored in your home directory (on Unix and Mac OS X systems), you can also use `mysql_read_default_file=$ENV{HOME}/.my.cnf`.

■ To learn more about configuration files, see www.mysql.com/doc/O/p/Option_files.html.

MySQL and Java

Over the past several years, Java has emerged as one of the most popular programming languages, thanks largely to its platform independence. You can use Java to create applets that run on Web pages, to write Java Server Pages (JSPs), or to develop stand-alone applications.

Because Java always uses JDBC (Java Database Connectivity) to connect to a database, if you write your code properly and adhere to SQL standards, your Java applications can be easily ported from platform to platform and database application to database application.

Like the previous two chapters, this one will not teach Java proper, though I will explain how and why I'm writing the scripts I'm writing. Beginning users should be able to write simple Java applications from these instructions. For the most part, the focus will be on using JDBC and the MM.MySQL driver to interact with a MySQL database. The MySQL manual itself has little to offer on the subject, but you can check the JDBC and MM.MySQL documentation for more information on each (Appendix C, "Resources," includes links to both).

Installing Java Support for MySQL

To be able to access a MySQL database from a Java application, you will need two items (aside from MySQL itself):

◆ Java SDK version 1.1 or higher (which includes JDBC)

◆ MM.MySQL

Installing Java itself is beyond the scope of this book but fortunately not a daunting task for the average user. Most developers will be satisfied with using the Java 2 Platform, Standard Edition (J2SE), which can be downloaded from http://java.sun.com. Mac OS X users benefit from Apple's tight integration of Java into the operating system (Mac OS X version 10.1.5 comes with version 1.3.1 of J2SE), whereas Windows has intermittently supported the technology over its evolution.

In this section, I will demonstrate how to make the MM.MySQL driver usable with your current Java setup.

To install MM.MySQL:

1. Download the current version of MM.MySQL from http://mmmysql. sourceforge.net (**Figure 8.1**).

   Currently Mark Matthews, the creator of the driver, has version 2.0.14 of the driver available for download as a jar file.

2. Unjar the downloaded file using one of these applications:

   ▲ jar xvf /path/to/filename.jar (command line)

   ▲ StuffIt (Macintosh)

   ▲ WinZip (Windows)

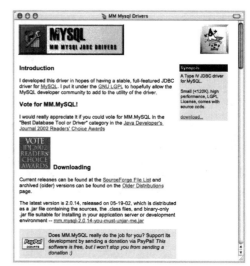

Figure 8.1 The MM.MySQL driver is hosted at SourceForge.net, along with thousands of other open source projects.

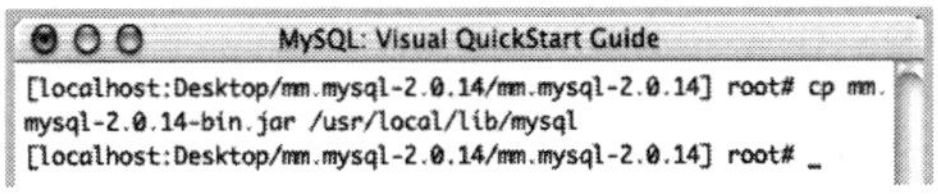

Figure 8.2 To make use of the JDBC driver, it must be stored in a logical location and the classpath must be adjusted accordingly (Figure 8.3).

The *jar* extension indicates that the file is a Java archive that will need to be expanded, much like a Stuffed (`.sit`) or Zipped (`.zip`) archive. You can do this using the specific Java tool, *jar*, or with almost any other extraction application.

At the time of this writing, the MM.MySQL driver is available as one large jar file that must be unjarred. Once you've expanded the downloaded file, you will find the actual driver, which is also a jar file. The difference between these two jar files can be confusing, but fortunately the down-loaded file uses the phrase *you-must-unjar-me* in its name.

3. Move the driver to its new location (**Figure 8.2**).

```
cp mm.mysql-2.0.14-bin.jar /path/to
→ directory
```

The command above will move the file through the command prompt, or you can use Windows Explorer.

In reality, the location of the driver does not matter as long as the application that uses it can find it. Common locations could be

- ▲ `C:\java`
- ▲ `C:\Program Files\j2sdk1.4.01\lib\ext`
- ▲ `/usr/local/lib/mysql`
- ▲ `<JAVA_HOME/>jre/lib/ext`

These are all logical destinations, the last of which refers to the Java root directory on your computer. Another very easy option is to place the driver in the same directory as the scripts that will be using it.

continues on next page

4. Add your chosen location and file to your classpath, if necessary (**Figure 8.3**).

```
java set CLASSPATH=/path/to/
→ mm.mysql-2.0.14-bin.jar
```

If you decided to use the binary version of the driver, a statement like this one—entered at the command prompt—will tell Java how to find the driver. An easier option would be to specify the classpath when you run a script. Finally, if the driver is in the same directory as the script that will use it or if it is within the lib/ext directory of your Java root, you can skip this step.

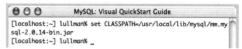

Figure 8.3 Setting the classpath is a crucial step in guaranteeing that your applications can use the driver.

✔ Tips

- For a deployed Web application, place the JDBC driver (the .jar file) in the WEB-INF/lib directory.

- For development purposes, you can also use the expanded mm.mysql class files by adding the org directory and its contents to your classpath, rather than the mm.mysql-2.0.14-bin.jar file.

- You can set multiple classpaths, which will most likely be required, by separating each with a semicolon.

- Be careful with all of your commands, class names, and file names, as Java is case-sensitive.

Connecting to the Database

Before I demonstrate how to use JDBC in more detail, it's best to confirm that you can successfully connect to the database. Frequently this can be the most taxing step in the whole process. It starts with stating that you want to use the SQL classes:

```
import java.sql.*;
```

Then, if you are using the JDBC DriverManager, you specify which `java.sql.Driver` class to use:

```
Class.forName("org.gjt.mm.mysql.Driver");
```

Next, you can established a connection to the database using the DriverManager:

```
Connection con = DriverManager.getConnection
→ (url, "username", "password");
```

The `url` value is a string that indicates the database, host name, and more, in the format *jdbc:protocol:subprotocol*, where *protocol* (in this case) would be `mysql`, and *subprotocol* would include the host name, the port, and the database name, like so (the square brackets indicate optional parameters):

```
jdbc:mysql://[hostname][:port]/
→ databasename
```

As an example, to connect to the *test* database, without specifying a host, your `url` would be

```
jdbc:mysql:///test
```

To specify the host and the port, use

```
jdbc:mysql://localhost:3306/test
```

At the end of the script, after all of the MySQL interaction has been completed, you should close the database connection and free up its resources using the connection's `close()` method:

```
con.close();
```

To connect to MySQL:

1. Create a new Java class in your text editor or Java development tool (**Script 8.1**).

   As long as you have Java installed, you can write the scripts in nearly any text editor. If you have a particular program for coding, compiling, and running Java, so much the better.

2. Use the sql classes and define the class.

   ```
   import java.sql.*;
   public class Connect {
       public static void main(String
       → args[]) throws Exception {
   ```

   The first application I will write will be called Connect and have just one main block of code to be executed. I'll use this basic format throughout the chapter.

Script 8.1 This simple Java class establishes a connection to a MySQL database.

```
1    import java.sql.*;
2
3    public class Connect {
4
5        public static void main(String args[]) throws Exception {
6            Connection con = null;
7
8            try {
9                String url = "jdbc:mysql:///test";
10               Class.forName("org.gjt.mm.mysql.Driver");
11               con = DriverManager.getConnection(url, "", "");
12
13               if (con != null) {
14                   System.out.println("A database connection has been established!");
15               }
16           }
17
18           finally {
19               if( con != null ) {
20                   try {
21                       con.close();
22                   } catch( Exception e ) {
23                       System.out.println(e.getMessage());
24                   }
25               }
26           }
27       }
28   }
```

3. Initialize the connection variable.

```
Connection con = null;
```

The con variable will be of type `java.sql.Connection`, as defined by the `java.sql.*` classes. Here I'm setting its initial value to `null`.

4. Establish a connection to the *test* database.

```
try {
    String url = "jdbc:mysql:///test";
    Class.forName("org.gjt.mm.mysql.
    → Driver");
    con = DriverManager.getConnection
    → (url, "", "");
```

The second line of this group defines the JDBC `url` variable (the address for connecting to the database). The third line dictates which driver should be loaded, and the final line attempts to make a connection, assigning the connection to the previously established con variable.

In this example I am not using a specific host name, user name, or password. This is fine as long as the permissions on your MySQL database allow for an unnamed user without a password from any host to connect to the *test* database. If the permissions would not allow for this, the Java application will fail here and you should change the settings accordingly. Using the proper user name, password, and host is critical to the success of your Java applications.

5. Print a message if the connection was made.

```
if (con != null) {
    System.out.println("A database
    → connection has been established!");
}
```

continues on next page

CONNECTING TO THE DATABASE

To a degree, this code is not really necessary because a failure to connect to the database will throw an error. On the other hand, should the connection be made, I'd like to indicate its success somehow.

6. Complete the try clause and wrap up the class.

```
}
finally {
if( con != null ) {
    try {
        con.close();
    } catch( Exception e ) {
        System.out.println
        → (e.getMessage());
    }
}
}
}
}
}
```

From the perspective of MySQL, the only relevant line here is `try { con.close(); }`, which closes an open database connection. If for some reason it cannot close the connection, the error message will be reported.

7. Save the file as `Connect.java`.

Per Java's syntax, you will need to make sure you name the file using the same spelling and capitalization as the name of the class.

8. Compile `Connect.java`.

There are two primary options for doing this:

▲ Type `javac /path/to/Connect.java` at a command prompt.

or

▲ Use your Java development application to compile the class.

Figure 8.4 Successfully running the application creates this message.

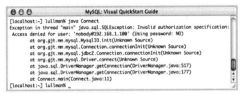

Figure 8.5 If Connect cannot connect to the database, an error will be reported (here, "Access denied for user...").

9. Run Connect (**Figures 8.4** and **8.5**).

Again, two choices:

▲ Type java Connect at a command prompt from within the same directory as the Connect.java file.

or

▲ Use your Java development application to run the class.

If you have not already added the driver to the default classpath, stored the driver in the same directory as Connect.java, or changed the classpath so that Java otherwise knows where to find the driver, you'll need to tell Java the driver's location when you run the file. To do so, at the command prompt you would instead type

```
java -cp .;/path/to/
→ mm.mysql-2.0.14-bin.jar Connect
```

✔ Tips

■ The org.gjt.mm.mysql.Driver class name refers to the location of the driver class files, which you'll find within the org/gjt/mm/mysql directory that comes with the MM.MySQL driver.

■ Sometimes if you specify localhost as the host, Java will replace this value with the IP address of the host (e.g., *192.168.1.1* or *127.0.0.1*), which may interfere with the permissions as established in the MySQL database.

■ You can add extra parameters to your url string by using this format:

```
jdbc:mysql:///test?name=value&name2=
→ value2.
```

For example:

```
jdbc:mysql:///test?user=John&password=
→ Javaman
```

CONNECTING TO THE DATABASE

Executing Simple Queries

Once you've been able to successfully connect to the database, you can start interacting with it. For beginners, the easiest first thing to do is to execute a simple query—one that alters a database without returning any results. Queries that begin with INSERT, ALTER, CREATE, DELETE, or UPDATE fall into this category.

Running a simple query is a two-step process. First you create a statement variable that will be used to run the query, then you execute a query using the statement variable. Commonly your code might look like this:

```
Statement stmt;

stmt = con.createStatement();

stmt.executeUpdate("DELETE FROM tablename
→ WHERE column = 'value'");

stmt.close();
```

The createStatement() method creates an open channel through which queries can be run. The executeUpdate() method actually runs the query on the database, and then the close() method will free up the resources assigned to the open connection. As a basic example of this, I'll write an application that takes command-line arguments for populating the *clients* table in the *accounting* database.

To execute a simple query:

1. Create a new Java application in your text editor or Java development tool (**Script 8.2**).

```
import java.sql.*;

public class Insert {

    public static void main(String
    → args[]) throws Exception {
```

The beginning part of this script differs from Script 8.1 only in the name of the class, changing *Connect* to *Insert*.

2. Initialize the variables.

```
Connection con = null;
Statement stmt = null;
```

Along with a connection variable, simple queries will require a variable of type `Statement`.

continues on next page

Script 8.2 The `Insert` Java class takes three command-line arguments and adds them as the client name, contact's first name, and contact's last name in the *clients* table.

```
                                            script
1    import java.sql.*;
2
3    public class Insert {
4
5        public static void main(String args[]) throws Exception {
6            Connection con = null;
7            Statement stmt = null;
8
9            try {
10               String url = "jdbc:mysql:///accounting";
11               Class.forName("org.gjt.mm.mysql.Driver");
12               con = DriverManager.getConnection(url, "username", "password");
13
14               stmt = con.createStatement();
15               stmt.executeUpdate("INSERT INTO clients (client_name, contact_first_name, contact_
                 last_name) VALUES ('" + args[0] + "', '" + args[1] + "', '" + args[2] + "')");
16               System.out.println("The values were added to the database!");
17           }
18
19           catch (SQLException e) {
20               e.printStackTrace();
21           }
22
23           finally {
24               if ( con != null ) {
25                   try {
26                       con.close();
27                       stmt.close();
28                   } catch( Exception e ) {
29                       System.out.println(e.getMessage());
30                   }
31               }
32           }
33       }
34   }
```

3. Establish a connection to the *accounting* database.

```
try {
    String url = "jdbc:mysql:///
    ⇢ accounting";
    Class.forName("org.gjt.mm.mysql.
    ⇢ Driver");
    con = DriverManager.getConnection
    ⇢ (url, "username", "password");
```

There are three very significant changes you'll need to make in this script compared with the previous one: the database name (from *test* to *accounting*), the user name, and the password. Be certain to use a user/password combination that has permission to connect to and modify the *accounting* database.

4. Execute an INSERT query.

```
stmt = con.createStatement();
stmt.executeUpdate("INSERT INTO clients
⇢ (client_name, contact_first_name,
⇢ contact_last_name) VALUES ('" +
⇢ args[0] + "', '" + args[1] + "', '" +
⇢ args[2] + "')");
System.out.println("The values were
⇢ added to the database!");
```

The first step is to establish the `stmt` variable based upon the `createStatement()` method of the `con` connection variable. Then the query is fed as an argument to the `executeUpdate()` method. In this example, I'll be adding a client's name along with a contact's first and last name. These values will be retrieved as command-line arguments typed when the application is run. To access their values, I refer to `args[0]` through `args[2]`, which is established in the initial class line.

5. Complete the `try` clause and catch any errors that might have occurred.

```
}
catch (SQLException e) {
    e.printStackTrace();
}
```

Figure 8.6 I can use Java to add records to a database by typing new values on the command line as I run the application.

The catch block of code will report on any errors caught by MySQL when executing the query. It's similar in usage and result to the System.out.println(e.getMessage()) line used in the Connect class.

6. Wrap up the class.

```
finally {
if( con != null ) {
    try {
        con.close();
        stmt.close();
    } catch( Exception e ) {
    System.out.println(e.getMessage());
    }
}
}
}
}
```

One addition to this script is that I now formally close the stmt variable as well as con. Closing these frees up the resources they require while the application is running.

7. Save the file as Insert.java.

8. Compile Insert.java.

9. Run Insert (**Figure 8.6**).

To run the application, follow the steps as explained in the previous section of this chapter, but be sure to add the three requisite arguments (for the client name, contact first name, and contact last name):

```
java -cp .;/path/to/mm.mysql-2.0.14-bin.jar Insert client contact1 contact2
```

✔ Tip

■ To use spaces within the command-line arguments fed to a Java application, quote the entire string to distinguish it from the other arguments (see Figure 8.6).

Retrieving Query Results

While a simple query is easy to execute (as in the previous example), the more complicated queries that select records from a database will require slightly more complicated Java applications.

First of all, instead of using the executeUpdate() function, you'll need to run the query through the executeQuery() method. This function returns a ResultSet variable, which will be used to access each returned row. The easiest way to do so is to use a while loop and the next() method:

```
while (results.next()) {
// Do something with the results.
}
```

One way of managing the results is to assign the column values to variables, based upon the value type. The getInt() function will retrieve an integer value and getString() manages text. Both of these will accept either the column name or number (indexed starting at 1) as an argument.

```
while (rs.next()) {
    int key = rs.getInt("id");
    String value = rs.getString
    → ("stringcolumnname");
}
```

To retrieve query results:

1. Create a new Java application in your text editor or Java development tool (**Script 8.3**).

   ```
   import java.sql.*;
   public class Select {
       public static void main(String
       → args[]) throws Exception {
   ```

2. Initialize the variables.

   ```
   Connection con = null;
   Statement stmt = null;
   ResultSet rs = null;
   ```

   The application will introduce a new variable called rs of type ResultSet. This variable will be used to access the results of the query.

   continues on next page

Script 8.3 The Select class runs a basic query on a table and displays the results.

```
1    import java.sql.*;
2
3    public class Select {
4
5        public static void main(String args[]) throws Exception {
6            Connection con = null;
7            Statement stmt = null;
8            ResultSet rs = null;
9
10           try {
11               String url = "jdbc:mysql:///accounting";
12               Class.forName("org.gjt.mm.mysql.Driver");
13               con = DriverManager.getConnection(url, "username", "password");
14
15               stmt = con.createStatement();
16               rs = stmt.executeQuery("SELECT client_id, client_name FROM clients LIMIT 5");
17
18               while (rs.next()) {
19                   int key = rs.getInt("client_id");
20                   String value = rs.getString("client_name");
21
22                   System.out.println(key + ": " + value + "\n");
23               }
24           }
25
```

Script continues on next page

3. Establish a connection to the *accounting* database.

```
try {
    String url = "jdbc:mysql:///
    → accounting";
    Class.forName("org.gjt.mm.mysql.
    → Driver");
    con = DriverManager.getConnection
    → (url, "username", "password");
```

Again, be certain to use a user/password combination that has permission to connect to and select from the *accounting* database.

4. Execute a SELECT query.

```
stmt = con.createStatement();
stmt.executeQuery("SELECT client_id,
→ client_name FROM clients LIMIT 5");
```

Like before, the first step is to establish the stmt variable based upon the createStatement() method of the con connection variable. Then the query is fed as an argument to the executeQuery() method, rather than the executeUpdate() used previously. For demonstration purposes, this query will display five records of client information. Naturally, you can run any sort of SELECT query from Java, as long as it is SQL2 compliant.

5. Print out the returned rows.

```
while (rs.next()) {
    int key = rs.getInt("client_id");
    String value = rs.getString
    → ("client_name");
    System.out.println(key + ": " +
    → value + "\n");
}
```

This loop will retrieve every record returned by the query (which should be five at the most). Then I use the getInt() and getString() methods to retrieve the value of an integer and a string column type, respectively. To use these, I refer to the column name specifically.

Script 8.3 *continued*

```
 script
26          catch (SQLException e) {
27              e.printStackTrace();
28          }
29
30          finally {
31              if (rs != null) {
32                  try {
33                      rs.close();
34                  } catch (SQLException e) {
35                      e.printStackTrace();
36                  }
37              }
38              if (stmt != null) {
39                  try {
40                      stmt.close();
41                  } catch (SQLException e) {
42                      e.printStackTrace();
43                  }
44              }
45              if (con != null) {
46                  try {
47                      con.close();
48                  } catch (SQLException e) {
49                      e.printStackTrace();
50                  }
51              }
52          }
53      }
54  }
```

6. Complete the **try** clause and catch any errors that might have occurred.

```
}
catch (SQLException e) {
    e.printStackTrace();
}
```

7. Wrap up the class, closing all resources.

```
finally {
    if (rs != null) {
        try {
            rs.close();
        } catch (SQLException e) {
            e.printStackTrace();
        }
    }
    if (stmt != null) {
        try {
            stmt.close();
        } catch (SQLException e) {
            e.printStackTrace();
        }
    }
    if (con != null) {
        try {
            con.close();
        } catch (SQLException e) {
            e.printStackTrace();
        }
    }
}
}
}
```

continues on next page

RETRIEVING QUERY RESULTS

Especially when dealing with SELECT queries, freeing up the resources of a statement and a result set is a good programming practice. This will be more and more true as your queries become more complex. In the final clause, I attempt to close the result set, statement, and connection (in that order), if each has a value.

8. Save the file as Select.java, compile, and run the application (**Figure 8.7**).

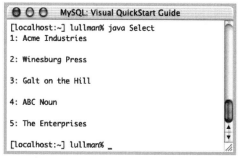

Figure 8.7 The Select class will run a query and display the results.

✔ Tips

■ As of JDBC 2.0, you can scroll through result sets using next()—as demonstrated in this section—and previous().

■ When using the getInt() and getString() functions, referring to columns by their index is faster than referring to columns by name.

■ The getMetaData() function can be used to find out information about a particular column, such as its name, data type, etc.

Using Property Files

Throughout this chapter I have made it a practice to hard code the database name, user name, and password into each application I wrote. While this will work, it's not an ideal solution in terms of both programming and security.

With this in mind, I'd like to introduce one final concept, called a property file. A property file is much like a configuration file that a PHP programmer might write or a .my.cnf file used by Perl: It lists all the application-specific criteria. Then, should any key piece of information change, such as the database name, the database application being used, or the password, an alteration to the property file will stand as a change to the parameters of every script using it. More importantly for Java users, changes can be made to the property file without requiring that the class be recompiled.

A property file is a basic text file with lines in the format of *name=value*. Normally you would save this file with the `.properties` extension for Java uses.

Once you've written a property file, you can use the `ResourceBundle` class (from the `java.util` package) to access it:

```
ResourceBundle bundle =
→ ResourceBundle.getBundle
→ ("PropertyFileName");
String name = bundle.getString("name");
```

Notice that you refer to the filename, without its extension, when setting the `ResourceBundle` variable.

With this in mind, I'll create a basic property file for all of the scripts in this chapter to use. I'll also modify `Connect.java` to make use of the property file.

To use a property file:

1. Create a new text document in a text editor (**Script 8.4**).

2. Assign the *Driver*, *URL*, *User*, and *Password* values.

   ```
   Driver=org.gjt.mm.mysql.Driver
   URL=jdbc:mysql:///accounting
   User=username
   Password=password
   ```

   This property file will record these four parameters. (You could also add the host name to the URL, should you choose.) Notice that you do not want to quote any of these values.

3. Save the file as `Accounting.properties`.

   You will want to save this file in the same directory as the scripts that will be using it.

   Now that the property file has been created, I'll alter `Connect.java` to use it.

4. Open `Connect.java` (Script 8.1) in your text editor or Java development application.

5. Import the `java.util.*` classes, after line 1 (**Script 8.5**).

   ```
   import java.util.*;
   ```

   The `java.util` package contains the `ResourceBundle` class. Importing all of the `java.util` classes will allow the application to use the `ResourceBundle` to retrieve values from an external source.

Script 8.4 The property file will store application variables in a separate document.

```
1   Driver=org.gjt.mm.mysql.Driver
2   URL=jdbc:mysql:///accounting
3   User=username
4   Password=password
```

6. Change the original line 3 to reflect the new class name.

`public class Connect2 {`

For ease of demonstration, I'll be changing the name of the class and therefore need to change that value here. This step is optional.

7. Alter the original line 6 to establish a ResourceBundle variable.

`ResourceBundle bundle =`
`→ ResourceBundle.getBundle`
`→ ("Accounting");`

The appropriately named `bundle` variable will be used to access all of the information stored in the property file.

continues on next page

Script 8.5 The modified `Connect.java` (which I've renamed as `Connect2`) no longer uses hard-coded connection values.

```
1    import java.sql.*;
2    import java.util.*;
3
4    public class Connect2 {
5
6        public static void main(String args[]) throws Exception {
7            Connection con = null;
8            ResourceBundle bundle = ResourceBundle.getBundle("Accounting");
9
10           try {
11               String url = bundle.getString("URL");;;
12               Class.forName(bundle.getString("Driver"));
13               con = DriverManager.getConnection(url, bundle.getString("User"), bundle.getString
                 ("Password"));
14
15               if (con != null) {
16                   System.out.println("A database connection has been established!");
17               }
18           }
19
20           finally {
21               if( con != null ) {
22                   try { con.close(); }
23                   catch( Exception e ) { }
24               }
25           }
26       }
27   }
```

8. Modify the `try` clause to get values from the bundle.

```
try {
String url = bundle.getString("URL");;
Class.forName(bundle.getString
→ ("Driver"));
con = DriverManager.getConnection
→ (url, bundle.getString("User"),
→ bundle.getString("Password"));
if (con != null) {
System.out.println("A database
→ connection has been established!");
}
}
```

In this section of the application, Java will use fetched values for the driver, URL, user name, and password, rather than hard-coded values. With this structure, the script can stay the same from platform to platform and from database application to database application by only modifying the property file.

9. Save the file as `Connect2.java`, compile, and run the class (**Figure 8.8**).

If you did not change the name of the class, save the file as `Connect.java` instead. Regardless, be sure to save the file in the same directory as the `Accounting.properties` file.

✔ Tip

■ Using the `ResourceBundle` class like this is admittedly a kludge solution. Another, perhaps more likely option, would be to use the `Properties` class instead, although it's a slightly more involved method.

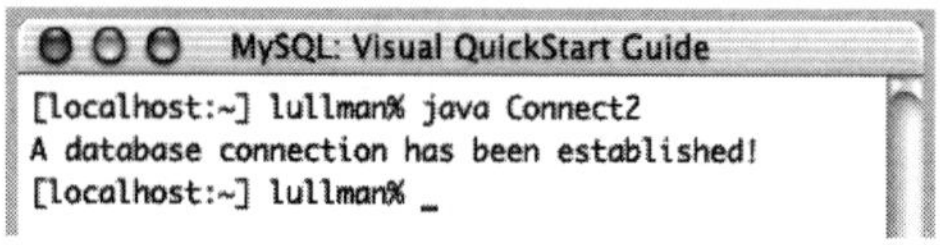

```
[localhost:~] lullman% java Connect2
A database connection has been established!
[localhost:~] lullman% _
```

Figure 8.8 Connect2 is different from its predecessor (see Figure 8.4) only in how it maintains the connection variables.

DATABASE PROGRAMMING TECHNIQUES

This, the final programming chapter of the book, will show you some specific ways of using programming languages to interface with MySQL. The previous three chapters demonstrated how to do basic MySQL interactions with PHP, Perl, and Java, but the focus here is more on database programming theory rather than information specific to MySQL. The particulars to be discussed include storing and retrieving binary data, creating a basic search engine, generating query result pages, and database security.

The techniques demonstrated in this chapter cover a handful of what I believe are the more commonly mentioned programming topics. I'll be demonstrating one workable solution to each of the quandaries. While you will most likely find yourself using slight variants on these techniques, following the steps for each topic should give you a sufficient sense of the theory behind them.

I'll use one of the previously discussed languages (primarily PHP and Perl) for each example, but you should be able to recognize and translate the techniques to whichever language you are using. (As time allows and demand merits it, I'll post versions of these scripts in other languages on the book's Web site at www.dmcinsights.com/mysql).

Storing and Retrieving Binary Data

One of the more common questions people ask regarding MySQL is how to store and retrieve binary data in a database. Binary data includes items such as an image, a PDF file, and so forth, as opposed to the simple text strings and numbers that are normally filed. To store binary data in your database you should first make a column of type BLOB.

```
CREATE TABLE tablename (
id INT UNSIGNED NOT NULL AUTO_INCREMENT,
binary_item BLOB
)
```

MySQL supports different sizes of BLOBs— TINYBLOB, MEDIUMBLOB, and BLOB—even though the SQL standard does not. In truth, a field of type BLOB is exactly like a TEXT field, except that it is case-sensitive, whereas TEXT fields are case-insensitive.

Once you've established a field that can take binary data, you could use the LOAD_FILE() function to fill it and SELECT to retrieve the file again.

```
INSERT INTO tablename SET image=LOAD_FILE
→ ('/path/to/file.ext')
SELECT image FROM tablename
```

Another and more reliable option is to use your programming language to read in the binary file, and then store this in the database. To demonstrate this method, I'll create a PHP script that uploads an image from a form and then displays it in a Web page. This script will assume that you are using PHP 4.2, the most current version available at the time of this writing. If you are using an earlier version, you may need to change your variable names accordingly.

Should You Store Binary Data?

There is some debate among database developers about whether or not you should store binary data in your database. The alternative would be to store the file on the server in a convenient location, then store the filename in the database. There are pros and cons to both methods.

On the one hand, storing binary data in a database allows you to back it up at the same time as you back up the rest of the data. It also makes those files accessible to anyone with access to the database. On the other hand, you'll need to write extra SQL and code in order to store and retrieve this information, and there may be a performance hit.

In the end, it's really up to the developer and the needs of the application as to which method you use, but it's great that MySQL offers different options. You should experiment with both processes to see which you like the best.

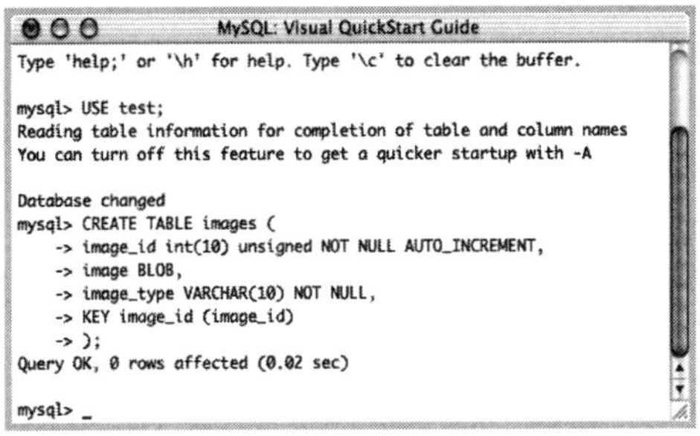

Figure 9.1 To begin this example, I make a new table using the mysql monitor.

To store and retrieve binary data:

1. Create the necessary table (**Figure 9.1**).

   CREATE TABLE images (

   image_id int(10) unsigned NOT NULL
   → AUTO_INCREMENT,

   image BLOB,

   image_type VARCHAR(10) NOT NULL,

   KEY image_id (image_id)

   );

   For demonstration purposes, I'll be creating a new *images* table within the *test* database. If you decide to change the structure of your table, you will need to change the query in the PHP script later in these steps.

2. Create a new PHP script in your text editor (**Script 9.1**).

   <!DOCTYPE html PUBLIC "-//W3C//DTD
   → XHTML 1.0 Transitional//EN"

   "http://www.w3.org/TR/2000/REC-
   → xhtml1-20000126/DTD/xhtml1-
   → transitional.dtd">

   <html
   xmlns="http://www.w3.org/1999/xhtml">

   <head>

   <title>Storing Images in MySQL</title>

   </head>

   <body>

   <?php

   This page will use a combination of XHTML and PHP to display a form, then handle a file upload. This is a standard XHTML header, followed by the initial PHP tag.

   continues on next page

3. Check if the form has been submitted.

```
if (isset($_POST['submit'])) {
```

Since this script will both display and
handle a form, one main conditional will
determine which action it is currently
doing. This first part will be run only if
the form was submitted (and the POST
variable submit has a value).

As an added level of security, you might
want to check at this point that a file was
uploaded (since it's possible to submit
the form without uploading an image).

Script 9.1 The store_binary.php script allows the user to select an image that will be stored in the database.

```
1   <!DOCTYPE html PUBLIC "-//W3C//DTD XHTML 1.0 Transitional//EN"
2          "http://www.w3.org/TR/2000/REC-xhtml1-20000126/DTD/xhtml1-transitional.dtd">
3   <html xmlns="http://www.w3.org/1999/xhtml">
4   <head>
5       <title>Storing Images in MySQL</title>
6   </head>
7   <body>
8   <?php
9
10  // ***** store_binary.php *****
11  // ***** Script 9.1 *****
12  // This script stores an image in the database.
13
14  if (isset($_POST['submit'])) { // If the form has been submitted...
15
16      // Database-specific information:
17      DEFINE (DB_USER, "username");
18      DEFINE (DB_PASSWORD, "password");
19      DEFINE (DB_HOST, "localhost");
20      DEFINE (DB_NAME, "test");
21
22      // Connect to MySQL:
23      $db_connection = mysql_connect (DB_HOST, DB_USER, DB_PASSWORD) or die ('Could not connect to
        MySQL: ' . mysql_error());
24
25      // Select the database:
26      mysql_select_db (DB_NAME) or die ('Could not select the database: ' . mysql_error());
27
28      // Read the uploaded file.
29      $image = addslashes(fread(fopen($_FILES['the_file']['tmp_name'], "r"), $_FILES['the_file']
        ['size']));
30
31      // Generate the query.
32      $query = "INSERT INTO images VALUES (0, '$image', '{$_FILES['the_file']['type']}')";
```

Script continues on next page

4. Establish a database connection.

```
DEFINE (DB_USER, "username");
DEFINE (DB_PASSWORD, "password");
DEFINE (DB_HOST, "localhost");
DEFINE (DB_NAME, "test");
$db_connection = mysql_connect
→ (DB_HOST, DB_USER, DB_PASSWORD) or
→ die ('Could not connect to MySQL: ' .
mysql_error());
mysql_select_db (DB_NAME) or die
→ ('Could not select the database: ' .
→ mysql_error());
```

These steps should be familiar to those who worked their way through Chapter 6, "MySQL and PHP." If desired, you could place all of the database connection information in a separate configuration file and just include that here.

continues on next page

Script 9.1 *continued*

```
33
34      // Execute the query and report on its success.
35      if (mysql_query ($query)) {
36          echo 'Image number ' . mysql_insert_id() . ' has been stored!';
37      } else {
38          echo 'The image could not be stored in the database! ' . mysql_error();
39      }
40
41      // Close the database connection.
42      mysql_close();
43
44  } else { // Display the form.
45  ?>
46      <form action="store_binary.php" method="post" enctype="multipart/form-data">
47      <input type="hidden" name="MAX_FILE_SIZE" value="100000" />
48      Select a file to upload: <input type="file" name="the_file" />
49      <br />
50      <input type="submit" name="submit" value="Submit!" />
51      </form>
52      <?php
53  }
54  ?>
55  </body>
56  </html>
```

5. Read the uploaded image file into a string.

```
$image =
addslashes(fread(fopen($_FILES
→ ['the_file']['tmp_name'], "r"),
→ $_FILES['the_file']['size']));
```

This is the most important line in the entire script. In this one step, the uploaded file (referred to by $_FILES['the_file'] ['tmp_name']) is read into a string called $image. To read the image, it is opened using the fopen() function, with the size of the file as the amount to read. The opened file is read with fread() and then run through the addslashes() function for security and reliability when inserting it into the database.

6. Query the database and report on its success.

```
$query = "INSERT INTO images VALUES
→ (0, '$image', '{$_FILES['the_file']
→ ['type']}')";
if (mysql_query ($query)) {
    echo 'Image number ' . mysql_insert_
    → id() . ' has been stored!';
} else {
    echo 'The image could not be stored in
    → the database! ' . mysql_error();
}
```

The query is very basic and inserts a new record into the *images* table. The data includes: 0, for the auto-incremented primary key; the $image string that is the image data itself; and the image type, based upon the MIME type of the file uploaded. Another logical thing you could store in the database would be the image size in pixels.

This is another place where, if you really want to be careful, you could check to make sure that $image has a value before inserting it into the database (in other words, that the image was successfully read).

Figure 9.2 This HTML form will allow users to select an image on their hard drive that will be stored in the database.

Figure 9.3 After the script has stored the image, it will indicate what image number it is. This number will be used to view the image again (Figure 9.4).

7. Close the database connection and compete the main conditional displaying the form.

```
mysql_close();
} else {
?>
    <form action="store_binary.php"
    → method="post" enctype="multipart/
    → form-data">
    <input type="hidden" name=
    → "MAX_FILE_SIZE" value="100000" />
    Select a file to upload: <input type=
    → "file" name="the_file" />
    <br />
    <input type="submit" name="submit"
    → value="Submit!" />
    </form>
    <?php
}
```

The most important pieces of this form are the form's action (referring back to this same script), its enctype (which allows for a file to be uploaded), and the name of the file being uploaded (which should match the name used earlier in the script).

You should also adjust the MAX_FILE_SIZE value based upon how large of an image you will want to store. In my example, up to an 97-Kbyte image will work just fine.

8. Complete the script.

```
?>
</body>
</html>
```

9. Save the script as store_binary.php, upload it to your Web server, and test in your Web browser (**Figures 9.2** and **9.3**).

Now that I've written a script for storing images in a database, I'll create another that will retrieve and display the image in a Web browser.

continues on next page

10. Create a new PHP script (**Script 9.2**).

```
<?php
```

11. Check that an image number was appended to the URL.

```
if (isset($_GET['i'])) {
```

This page will be called by using the syntax *view_image.php?i=x*, where *x* refers to the image_id in the database for the corresponding image. This conditional just checks for i's value before attempting to retrieve the image.

Script 9.2 The view_image.php script retrieves an image from a database and sends it to the Web browser.

```
1    <?php
2
3    // ***** view_image.php *****
4    // ***** Script 9.2 *****
5    // This script displays an image stored in the database.
6
7    if (isset($_GET['i'])) { // If there is an image number, display it.
8
9        // Database-specific information:
10       DEFINE (DB_USER, "username");
11       DEFINE (DB_PASSWORD, "password");
12       DEFINE (DB_HOST, "localhost");
13       DEFINE (DB_NAME, "test");
14
15       // Connect to MySQL:
16       $db_connection = mysql_connect (DB_HOST, DB_USER, DB_PASSWORD) or die ('Could not connect to
         MySQL: ' . mysql_error());
17
18       // Select the database:
19       mysql_select_db (DB_NAME) or die ('Could not select the database: ' . mysql_error());
20
21       // Retrieve the image information.
22       $query = "SELECT image, image_type FROM images WHERE image_id={$_GET['i']}";
23       if ($query_result = mysql_query ($query)) {
24           $image = mysql_fetch_array($query_result);
25           header ("Content-type: $image[1]");
26           echo $image[0];
27       }
28
29       // Close the database connection.
30       mysql_close();
31
32   }
33   ?>
```

12. Connect to the database.

```
DEFINE (DB_USER, "username");
DEFINE (DB_PASSWORD, "password");
DEFINE (DB_HOST, "localhost");
DEFINE (DB_NAME, "test");
$db_connection = mysql_connect
→ (DB_HOST, DB_USER, DB_PASSWORD) or
→ die ('Could not connect to MySQL: ' .
→ mysql_error());
mysql_select_db (DB_NAME) or die
→ ('Could not select the database: ' .
→ mysql_error());
```

13. Retrieve the image from the database.

```
$query = "SELECT image, image_type FROM
→ images WHERE image_id={$_GET['i']}";
if ($query_result = mysql_query
→ ($query)) {
    $image = mysql_fetch_array
    → ($query_result);
    header ("Content-type: $image[1]");
    echo $image[0];
}
```

The query returns the image and image type information from the table based upon the image_id value (which corresponds to i, passed to the script). If the query is successful, an array of information is assigned to the $image variable. Then, a call of the header() function will tell the browser what type of data to expect, based upon the stored image type of the image. Afterward, the original image information is sent to the browser.

14. Complete the script.

```
mysql_close();
}
?>
```

continues on next page

STORING AND RETRIEVING BINARY DATA

15. Save the file as `view_image.php`, upload it to your Web server, and test in a Web browser (**Figure 9.4**). Be certain to append the image number to the URL, for example: www.someaddress.com/view_image.php?i=1.

✔ Tips

■ To store a binary object in a MySQL database, the file must be present on the server (it cannot be loaded remotely).

■ When using the `LOAD_FILE()` function, the MySQL user attempting to load the file must have `FILE` privileges on the database (which is one of the reasons I chose not to use this method here).

■ You can use the `view_image.php` script to display images anywhere within a Web page by using the code `<img src="view_image.php?i=89" />`.

■ If the image is not being uploaded and stored in the database, make sure that it is small enough (less than about 100 Kbytes). If the image is only partially displaying in the browser window, change the image column type to a larger form of `BLOB`.

Figure 9.4 The `view_image.php` script retrieves an image from the database and sends it to the Web browser.

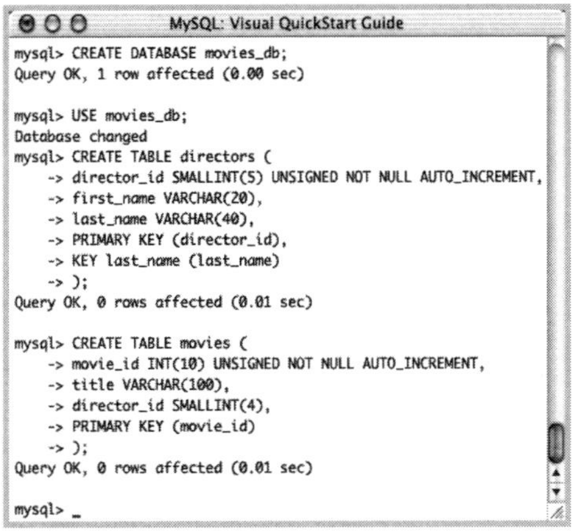

Figure 9.5 For the example in this section, I'll create the *movies_db* database.

Creating a Search Engine

One of the most useful aspects of storing information in a database is the ability to use those records as the basis for a search engine. Search engines dominate the Web (e.g., Google) and are frequently an added bonus in many applications and operating systems.

Once you've stored information in a database, there are two ways to turn it into a search engine:

◆ Use a full-text index and full-text searching.

◆ Manually write appropriate queries for searching the database.

For larger applications with substantial data, the full-text method is preferred; that's discussed in Chapter 11, "Advanced MySQL." As a more generic example, I'll demonstrate how to use Perl to create a basic search engine.

To create a search engine:

1. Create a new database (**Figure 9.5**).

   CREATE DATABASE movies_db;

   USE movies_db;

   CREATE TABLE directors (

   director_id SMALLINT(5) UNSIGNED NOT
   → NULL AUTO_INCREMENT,

   first_name VARCHAR(20),

   last_name VARCHAR(40),

   PRIMARY KEY (director_id),

   KEY last_name (last_name)

   );

   CREATE TABLE movies (

   movie_id INT(10) UNSIGNED NOT NULL
   → AUTO_INCREMENT,

   title VARCHAR(100),

   director_id SMALLINT(4),

   PRIMARY KEY (movie_id)

   );

continues on next page

For this example, I'll be using the *movies_db* database, which is also an example in other chapters. If you have not yet created the database, you can use the SQL above to do so now.

2. Populate the tables (**Figure 9.6**).

   If your database does not have at least several records in it, run some INSERT queries to give it some records (which will be searched shortly).

   Now that a database has been established, I'll write a Perl script that takes up to two user-entered keywords and uses them to search *movies_db*.

3. Create a new Perl script in your text editor (**Script 9.3**).

   ```
   #!/usr/bin/perl
   use DBI;
   use strict;
   ```

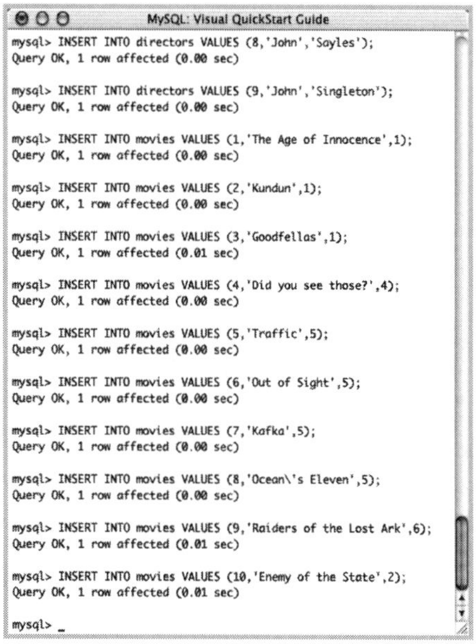

Figure 9.6 To perform searches on the database, I need to add some records first.

Script 9.3 The `search_movies.pl` Perl script demonstrates the technique behind a basic search engine.

```
1    #!/usr/bin/perl
2
3    # Script 9.3, 'search_movies.pl'
4
5    # Use what needs to be used.
6    use DBI;
7    use strict;
8
9    # Connect to the database.
10   my $user;
11   my $password;
12   my $dbh = DBI->connect('DBI:mysql:movies_db;mysql_read_default_file=/Users/lullman/.my.cnf',
     $user, $password, {RaiseError => 1});
13
14   # If a connection was made, run the query.
15   if ($dbh) {
16
17       # Get the keywords.
18       print "Enter a keyword to be searched: ";
19       my $term1 = <STDIN>;
20       print "Enter a second keyword to be searched: ";
21       my $term2 = <STDIN>;
22
23       # Create the SQL statement.
```

Script continues on next page

4. Establish a connection to the database.

```
my $user;
my $password;
my $dbh = DBI->connect('DBI:mysql:
→ movies_db;mysql_read_default_file=
→ /Users/lullman/.my.cnf', $user,
→ $password, {RaiseError => 1});
```

Following the steps I outlined toward the end of Chapter 7, "MySQL and Perl," I'll be using a .my.cnf file to store the database access information. You can also hard code these values here, should you prefer.

5. Start the main conditional.

```
if ($dbh) {
```

If the script was able to connect to the database, it'll proceed through the rest of the steps.

continues on next page

Script 9.3 *continued*

```
24    my $sql = "SELECT CONCAT(directors.first_name, ' ', directors.last_name) AS Director, title
      AS Title FROM directors, movies WHERE directors.director_id=movies.director_id";
25
26    # Add the keywords to the SQL statement.
27    if (length($term1) > 1) {
28        chop($term1);
29        $sql .= " AND ( (directors.last_name LIKE '%$term1%' OR directors.first_name LIKE
          '%$term1%' OR movies.title LIKE '%$term1%')";
30
31        if (length($term2) > 1) {
32            chop($term2);
33            $sql .= " AND (directors.last_name LIKE '%$term2%' OR directors.first_name LIKE
              '%$term2%' OR movies.title LIKE '%$term2%')";
34        }
35
36        $sql .= ")";
37    }
38
39    # Run the query.
40    my $query = $dbh->prepare ($sql);
41    my @row;
42    my $n;
43    if (defined($query)) {
44        print "\n";
```

Script continues on next page

CREATING A SEARCH ENGINE

6. Obtain the keywords to be searched.

```
print "Enter a keyword to be searched: ";
my $term1 = <STDIN>;
print "Enter a second keyword to be
→ searched: ";
my $term2 = <STDIN>;
```

In this example, I will give the user the option of entering up to two keywords that will be searched across the director and movie tables. To modify the complexity of this script, begin by altering the inputs here (perhaps by letting the user specify the table or column to be searched).

Script 9.3 *continued*

```
45          $query->execute();
46          for ($n=0; $n < $query->{'NUM_OF_FIELDS'}; $n++) {
47              print @{$query->{'NAME'}}[$n];
48              print "\t";
49          }
50          print "\n";
51          while (@row = $query->fetchrow_array()) {
52              foreach (@row) {
53                  print "$_ \t";
54              }
55              print "\n";
56          }
57      } else {
58          print "The query was not executed because MySQL reported " . DBI->errstr() . ". \n";
59      }
60      print "\n";
61
62      # Close the query and disconnect from the database.
63      $query->finish();
64      $dbh->disconnect;
65
66  } else {
67      print "Could not connect to the database! \n";
68  }
```

7. Begin the SQL query.

```
my $sql = "SELECT CONCAT
→ (directors.first_name, ' ',
→ directors.last_name) AS Director,
→ title AS Title FROM directors, movies
→ WHERE directors.director_id=
→ movies.director_id";
```

The query in this example will return the director's name and movie title for each record that matches the search. For easy formatting purposes, I use the AS alias to change the name of the two returned values (to Director and Title). You'll see where this formatting comes into play when the script is run.

8. Add the keywords to the query.

```
if (length($term1) > 1) {
    chop($term1);
    $sql .= " AND ( (directors.last_name
→ LIKE '%$term1%' OR directors.
→ first_name LIKE '%$term1%' OR
→ movies.title LIKE '%$term1%')";
    if (length($term2) > 1) {
        chop($term2);
        $sql .= " AND (directors.last_
→ name  LIKE '%$term2%' OR
→ directors.first_name LIKE
→ '%$term2%' OR movies.title
→ LIKE '%$term2%')";
    }
        $sql .= ")";
}
```

The *movies_db* database has three fields that are likely candidates for searching: directors.first_name, directors.last_name, and movies.title. For my search I will run a LIKE '%keyword%' conditional on each of these. Further, I will assume that a record must contain both keywords for a match to be made, if two keywords are entered.

continues on next page

CREATING A SEARCH ENGINE

To achieve this query structure, I first check that both keywords have a value (so I'm not assuming the user entered anything) and then chop off the last character of each (the carriage return). Finally it's just a matter of appending the extra clauses to the existing query.

This section of the script is at the heart of search engine theory. For that matter, there is also plenty of room for alterations or improvements, including limiting the searches to specific columns, allowing for more keywords, and changing the binary method of the search (i.e., should keywords be joined by an **AND** clause or an **OR** one).

9. Run the query and display the results.

```
my $query = $dbh->prepare ($sql);
my @row;
my $n;
if (defined($query)) {
    print "\n";
    $query->execute();
    for ($n=0; $n < $query->
    → {'NUM_OF_FIELDS'}; $n++) {
        print @{$query->{'NAME'}}[$n];
        print "\t";
    }
    print "\n";
    while (@row = $query->
    → fetchrow_array()) {
        foreach (@row) {
            print "$_ \t";
        }
        print "\n";
    }
} else {
    print "The query was not executed
    → because MySQL reported " . DBI->
    → errstr() . ". \n";
}
print "\n";
```

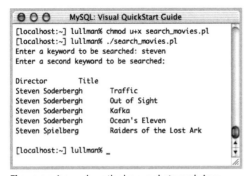

Figure 9.7 A search on the keyword *steven* brings up every movie directed by Steven Soderbergh or Spielberg. It would also return movies with the word in the title or by a director whose last name is *Stevens*.

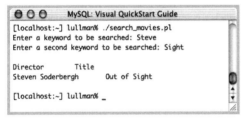

Figure 9.8 With this Perl script, a two-keyword search will narrow the results returned.

This structure for displaying the query results is virtually identical to the one demonstrated in browse_table.pl, back in Chapter 7 (Script 7.4). I've changed the formatting ever so slightly, but the remainder of the process should be familiar.

10. Tidy up the MySQL resources and finish the script.

```
$query->finish();

$dbh->disconnect;

} else {

    print "Could not connect to the
    ➝ database! \n";

}
```

The `else` part of this script is enacted should it not be able to connect to the database (see the `if ($dbh)` conditional).

11. Save the script as `search_movies.pl` (save the script in the same directory as `.my.cnf` if you are using it, too), and test (**Figures 9.7** and **9.8**).

✔ Tips

■ One of the benefits of using full-text searching as opposed to this method is that it returns the results weighted by relevance.

■ To improve the efficiency of searches on string values in a database, index the columns being searched.

Making Query Result Pages

Except for limited queries on small databases, most SELECT statements will return tens, hundreds, or even thousands of records. When printing these records (to a Web page or wherever), you will presumably not want to display them all at one time. In such cases, you will need to make query result pages so that page one will display the first 25 records, page two the next 25, and so forth until all of the records have been displayed.

Depending upon the programming language being used and the needs of the application, there are two logical ways of developing query result pages:

◆ Assign the query's resource link to a variable that gets passed from page to page (see the sidebar "Using a Resource Link").

◆ Reapply the query on each page, changing the start and end points (the LIMITs) accordingly.

The second method is sufficient for most purposes and I'll demonstrate it using PHP. As my example, the script will browse through all of the records in the *movies_db* database (created in the previous section of this chapter) by movie title.

Using a Resource Link

Assuming that you are using a programming language that does not automatically close a database connection when a script runs (or that allows for permanent connections), you can simplify the steps outlined in this section. Here's how:

Normally when you query a database, the result of that query can be assigned to a variable. The value of this variable is essentially a link to the database for that particular query. Normally data is retrieved within a loop, fetching a record through this link with each iteration. But, if you can get the link to exist beyond the scope of a single script, it can be passed from page to page, allowing you to access rows as needed, without requerying the database every time.

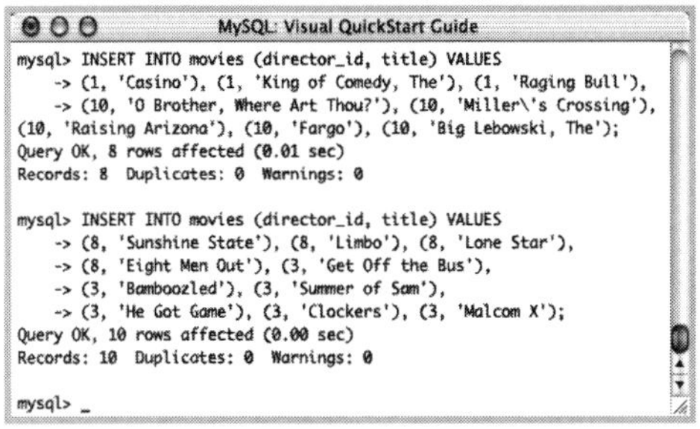

Figure 9.9 For the query result page to be more effective, I'm adding several more records to the database.

To create a query result page:

1. Create and populate the *movies_db* database, if necessary (**Figure 9.9**).

   If you had already created the database (see step 1 in the previous section), you can either skip this step or add more records (the more the merrier).

2. Begin a new PHP script in your text editor (**Script 9.4**).

   ```
   <!DOCTYPE html PUBLIC "-//W3C//DTD
   → XHTML 1.0 Transitional//EN"
   "http://www.w3.org/TR/2000/
   → REC-xhtml1-20000126/DTD/xhtml1-
   → transitional.dtd">
   <html xmlns="http://www.w3.org/
   → 1999/xhtml">
   <head>
       <title>Browse the Movie Titles</
       → title>
   </head>
   <body>
   <?php
   ```

   continues on next page

Script 9.4 This PHP script demonstrates how easy professional-caliber query result pages can be.

```
1    <!DOCTYPE html PUBLIC "-//W3C//DTD XHTML 1.0 Transitional//EN"
2           "http://www.w3.org/TR/2000/REC-xhtml1-20000126/DTD/xhtml1-transitional.dtd">
3    <html xmlns="http://www.w3.org/1999/xhtml">
4    <head>
5        <title>Browse the Movie Titles</title>
6    </head>
7    <body>
8    <?php
9
10   // ***** browse_movies.php *****
11   // ***** Script 9.4 *****
12   // This script generates query result pages of movie titles in the movies_db database.
13
14   // Number of records to show per page:
15   $display_number = 5;
16
17   // Database-specific information:
18   DEFINE (DB_USER, "username");
19   DEFINE (DB_PASSWORD, "password");
```

Script continues on next page

3. Establish the number of records to show per page.

`$display_number = 5;`

For convenience sake, I prefer to set this number as a variable. This way I can change how the script works by changing only one value (even though the number will be used several times over the course of the script).

Script 9.4 *continued*

```
script
20    DEFINE (DB_HOST, "localhost");
21    DEFINE (DB_NAME, "movies_db");
22
23    // Connect to MySQL:
24    $db_connection = mysql_connect (DB_HOST, DB_USER, DB_PASSWORD) or die ('Could not connect to
      MySQL: ' . mysql_error());
25
26    // Select the database:
27    mysql_select_db (DB_NAME) or die ('Could not select the database: ' . mysql_error());
28
29    // Determine how many records there are.
30    if (isset($_GET['np'])) {
31        $num_pages = $_GET['np'];
32    } else {
33        $query = "SELECT CONCAT(directors.first_name, ' ', directors.last_name) AS Director, title
          AS Title FROM directors, movies WHERE directors.director_id=movies.director_id ORDER BY
          movies.title ASC";
34        $query_result = mysql_query ($query) or die (mysql_error());
35        $num_records = @mysql_num_rows ($query_result);
36
37        if ($num_records > $display_number) {
38            $num_pages = ceil ($num_records/$display_number);
39        } else {
40            $num_pages = 1;
41        }
42    }
43
44    // Determine where in the database to start returning results.
45    if (isset($_GET['s'])) {
46        $start = $_GET['s'];
47    } else {
48        $start = 0;
49    }
50
51    // Retrieve and display the records.
52    $query = "SELECT CONCAT(directors.first_name, ' ', directors.last_name) AS d, title FROM direc-
      tors, movies WHERE directors.director_id=movies.director_id ORDER BY movies.title ASC LIMIT
      $start, $display_number";
```

Script continues on next page

4. Connect to the database.

```
DEFINE (DB_USER, "username");
DEFINE (DB_PASSWORD, "password");
DEFINE (DB_HOST, "localhost");
DEFINE (DB_NAME, "movies_db");
$db_connection = mysql_connect
(DB_HOST, DB_USER, DB_PASSWORD) or die
  → ('Could not connect to MySQL: ' .
  → mysql_error());
mysql_select_db (DB_NAME) or die
  → ('Could not select the database: ' .
  → mysql_error());
```

As always, you could place this information in a separate configuration file for added security.

continues on next page

Script 9.4 *continued*

```
script
53    $query_result = mysql_query ($query) or die (mysql_error());
54
55    // Display all of the records:
56    while ($row = mysql_fetch_array ($query_result, MYSQL_ASSOC)) {
57        echo "{$row['d']} <i>{$row['title']}</i><br />\n";
58    }
59
60    // Make the links to other pages, if necessary.
61    if ($num_pages > 1) {
62
63        echo '<hr width="50%" align="left" />';
64
65        // Determine what page the script is on.
66        $current_page = ($start/$display_number) + 1;
67
68        // If it's not the first page, make a Previous button.
69        if ($current_page != 1) {
70            echo '<a href="browse_movies.php?s=' . ($start - $display_number) . '&np=' . $num_pages .
                 '">Previous</a> ';
71        }
72
73        // Make all the numbered pages.
74        for ($i = 1; $i <= $num_pages; $i++) {
75            if ($i != $current_page) {
76                echo '<a href="browse_movies.php?s=' . (($display_number * ($i - 1))) . '&np=' .
                     $num_pages . '">' . $i . '</a> ';
77            } else {
78                echo $i . ' ';
```

Script continues on next page

MAKING QUERY RESULT PAGES

5. Determine how many pages will need to be used to display all of the records.

```
if (isset($_GET['np'])) {
    $num_pages = $_GET['np'];
} else {
    $query = "SELECT CONCAT
    → (directors.first_name, ' ',
    → directors.last_name) AS Director,
    → title AS Title FROM directors,
    → movies WHERE directors.director_
    → id=movies.director_id ORDER BY
    → movies.title ASC";
    $query_result = mysql_query ($query)
    → or die (mysql_error());
    $num_records = @mysql_num_rows
    → ($query_result);
    if ($num_records > $display_number) {
        $num_pages = ceil ($num_records/
        → $display_number);
    } else {
        $num_pages = 1;
    }
}
```

Script 9.4 *continued*

```
script
79          }
80      }
81
82      // If it's not the last page, make a Next button.
83      if ($current_page != $num_pages) {
84          echo '<a href="browse_movies.php?s=' . ($start + $display_number) . '&np=' . $num_pages .
            '">Next</a> ';
85      }
86
87  }
88
89  // Free up the resources.
90  mysql_free_result($query_result);
91  mysql_close();
92  ?>
93  </body>
94  </html>
```

This is the first step in generating query result pages: seeing how many records will be displayed and therefore how many pages will be needed. If the URL has an *np* value (for the number of pages), this means that the number has already been calculated and does not need to be determined again. If *np* does not have a value, it will need to be derived.

To calculate the number of pages, the query is run once on the database and the number of rows is fetched. If there are more rows than will fit on one page, I divide the number of rows by the number of rows to display per page and round this value up to the next highest integer. Otherwise, one page will suffice.

6. Determine with what record the query should start displaying.

```
if (isset($_GET['s'])) {
    $start = $_GET['s'];
} else {
    $start = 0;
}
```

The query itself will use a `LIMIT` clause to show up to `$display_number` records per page. For this reason I need to determine whether the `LIMIT` should start at 0 (which is the first record) or elsewhere. If the *s* value (for *start*), appended to the URL, has a value, the query will use it. Otherwise, it will begin at 0.

continues on next page

MAKING QUERY RESULT PAGES

7. Display all of the records for this particular page.

```
$query = "SELECT CONCAT
→ (directors.first_name, ' ',
→ directors.last_name) AS d, title
→ FROM directors, movies WHERE
→ directors.director_id=
→ movies.director_id ORDER BY
→ movies.title ASC LIMIT $start,
→ $display_number";
$query_result = mysql_query ($query) or
→ die (mysql_error());
while ($row = mysql_fetch_array
→ ($query_result, MYSQL_ASSOC)) {
    echo "{$row['d']} <i>{$row['title']}
    → </i><br />\n";
}
```

The query in this step needs to be exactly like the query used to determine the number of rows and pages except for the addition of the LIMIT clause. This clause gives the page the ability to show a continuous sequence of results over the course of several pages. For example, upon first viewing the page, the user will see records 1-5 (retrieved by adding LIMIT 0, 5—which is $start and $display_number, accordingly—to the end of the query). The second page would have a limit of 5, 5; the third 10, 5; and so forth.

Aside from the query itself, this section of the script merely displays the record in a basic format.

8. Begin making hyperlinks to the other query result pages.

```
if ($num_pages > 1) {
    echo '<hr width="50%" align="left"
→ />';
    $current_page = ($start/$display_
→ number) + 1;
```

If the query requires multiple pages, I'll need to make links so that the user can browse through them all. In this example, the navigation will have a previous link, a next link, and numbered links for every page (with the current page unlinked).

To calculate the current page, I add 1 to the division of the start number divided by the display number. For example, the first page will have a $start of 0 and a $display_number of 5. Zero divided by 5 is zero, plus 1 is 1. Hence, it's the first page. The fourth page will have a $start value of 15 (because it's showing the fourth group of five records from the database) and a $display_number of 5 still.

9. Create the *Previous* link.

```
if ($current_page != 1) {
    echo '<a href="browse_movies.php?
→ s=' . ($start - $display_number) .
→ '&np=' . $num_pages . '">Previous
→ </a> ';
}
```

If it is not the first page, I want to make a link to the previous page. The link is a URL of the format *browse_movies.php?s=x&np=y* where *s* is the number to start with and *np* is the number of total pages. The *x* value will be based upon the current start value minus the number of records to display per page (in other words, the previous page should begin $display_number of records prior to this one). The *y* value will be based upon the calculated number of pages.

continues on next page

MAKING QUERY RESULT PAGES

10. Generate the numbered links.

```
for ($i = 1; $i <= $num_pages; $i++) {
    if ($i != $current_page) {
        echo '<a href="browse_movies.
        → php?s=' . (($display_number *
        → ($i - 1))) . '&np=' . $num_
        → pages . '">' . $i . '</a> ';
    } else {
        echo $i . ' ';
    }
}
```

So that the user can immediately jump through the list of movies, I want to make numbered links. To do so, I loop through the numbers 1 to the total number of pages, creating a link for each number except for the current page (no reason to link a page to itself). The *s* value here is calculated as $i minus 1, multiplied by the number of records displayed per page. For the second page, $i minus 1 is 1, times 5 is 5, meaning that the second page should begin with the second group of five records out of the database.

11. Make the *Next* page link.

```
if ($current_page != $num_pages) {
    echo '<a href="browse_movies.
    → php?s=' . ($start + $display_
    → number) . '&np=' . → $num_pages .
    → '">Next</a> ';
}
```

Every page except for the final one will have a *Next* link.

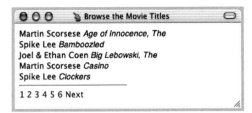

Figure 9.10 Upon first viewing browse_movies.php, the first five movies in the database (alphabetical by title) are displayed, along with links to the other pages.

Figure 9.11 Clicking on any numbered link brings the user to that page.

Figure 9.12 The last page will not have a *Next* link, just as the first does not have a *Previous* link (Figure 9.10).

12. Close the links conditional, the database connection, and complete the HTML page.

```
}
mysql_free_result($query_result);
mysql_close();
?>
</body>
</html>
```

13. Save the file as browse_movies.php, upload it to your Web server, and test in a Web browser (**Figures 9.10**, **9.11**, and **9.12**).

✔ Tip

■ One potential flaw in this system is that if the database changes between the different executions of the query, it could throw off the result pages.

Database Security

Security is an important topic and not one that can be overstated. A database is predicated upon the notion of data integrity, and the amount and type of security you use in your applications only undermines or enforces that concept.

Database security involves three primary concepts when you're using a programming language as the interface. First, you should be careful to establish the proper users and privileges so that, for example, scripts that are only selecting records have only SELECT privileges, and scripts are not run as a root user. Second, you should safely store or protect this user and password information. Third, you should validate submitted data before storing it in a database. This is both a security and data integrity issue.

Table 9.1 lists different security-related functions and operators for the PHP and Perl. Regular expressions are perhaps the best way to validate user-submitted information, but they can be tedious and are not for the beginning user.

Security Tools		
FUNCTION	LANGUAGE	PURPOSE
addslashes()	PHP	Escapes problematic characters.
ereg()	PHP	Checks data against a regular expression.
is_numeric()	PHP	Confirms that a value is a number.
mysql_escape_string()	PHP	Escapes a string specifically for using in a MySQL query.
s//	Perl	Checks data against a regular expression.
q{}	Perl	Used to escape single quotation marks.

Table 9.1 These are some of the most common API functions and tools for improving the security of your database applications.

Figure 9.13 The original search_movies.pl would go haywire if the user used an apostrophe in a keyword.

Figure 9.14 After applying regular expressions to the keywords, the Perl script works without a hitch (compare with Figure 9.13).

The following task demonstrates how to use regular expressions in Perl to escape single quotation marks. To learn more about regular expressions, see Chapter 11, "Advanced MySQL," or search online for other references.

To increase the security of a Perl script:

1. Open search_movies.pl (Script 9.3) in your text editor.

   As it stands, one of the flaws in the original script is that if a user puts an apostrophe in a keyword, it will render the script unusable (**Figure 9.13**). This is because the single quotation mark in the keyword will conflict with the balance of single quotation marks in the query, and MySQL will report an error.

2. After line 28 of the original script, add (**Script 9.5**):

   ```
   $term1 =~ s/'/\\'/;
   ```

   This is an application of regular expressions within Perl. It states that the value of $term1 should be equal to the value of $term1 after replacing every single quotation mark with an escaped single quotation mark (\\'). You'll need to use two backslashes to achieve this effect, as the first one escapes the second.

3. After line 32 of the original script, add:

   ```
   $term2 =~ s/'/\\'/;
   ```

   I simply apply the same regular expression to the second term so that both are safe to use in a query.

4. Save the file (I saved mine as search_movies2.pl to distinguish it) and test (**Figure 9.14**).

✔ Tip

- If you want to escape double quotation marks in the keywords, use these lines:

  ```
  $term1 =~ s/"/\\"/;
  $term2 =~ s/"/\\"/;
  ```

Script 9.5 This modification of the original `search_movies.pl` script will guard against SQL errors by escaping single quotation marks.

```
                                        script
1    #!/usr/bin/perl
2
3    # Script 9.5, 'search_movies2.pl'
4
5    # Use what needs to be used.
6    use DBI;
7    use strict;
8
9    # Connect to the database.
10   my $user;
11   my $password;
12   my $dbh = DBI->connect('DBI:mysql:movies_db;mysql_read_default_file=/Users/lullman/.my.cnf',
     $user, $password, {RaiseError => 1});
13
14   # If a connection was made, run the query.
15   if ($dbh) {
16
17       # Get the keywords.
18       print "Enter a keyword to be searched: ";
19       my $term1 = <STDIN>;
20       print "Enter a second keyword to be searched: ";
21       my $term2 = <STDIN>;
22
23       # Create the SQL statement.
24       my $sql = "SELECT CONCAT(directors.first_name, ' ', directors.last_name) AS Director, title
         AS Title FROM directors, movies WHERE directors.director_id=movies.director_id";
25
26       # Add the keywords to the SQL statement.
27       if (length($term1) > 1) {
28           chop($term1);
29           $term1 =~ s/'/\\'/;
30           $sql .= " AND ( (directors.last_name LIKE '%$term1%' OR directors.first_name LIKE
             '%$term1%' OR movies.title LIKE '%$term1%')";
31
32           if (length($term2) > 1) {
33               chop($term2);
34               $term2 =~ s/'/\\'/;
35               $sql .= " AND (directors.last_name LIKE '%$term2%' OR directors.first_name LIKE
                 '%$term2%' OR movies.title LIKE '%$term2%')";
36           }
37
38           $sql .= ")";
39       }
40
41       # Run the query.
42       my $query = $dbh->prepare ($sql);
43       my @row;
44       my $n;
45       if (defined($query)) {
```

Script continues on next page

Script 9.5 *continued*

```
46          print "\n";
47          $query->execute();
48          for ($n=0; $n < $query->{'NUM_OF_FIELDS'}; $n++) {
49              print @{$query->{'NAME'}}[$n];
50              print "\t";
51          }
52          print "\n";
53          while (@row = $query->fetchrow_array()) {
54              foreach (@row) {
55                  print "$_ \t";
56              }
57              print "\n";
58          }
59      } else {
60          print "The query was not executed because MySQL reported " . DBI->errstr() . ". \n";
61      }
62      print "\n";
63
64      # Close the query and disconnect from the database.
65      $query->finish();
66      $dbh->disconnect;
67
68  } else {
69      print "Could not connect to the database! \n";
70  }
```

MySQL
ADMINISTRATION

After you have gone through all of the effort of installing MySQL, running it, creating databases, and even programming applications using PHP, Perl, or Java, you'll need to begin administering the software. Administration involves several aspects, from the obvious backing up of data to improving security and performance. Fortunately the reliability of MySQL demands little in the way of maintenance, but should the need arise, this, too, is easily accomplished.

To demonstrate the different techniques involved, I will use a combination of Windows 2000, Red Hat Linux, and Mac OS X operating systems, since the techniques are the same on all three. You will also see that in newer versions of MySQL what used to be accomplished with a separate utility (e.g., mysqldump) can now be managed within the mysql monitor using SQL. In those cases, I will primarily discuss the dedicated application, but I will also include a sidebar on the corresponding SQL.

MySQL Data Files

As you begin to fill up your databases with information, it becomes more and more important to regularly back up this data. MySQL stores all of the information constituting a database—both the structure and the contents—as a series of files on the server's hard drive. Depending upon your operating system, the installation type, and the configuration settings, these files will most likely be in one of the following:

◆ C:\mysql\data

◆ /usr/local/mysql/data

◆ /usr/local/var

◆ /var/lib/mysql

If you do not know where your installation of MySQL is keeping the data, run this command—using the root username and password—from the appropriate directory (e.g., /usr/local/mysql/bin or C:\mysql\bin) (**Figure 10.1**).

mysqladmin -u root -p variables

Within the main data directory, MySQL will create a new subdirectory for each database. Within these folders you will find the actual database files. For example, if your database is called *alpacas*, you will find all of that data-base's information stored in C:\mysql\data\alpacas. Each table in the database will be represented by three files (**Figure 10.2**):

◆ *tablename.frm*, which details the structure of the table: column names, column types, and so forth

◆ *tablename.MYD*, which is the data stored in the table

◆ *tablename.MYI*, which records the table's indexes

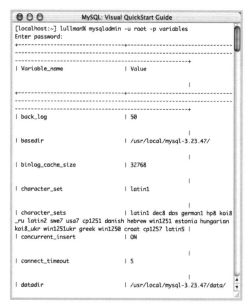

Figure 10.1 Running the mysqladmin variables command will create a listing of MySQL's settings, including the *datadir*, where your database files are stored.

Figure 10.2 The database files—three for each table—are stored within a directory named the same as the database itself.

MySQL: Visual QuickStart Guide

```
[localhost:~] lullman% mysqladmin -u root -p shutdown
Enter password:
[localhost:~] lullman%
```

Figure 10.3 Whenever you will be manually manipulating MySQL's files, you'll need to shut down MySQL first.

This structure applies to all MyISAM tables, the default table type for MySQL (ISAM stands for Indexed Sequential Access Method). Backing up the data from a database can be as simple as making copies of these files.

To copy the data directory:

1. Stop the mysql server using one of these commands (**Figure 10.3**):
   - ▲ `mysqladmin -u root -p shutdown` (Unix/Mac OS X)
   - ▲ `NET STOP mysql` (Windows as a service)
   - ▲ `/etc/rc.d/init.d/mysqld stop` (Red Hat Linux)

   These methods of stopping the server were discussed in Chapter 2, "Running MySQL." You may need to be within a particular directory (like `/usr/local/mysql/bin` or `C:\mysql\bin`) to call mysqladmin, depending upon your system configuration.

   When manually copying the files from a database, it's important to shut down the server so that there's no possibility of the database being altered while you are working with the files.

continues on next page

2. Copy the files to their new destination (**Figure 10.4**).

cd /path/to/mysql/

tar -cvf /path/to/destination/data.tar
→ data

cd /path/to/destination/

tar -xf data.tar

These four lines of code will work on Unix and Mac OS X. (On Windows you can copy and move the files using the Windows Explorer.) The second line will create a tarball (a compressed package) of all of the files within the **data** directory, storing this package in the destination directory. The fourth line will decompress the tarball, recreating the data directory in its new location. (The other two lines are for moving yourself to the proper directories; change the particulars to match your server's setup.)

In order to perform these two operations, you will most likely need to be logged in with root-level permissions.

3. Reset the permissions on the moved files (**Figure 10.5**).

chown -R mysql data/*

For MySQL to be able to write to the databases, you'll need to change the ownership of these files. Since the mysqld server is normally run as the *mysql* user, the **data** directory should belong to this user as well. To be really precise, you could set the permissions for the mysql user and group with chown -R mysql.mysql.

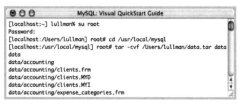

Figure 10.4 On Unix and Mac OS X systems, you can use the tar command to copy the data files.

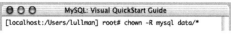

Figure 10.5 The final step after moving database files is to reestablish the proper permissions.

The above command will work for most operating systems; on Windows, you'll need to right-click on the directory and set the permissions using the menus that appear (which will differ based upon the version of Windows). That being said, because of the way permissions work on Windows, you may not need to mess with them at all.

4. Restart MySQL.

✔ Tips

- If you are moving database files to a directory where similarly named files exist (in other words, where there already is a database with the same name), you will need to drop or rename the older database before moving the new files.

- Within the main data directory you will also find files used by MySQL in general. These include error and other logs. You will learn more about them later in this chapter.

- To ensure flawless backing up of your data, ideally the database should be locked (more on this in Chapter 11, "Advanced MySQL") or, in this case, the mysqld server should be stopped before proceeding.

Backing Up Databases

Another option in backing up your database is to use MySQL's built-in mysqldump utility. Instead of copying the specific files, you can use mysqldump to recreate the SQL queries used to build—and more importantly, to populate—the tables and data. An added benefit of this formal backup is that your databases can be easily transferred to another operating system or even another database application by importing the SQL queries there.

The syntax for mysqldump is

`mysqldump [options] databasename`

The [options] section is, naturally, optional, but common arguments to use would include the following:

- --add-drop-table, which adds code to the mysqldump output so that it will delete a table before creating it

- -d, which specifies that the database structure should be dumped but not the data itself

- -t, which specifies that the data should be dumped but not the data structure

- -T, which allows you to indicate a directory where the output should be stored as a series of files

This last option is particularly useful since mysqldump will otherwise send all of the output to the screen, where it is far more difficult to manage. As an example, the following will create two files in the C:\backup directory for each table in *databasename*:

`mysqldump -u root -p -T C:\backup`
`→ databasename`

An SQL Equivalent, Part 1

With newer versions of MySQL you can back up the database—as mysqldump would—using SQL within the mysql monitor. The proper terminology for doing so is

`BACKUP TABLE tablename TO '/path/to/`
`→ directory'`

This query will send all of the data in *tablename* to the specified directory as a series of *.frm*, *.MYD*, and *.MYI* files. You can backup multiple tables by separating each table name by a comma.

Yet another SQL option is to use a `SELECT INTO` query:

`SELECT * INTO OUTFILE '/path/to/`
`→ filename.txt' FROM tablename`

This structure will allow you to create a more specialized query and store the results in a text file. This method will only store the data, not the structure of a table.

Two caveats with using SQL to backup your databases are that MySQL must have permission to create the file in the directory that you name and that you must be logged in as a user with `FILE` permissions (which may also mean you can only do this while working directly on the server). For these reasons, you may find using the mysqldump utility easier.

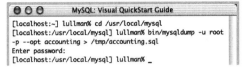

```
[localhost:~] lullman% cd /usr/local/mysql
[localhost:/usr/local/mysql] lullman% bin/mysqldump -u root
-p --opt accounting > /tmp/accounting.sql
Enter password:
[localhost:/usr/local/mysql] lullman% _
```

Figure 10.6 Using mysqldump with the --opt argument will create one text file as a backup of the entire named database.

In general, the easiest, most fail-safe configuration option for mysqldump is to use --opt. This setting will automatically initiate a standard set of parameters, and instead of making several files, it will create one large text file. In this case you should specify the filename to be created as a backup, rather than a directory:

mysqldump --opt databasename < /path/to/
→ filename.sql

To demonstrate backing up a database, I'll begin by dumping the *accounting* files, which have been developed throughout the course of this book.

To use mysqldump:

1. Log onto your system from a command-line interface.

2. Move to the mysql/bin or just mysql directory, depending upon your operating system.

   cd /usr/local/mysql (Unix)

   cd C:\mysql\bin (Windows)

3. Back up the *accounting* database as a whole (**Figure 10.6**).

   Type either

   ▲ mysqldump -u root -p --opt
      → accounting > /tmp/accounting.sql
      or

   ▲ bin/mysqldump -u root -p --opt
      → accounting > /tmp/accounting.sql

   This code (use the appropriate syntax for your server) will dump both the structure and the contents of the *accounting* database as a series of SQL commands stored within the /tmp/accounting.sql file. If you are using Windows, you can choose another directory, such as C:\backup (if it exists).

   continues on next page

While you do not necessarily need to be the root user to use mysqldump, you will need to be a user with access to the database being backed up.

4. Backup up the *accounting* database as a series of files (**Figure 10.7**).

   `mysqldump -u root -p -T /tmp accounting`

   With the -T option mysqldump will create two text files for each table: one, `tablename.sql`, would recreate the table's structure, and the second, `tablename.txt`, would repopulate the records of that table.

5. View the contents of the /tmp directory (**Figure 10.8**).

   `ls /tmp`

   The /tmp directory now contains the `accounting.sql` file, which is a dump of the entire database, and several `.txt` and `.sql` files which combined represent each table.

✔ Tips

- Remember that the mysql daemon must be running in order to use mysqldump.

- To see the result of using mysqldump, view one of the created files by opening it in a text editor.

- If you find yourself using the mysqldump application a lot, it would be well worth your time to read the section of the manual on it in order to learn about all of the configuration options.

- You can backup every database at once using

  `mysqldump --opt --all-databases > /path/`
  `→ to/file.sql`

- One of the advantages of using mysqldump to backup your files is that you can set up a cron (on Unix and Mac OS X) or a service (on Windows) to automatically run mysqldump every day.

Figure 10.7 The -T option with mysqldump differs from --opt in that it will create multiple files constituting a backup, rather than one.

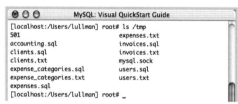

Figure 10.8 The /tmp directory now contains the *accounting* database backed up in two different ways.

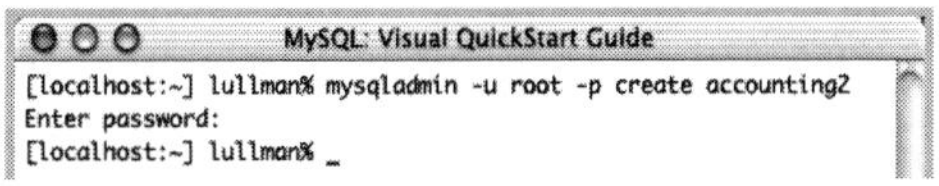

Figure 10.9 In order to practice using batch files without altering my existing database, I'll create a new database with mysqladmin.

Using Batch Files

For the most part, throughout the course of this book I have run queries directly in the mysql monitor. The MySQL software also allows you to run queries on the server without entering the mysql client itself or using an API. To do so is to use mysql in what is called *batch mode*. Instead of entering queries directly, you can store them in a text file and then run the text file in mysql:

bin/mysql -u username -p < '/path/to/
→ filename.txt'

Since you will presumably be running the queries on a particular database, you will often use the -D option to select it:

bin/mysql -u username -p -D databasename <
→ '/path/to/filename.txt'

As just one example of this technology, I will run the table-creation SQL statements (created in the previous section of this chapter) through the mysql client to recreate the *accounting* database.

To use batch files:

1. Create a new accounting database, if necessary (**Figure 10.9**).

   mysqladmin -u root -p create accounting2;

   Because you will encounter problems attempting to create tables when a table with the same name exists, you will need to create a new *accounting* database where there was not one or make a new database to work with before proceeding. If you want to practice these steps without affecting the existing *accounting* database, create an *accounting2* database to use.

   If you used the --add-drop-tables option when running mysqldump, the SQL will automatically first delete the table, and then recreate it.

continues on next page

Using Batch Files

2. Recreate the *expenses* table
(**Figure 10.10**).

bin/mysql -u root -p -D accounting2 <
→ '/tmp/expenses.sql'

The expenses.sql file, created when I ran
mysqldump, contains the CREATE TABLE
expenses… SQL. Loading it into mysql
from the command line saves me the
hassle of retyping the lengthy query.

3. Recreate the *expense_categories* table
(**Figure 10.11**).

bin/mysql -u root -p -D accounting2 <
→ '/tmp/expense_categories.sql'

To create another table, you can use the
same syntax as you did in step 2, but
refer to a different filename.

4. Recreate the remaining tables
(**Figure 10.12**).

bin/mysql -u root -p -D accounting2 <
→ '/tmp/invoices.sql'

bin/mysql -u root -p -D accounting2 <
→ '/tmp/clients.sql'

bin/mysql -u root -p -D accounting2 <
→ '/tmp/users.sql'

Now that all of the tables have been
recreated, you can repopulate them using
mysqlimport (see the next section of this
chapter).

Figure 10.10 To recreate the *expenses* table without
retyping my SQL, I can use the batch files created by
mysqldump.

Figure 10.11 I can continue loading batch files into
MySQL…

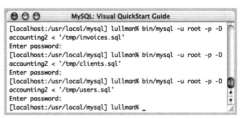

Figure 10.12 …until all of the tables have been
recreated.

✔ Tips

■ Another benefit of using mysql's batch mode is that you can establish crons (Unix) or services (Windows) to automatically run queries at set times.

■ To view the result of a batch file (what MySQL returns), add | more to your code. The line

```
bin/mysql -u username -p < '/path/to/
→ filename.txt' | more
```

will display the results one page at a time (press the space bar to see the subsequent pages or q to quit).

■ If you want to save the result of a batch file as its own text file, add > '/path/to/output.txt' to your code. The line

```
bin/mysql -u username -p < '/path/to/
→ input.txt' > '/path/to/output.txt'
```

creates a file containing the results of the queries.

USING BATCH FILES

Importing Data

Once you've learned how to back up your databases, you should understand how to reconstruct them. If you copied over the applicable files from the mysql/data directory, copying these files back will reestablish your information. This was demonstrated in the first part of the chapter. If you used the mysqldump utility, its counterpart, mysqlimport, will reinstate the databases. This application takes the data stored in a text file and inserts it into a table.

The syntax for using mysqlimport is

```
mysqlimport -u username -p databasename
→ '/path/to/filename.sql'
```

With mysqlimport, there are two assumptions: first, that the table the data is being inserted into already exists; and, second, that the text file containing the records to be inserted has the same name as the table.

As an example, I'll import the data from the *accounting* database, which was dumped earlier in this chapter.

To use mysqlimport:

1. Log onto your system from a command-line interface.

2. Move to the mysql/bin or just mysql directory, depending upon your operating system.
   cd /usr/local/mysql/bin (Unix)
   cd C:\mysql\bin (Windows)

An SQL Equivalent, Part 2

There are many different ways to import data into your database. These options include: using the mysqlimport utility, using batch files, and using SQL within the mysql monitor. For this last method there are two primary SQL commands. The first is RESTORE and the second is LOAD DATA.

RESTORE is the complement to the SQL term BACKUP and is used to recreate a table based upon files stored in a directory. The syntax is

```
RESTORE TABLE tablename FROM '/path/to/
→ directory'
```

With the RESTORE TABLE command, just like the BACKUP command, the operation can fail if MySQL cannot copy the file from the one directory to the other (e.g., from /tmp to /usr/local/mysql/data/accounting).

LOAD DATA INFILE is the complement of the SELECT ... INTO OUTFILE SQL query.

```
LOAD DATA INFILE '/path/to/
→ filename.txt' INTO TABLE tablename
```

To use the LOAD DATA technique, you will need FILE permissions, and you will need to start mysql with the --local-infile option if you are loading a file from a client machine to a separate server computer.

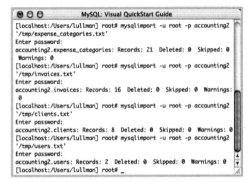

Figure 10.13 The mysqlimport utility can be used to insert records into a table from tab-delimited text files.

```
[localhost:/Users/lullman] root# mysqlimport -u root -p accounting2
'/tmp/expense_categories.txt'
Enter password:
accounting2.expense_categories: Records: 21 Deleted: 0 Skipped: 0
Warnings: 0
[localhost:/Users/lullman] root# mysqlimport -u root -p accounting2
'/tmp/invoices.txt'
Enter password:
accounting2.invoices: Records: 16 Deleted: 0 Skipped: 0 Warnings:
0
[localhost:/Users/lullman] root# mysqlimport -u root -p accounting2
'/tmp/clients.txt'
Enter password:
accounting2.clients: Records: 8 Deleted: 0 Skipped: 0 Warnings: 0
[localhost:/Users/lullman] root# mysqlimport -u root -p accounting2
'/tmp/users.txt'
Enter password:
accounting2.users: Records: 2 Deleted: 0 Skipped: 0 Warnings: 0
[localhost:/Users/lullman] root# _
```

Figure 10.14 The mysqlimport utility will report on the success of each operation, indicating the number of records added or if a problem occurred.

3. Import the records for the *expenses* table (**Figure 10.13**).

```
mysqlimport -u root -p accounting2
→ '/tmp/expenses.txt'
```

This code will take the records stored in the `expenses.txt` file (created by mysqldump) and insert them into the *expenses* table.

4. Import the data to the other tables (**Figure 10.14**).

```
mysqlimport -u root -p accounting2
→ '/tmp/expense_categories.txt'

mysqlimport -u root -p accounting2
→ '/tmp/invoices.txt'

mysqlimport -u root -p accounting2
→ '/tmp/clients.txt'

mysqlimport -u root -p accounting2
→ '/tmp/users.txt'
```

You will need to adjust these lines accordingly (for example, if you dumped the data into a different directory) and you will need to enter the password with each iterance.

✔ Tips

- The steps demonstrated in this and the previous sections could have been simplified by using `accounting.sql`—which contains all the SQL required to rebuild every table—as your batch file. Of course then there wouldn't have been cause to use mysqlimport, which you'll want to be familiar with!

- The mysqlimport utility is actually just an implementation of the `LOAD DATA INFILE` without directly using the mysql monitor.

- To ensure that the table is empty before inserting stored records, use the `-d` option with mysqlimport.

IMPORTING DATA

Database Maintenance

Part of administrating a database, besides
maintaining backups of the data, is checking
the integrity of the files. As with any file on a
server, it is possible for these items to become
corrupted. (In fact, there was a problem in
which earlier versions of the Linux kernel
corrupted MySQL files.) To check for and
repair corrupted files, use the myisamchk
utility, like so:

`myisamchk [options] table_filename`

One difference in using myisamchk, as
opposed to the other utilities described in
this chapter, is that you must feed the application the name of the actual table file as it
is on the server. This will normally be something like:

`/usr/local/mysql/data/databasename/`
`→ tablename.MYI`

or

`C:\mysql\data\databasename\tablename.MYI`

Also, myisamchk will only work on MyISAM
table types (see Chapter 11, "Advanced
MySQL," for information on other types).

There are three primary arguments
(options) to add when using myisamchk:

- -a, analyze the table
- -r, repair the table
- -e, perform extended repairs

The general advice is to use `myisamchk -a`
frequently and `myisamchk -r` periodically or
when prompted by `myisamchk -a`. If you run
into serious problems, use the more thorough
and time-consuming `myisamchk -e`. Which
setting you use and how often is dictated by
how active your database is and how frequently
its contents and/or structure will change.

An SQL Equivalent, Part 3

Once again, you have the option of performing maintenance using SQL within
the mysql monitor rather than the dedicated utility. To quickly analyze a table, use

`CHECK TABLE tablename`

Unlike myisamchk, this query will work
on both MyISAM and InnoDB table types.

You can change the level of checking
performed by changing the SQL to `CHECK
TABLE tablename EXTENDED`.

If the `CHECK TABLE` query indicates a
problem, run `REPAIR TABLE tablename
EXTENDED`.

```
● ● ●          MySQL: Visual QuickStart Guide
[localhost:/Users/lullman] root# myisamchk -a /usr/local/mysql/data/
accounting/expenses.MYI
Checking MyISAM file: /usr/local/mysql/data/accounting/expenses.MYI
Data records:     15  Deleted blocks:     0
myisamchk: warning: 1 clients is using or hasn't closed the table pr
operly
- check file-size
- check key delete-chain
- check record delete-chain
- check index reference
- check data record references index: 1
- check record links
MyISAM-table '/usr/local/mysql/data/accounting/expenses.MYI' is usab
le but should be fixed
[localhost:/Users/lullman] root# _
```

Figure 10.15 The myisamchk utility reports on the condition of MyISAM tables.

```
● ● ●          MySQL: Visual QuickStart Guide
[localhost:/Users/lullman] root# myisamchk -r /usr/local/mysql/data/
accounting/expenses.MYI
- recovering (with sort) MyISAM-table '/usr/local/mysql/data/account
ing/expenses.MYI'
Data records: 15
- Fixing index 1
[localhost:/Users/lullman] root# _
```

Figure 10.16 If myisamchk indicates there is a problem, it can be run again to make repairs.

To use myisamchk:

1. Log onto your system from a command-line interface.

2. Back up all of the existing data using the steps previously discussed.

   Since you could be affecting the data files themselves, it's always smart to back up everything before you use myisamchk. To do so, use one of the methods discussed earlier in the chapter.

3. Run a basic analysis of the *expenses* table (**Figure 10.15**).

   myisamchk -a /usr/local/mysql/data/
   → accounting/expenses.MYI

   In this first example, I'll check the expenses table of the original *accounting* database. Depending upon your system and configuration, you may or may not need to use the -u username -p options (e.g., to run it as a MySQL root user).

4. If you run into a problem, repair the table (**Figure 10.16**).

   myisamchk -r /usr/local/mysql/data/
   → accounting/expenses.MYI

   If myisamchk -a reported a problem (which it did in Figure 10.15), fix the table using myisamchk with the -r flag.

   continues on next page

5. Repeat these steps with the other tables (**Figure 10.17**).

```
myisamchk -a /usr/local/mysql/data/
→ accounting/*.MYI
```

To run a check on every table within a database, use the asterisk wild card. This will run myisamchk on the entire *accounting* database, reporting the condition of each table. Should a problem be reported, run myisamchk -r or myisamchk -e on the particular file.

6. Reload the databases (**Figure 10.18**).

```
mysqladmin -u root -p reload
```

This last step ensures that the mysqld server acknowledges the revamped tables.

✔ Tips

- Older versions of MySQL used the ISAM table type, which made files with the extensions .ISM and .ISD. Use the isamchk utility instead of the myisamchk on these table types, if you have them.

- Another way to inspect your tables is to use myisamchk -d. This will display information about your tables. If you see a high number of deleted blocks, run myisamchk -r.

- To run myisamchk on every table of every database, use myisamchk [options] /path/to/data/*/*.MYI.

- As with some of these other utilities, myisamchk can be run periodically from a cron or service.

Figure 10.17 To check the condition of every table in a database, use the *databasename*/*.MYI syntax.

Figure 10.18 After repairing the tables, the databases must be reloaded.

Improving Performance

MySQL was created with the express purpose of being a fast and reliable database. Still, there are ways to improve performance even within the existing framework of the software.

The first way to improve the performance of MySQL is to upgrade the server itself. The connection from the client to the server (via the Internet, for example) is one potential bottleneck, and the processor speed, amount of RAM, and type of hard drive all affect MySQL's performance. Since, in the end, MySQL is constantly reading and writing from files on the hard drive, it's easy to see how outdated or slow hardware can inhibit performance.

The second way to spruce things up is to manipulate how the MySQL server (mysqld) runs. You can do this by specifying different options, such as the following:

- key_buffer (memory allotted for indexes)

- max_connections (how many connections can be handled at one time)

- table_cache (table buffer)

More information on these parameters can be found in the MySQL manual. Remember that any option applied to `safe_mysqld` will be passed onto the mysqld daemon.

A third way to improve performance is to run the myisamchk utility on the databases at regular intervals. Besides the analysis and repair techniques shown in the previous section, you can also use `myisamchk --sort-index` to optimize your tables. Similarly, you could run the `OPTIMIZE` query within the mysql client.

To optimize a table:

1. Log into the mysql monitor and select the *accounting* database.

   mysql -u username -p

   USE accounting;

   As I've stated throughout this chapter, many of the administrative tasks can be accomplished using either the dedicated utility or via SQL. In this section, I'll demonstrate the SQL method first, and then use myisamchk.

2. Optimize the expenses table (**Figure 10.19**).

   OPTIMIZE TABLE expenses;

   After running this query, MySQL will indicate the status of the table.

3. Exit the mysql monitor.

   exit;

4. Run myisamchk on every table (**Figure 10.20**).

   myisamchk --sort-index /usr/local/
   → mysql/data/accounting/*.MYI

   The myisamchk utility is convenient for improving your table's performance, allowing you to run it on several tables at a time, but remember that it is restricted to the MyISAM table type.

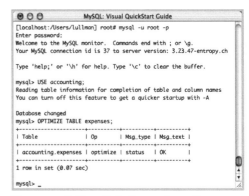

Figure 10.19 Table optimization can be easily accomplished with SQL.

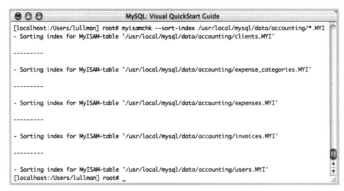

Figure 10.20 You can optimize every table—or every database—using the myisamchk utility.

IMPROVING PERFORMANCE

Figure 10.21 Starting mysqld with the `--log-update` option will have MySQL track changes made to your databases.

MySQL Logging

One subject that any database administrator should be familiar with is that of logs. There are two general types of logs MySQL uses: an error log, which records server problems, and a tracking log, which keeps a history of database alterations.

MySQL's error log will be located in the data directory and titled *hostname*`.err`. Normally this will mean that the file is either `/usr/local/mysql/data/localhost.err` or `C:\mysql\data\mysql.err`. The error log will record every error reported by the software, primarily when attempting to start mysqld. For this reason, checking the error log can greatly facilitate debugging any problems you have with running the server.

The second type of log, an update log, will record every change made to any database. In other words, it will track all of the SQL statements that have been run which affected the structure or contents of a table. In a way, this type of log is essentially a running back-up of the database.

To use and view logs:

1. Stop mysqld if it is currently running.

   Because I want to change how the mysqld server runs (namely, I want it to track changes made to databases), I'll need to stop it and restart it. If you are unsure as to how to stop mysqld, see Chapter 2, "Running MySQL."

2. Restart mysqld with the --log-update option (**Figure 10.21**).

   ```
   ./bin/safe_mysqld --user=
   → mysql --log-update &
   ```

continues on next page

MySQL Logging

The `--log-update` flag tells the mysqld process to record every action that alters the structure or contents of a database. As a default, mysqld is not started with this feature turned on.

3. Log into mysql and somehow alter the *accounting* database (**Figure 10.22**):

   `USE accounting;`

   `INSERT INTO expense_categories VALUES`
   `⇢ (NULL, 'Employee Benefits');`

   The myslqd server will only log queries that change the databases. Therefore, you need to perform an INSERT, UPDATE, DELETE, or ALTER query (SELECTs are not recorded). What you specifically do here is not as important so long as you alter the database some how.

4. Exit out of the monitor and view the log file in a text editor (**Figure 10.23**).

   `exit;`

   `vi /usr/local/mysql/data/localhost.001`

   The update logs are kept as files within the data directory, named as *hostname.num*. Therefore, the first update file will be called something like `localhost.001`. You can view it in a text editor using vi (Unix and Mac OS X) or with Notepad on Windows. (Type :q to exit the vi editor.)

Figure 10.22 To see how the update logs work, I'll need to execute some queries that affect the database.

Figure 10.23 The update log, `localhost.001`, records the relevant SQL queries, like USE and INSERT.

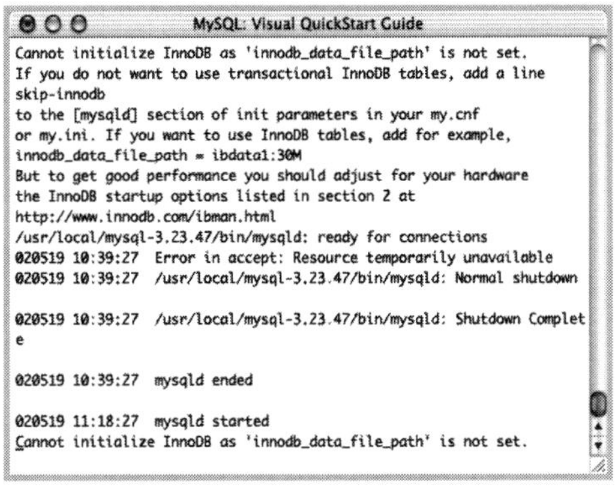
MySQL: Visual QuickStart Guide

```
Cannot initialize InnoDB as 'innodb_data_file_path' is not set.
If you do not want to use transactional InnoDB tables, add a line
skip-innodb
to the [mysqld] section of init parameters in your my.cnf
or my.ini. If you want to use InnoDB tables, add for example,
innodb_data_file_path = ibdata1:30M
But to get good performance you should adjust for your hardware
the InnoDB startup options listed in section 2 at
http://www.innodb.com/ibman.html
/usr/local/mysql-3.23.47/bin/mysqld: ready for connections
020519 10:39:27  Error in accept: Resource temporarily unavailable
020519 10:39:27  /usr/local/mysql-3.23.47/bin/mysqld: Normal shutdown

020519 10:39:27  /usr/local/mysql-3.23.47/bin/mysqld: Shutdown Complet
e

020519 10:39:27  mysqld ended

020519 11:18:27  mysqld started
Cannot initialize InnoDB as 'innodb_data_file_path' is not set.
```

Figure 10.24 The error log, `localhost.err`, records messages reported by the server.

5. View the hostname.err file (**Figure 10.24**).

   ```
   vi /usr/local/mysql/data/
   → localhost.err
   ```

   Repeat your action in step 4 to view the contents of the error log. This file should already be filled with some information, listing the history of problems which have occurred.

✔ Tips

- Do not be overzealous with your use of MySQL update logs, as they do slow down the performance of the database.
- Update logs rapidly take up space on your hard drive, especially if you have active databases.
- To reestablish the state of a database from an update log, run it as a batch file:

  `mysql -u root -p < localhost.001`

Security

As a brief conclusion to this chapter, I should mention a few of the security issues to consider when using and administrating your databases. A number of these have already been stated over the course of the book, but it's worth having in one location. Some administrative-level security tips include the following:

◆ Do not allow anonymous users to connect to MySQL.

◆ Always require a password to connect to MySQL.

◆ Require users to also specify a hostname. This limits from where users can and cannot access MySQL (although it can be more tedious).

◆ Run mysqld as a user other than root on Unix systems. This can be accomplished by starting MySQL with `safe_mysqld --user=username &`. Commonly administrators create a user called *mysql* expressly for this purpose.

◆ When storing sensitive information in a table, particularly passwords, protect the data first using either the `PASSWORD()` or `ENCODE()` function, as discussed in Chapter 5, "MySQL Functions."

◆ Assign each user the absolute minimum required privileges.

◆ Use the `--secure` and `--skip-name-resolve` options when starting mysqld (via safe_mysqld). (These are both more advanced options that should be used only if you fully understand them.)

◆ Validate user-submitted data before inserting it into a database.

◆ Limit the root user to localhost access only.

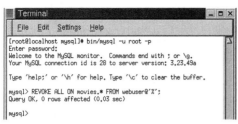

Figure 10.25 The REVOKE command, the opposite of GRANT, is the easiest way to remove or alter a user's permissions.

◆ Delete the test database, which, by default, any user can access.

◆ Delete unused user accounts, using the steps below.

To remove an existing user:

1. Log onto your system from a command-line interface.

2. Move to the mysql/bin or just mysql directory, depending upon your operating system (I'll use mysql with Red Hat Linux and append bin/ to the next line of code).

   cd /usr/local/mysql/bin (Unix)

   cd C:\mysql\bin (Windows)

3. Log into the mysql monitor.

   mysql -u username -p

4. Revoke the privileges of a user (**Figure 10.25**).

   REVOKE ALL ON movies.* FROM webuser@'%';

   For my example here, I will restrict the user *webuser*, created in Chapter 2, "Running MySQL," from accessing a particular database. Should you not have a *movies* database or a *webuser* user, change the SQL accordingly.

5. Exit out of mysql and reload the privileges with mysqladmin.

   exit;

   mysqladmin -u root -p reload

   Whether you are adding or deleting a user, the changes still do not take effect until you have reloaded the privileges.

   continues on next page

SECURITY

6. Test to see if the user can access the database (**Figure 10.26**).

`mysql -u webuser -p movies`

Because *webuser* has been denied the option of accessing the movies database, this command should be denied. The *webuser* can still access the *alpacas* database (also created in Chapter 2), though, based upon the previously created privileges.

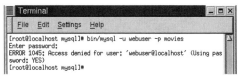

Figure 10.26 Once the user's permissions have been altered (and the privileges flushed), they can no longer access the database.

✔ Tip

■ Instead of exiting the mysql monitor and reloading MySQL, you can also enact any user/privileges changes within the mysql monitor using the SQL FLUSH PRIVILEGES.

11

ADVANCED MYSQL

This final chapter will cover a hodgepodge of topics that the beginning to intermediate MySQL user may not necessarily need, at least not at first. However, as your skills increase and the MySQL software develops, you'll find yourself using these technologies more and more. The topics I will discuss here include the InnoDB table type, how to use transactions, incorporating regular expressions, and performing full-text searches.

Some of these technologies are either fairly new to MySQL or are being incorporated more directly into future versions of the software. The latter is true for the InnoDB table type, which brings many industrial-level database features to MySQL. Some of the other techniques, such as regular expressions and full-text searching, you won't normally need, but when you do, they're irreplaceable. In this chapter, most of the demonstrations will be independent of the other information taught, and one in particular—InnoDB tables—will require special versions of the MySQL software.

Using InnoDB Tables

The MySQL software supports several different table types, including ISAM tables, which used to be the standard, and MyISAM, which is the current default. Along with these, MySQL can use InnoDB, BDB (Berkeley Database), HEAP, and temporary tables, each sporting different features and having different requirements. Of these various types, InnoDB is the most important (after the default MyISAM) and well worth your consideration. The InnoDB table type was developed by Innobase Oy (**Figure 11.1**). MySQL incorporated the technology by layering the MySQL software above an InnoDB base.

InnoDB tables are structured differently than MyISAM (they are stored as one file rather than three), but, most importantly, they allow you to perform transactions on your tables. I'll discuss transactions themselves and why they are important in the next section of this chapter.

To make an InnoDB table, you'll proceed through the normal `CREATE TABLE` SQL but conclude it with `TYPE=InnoDB`. This is true for assigning any table type, but when you do not specify a table type, MySQL assumes it to be MyISAM.

Most recent versions of the MySQL software come with the capability of using InnoDB tables, and MySQL 4 will integrate them even more so. I'll demonstrate how to begin creating InnoDB tables with MySQL, which does require some alterations to how MySQL is run.

Figure 11.1 The home page for the InnoDB software can be found at www.innodb.com.

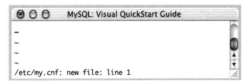

Figure 11.2 If you do not already have a copy of my.cnf on your server, you'll need to create a new one.

Figure 11.3 To begin using InnoDB tables, you'll need to make sure your my.cnf (or my.ini) file contains these lines.

To use InnoDB tables:

1. Create or edit your my.cnf file (**Figure 11.2**).

   vi /etc/my.cnf (Unix and Mac OS X)

   The my.cnf file is a configuration file for how MySQL runs. If one already exists, it would normally be found in /etc/my.cnf (Unix) or C:\ (Windows), and you can open it in any text editor. Otherwise, you'll need to create it from scratch.

   If C is not the bootable drive on your Windows operating system, you'll need to create a my.ini file and save it in your **WINDOWS** or **WINNT** directory instead.

   If you are using the WinMySQLadmin tool on Windows, you can edit the my.ini file within it. (Be sure to click "Save Modification" after making any changes.)

2. Add the following lines and save the file (**Figure 11.3**).

   [mysqld]

   innodb_data_home_dir = /usr/local/
   → mysql/data

   innodb_data_file_path = innodbdata:20M

   The first statement—the [mysqld] header —indicates that you want the following lines to apply to the mysqld application. The second line states where the InnoDB databases will be located (change this for your system as needed). Finally, the third lists a filename to be used and how large the file can be. InnoDB uses a single file (*tablename.frm*) for each table and then stores other database information in a general InnoDB file, named here.

   Also note that MySQL will need permission to create files in the specified directory, which should be true for your standard data folder.

   continues on next page

3. Stop mysqld.

`mysqladmin -u root -p shutdown`

Because you'll be making changes to how mysqld runs (in fact, which mysqld runs), you'll need to stop the existing process. If you are using Windows NT, 2000, or XP, and are running MySQL as a service, you can also use the tray-based traffic light icon to shut down the server (see Chapter 2, "Running MySQL").

4. Start mysqld or mysqld-max using either

▲ `./bin/safe_mysqld --user=mysql &` (Unix and Mac OS X, **Figure 11.4**)

or

▲ `C:\mysql\bin\mysqld-max --user=mysql` (Windows)

On non-Windows systems, restarting mysqld (using safe_mysqld) with a properly edited my.cnf file will enable you to use InnoDB tables. On Windows you'll need to specifically start the mysqd-max server. On Windows NT systems, add the `--standalone` flag as well. (Of course, in order for you to run mysqld-max, you would have had to install it along with the rest of the MySQL software.)

5. Enter the mysql monitor and create a new database (**Figure 11.5**).

`mysql -u root -p`

`CREATE DATABASE movies_db;`

`USE movies_db;`

These steps are the same as you've seen many times before. Even with InnoDB tables, MySQL will create a new directory for each new database, and the syntax for creating one is unchanged.

Instead of using an existing database, I'll be making a new one for storing movie information.

Figure 11.4 After editing the my.cnf file, restart the server so MySQL acknowledges the changes.

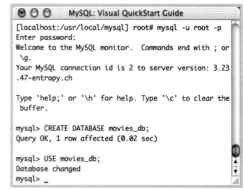

Figure 11.5 I'll be creating a new *movies_db* database on which to demonstrate InnoDB tables.

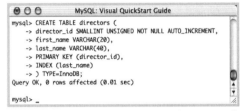

Figure 11.6 The first InnoDB table I'll be creating is *movies*.

```
MySQL: Visual QuickStart Guide
mysql> CREATE TABLE movies (
    -> movie_id INT UNSIGNED NOT NULL AUTO_INCREMENT,
    -> title VARCHAR(100),
    -> director_id SMALLINT(4),
    -> PRIMARY KEY (movie_id)
    -> ) TYPE=InnoDB;
Query OK, 0 rows affected (0.37 sec)

mysql> _
```

```
MySQL: Visual QuickStart Guide
mysql> CREATE TABLE directors (
    -> director_id SMALLINT UNSIGNED NOT NULL AUTO_INCREMENT,
    -> first_name VARCHAR(20),
    -> last_name VARCHAR(40),
    -> PRIMARY KEY (director_id),
    -> INDEX (last_name)
    -> ) TYPE=InnoDB;
Query OK, 0 rows affected (0.01 sec)

mysql> _
```

Figure 11.7 The second InnoDB table in the *movies_db* database contains all of the director information.

6. Create a new InnoDB table (**Figure 11.6**).

CREATE TABLE movies (

movie_id INT UNSIGNED NOT NULL
→ AUTO_INCREMENT,

title VARCHAR(100),

director_id SMALLINT(4),

PRIMARY KEY (movie_id)

) TYPE=InnoDB;

The first table, *movies*, will store the movie *title* and *director_id* (which, in turn, will be a primary key in the *directors* table). Naturally, there may be any number of other pieces of information you'd want to include, but I will use only the bare minimum here. After closing the initial parentheses (which ends the table column definitions section of the query), I indicate the table's type. If your system will not support the InnoDB type, you'll see an error message after running this command.

7. Create a second InnoDB table (**Figure 11.7**).

CREATE TABLE directors (

director_id SMALLINT(4) UNSIGNED NOT
→ NULL AUTO_INCREMENT,

first_name VARCHAR(20),

last_name VARCHAR(40),

PRIMARY KEY (director_id),

INDEX (last_name)

) TYPE=InnoDB;

The *directors* table, for the time being, just records a director's first and last name, correlated to an ID. I've added an index to the *last_name* column for improved performance, which you could also do with the *movies* table's *title* column. InnoDB tables can be indexed just as you would any other table type.

continues on next page

8. View the contents of the data directory
(**Figure 11.8**).

`ls -l /usr/local/mysql/data`

For Unix and Mac OS X users, the `ls`
command will reveal the contents of a
directory; in Windows, you can just use
Windows Explorer. If the above steps
worked without a problem, you should
see the `innodbdata` file here, along with
InnoDB-specific log files. Within the
`movies_db` directory you should also find
the `directors.frm` and `movies.frm` files.

✔ Tips

■ You can change an existing table's type
using the command
`ALTER TABLE tablename TYPE=InnoDB`.

■ If you are compiling your own version
of MySQL from the source files, use the
`--with-innodb` configuration option to
be able to use InnoDB tables.

■ InnoDB tables recognize foreign keys (i.e.,
you can define a field as a foreign key) and
will check for foreign key compliancy.
See www.mysql.com/doc/S/E/
SEC446.html for more information.

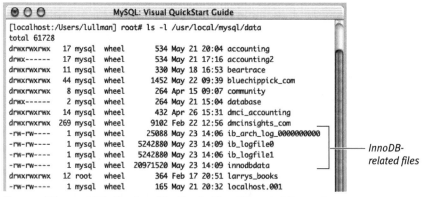

Figure 11.8 You can tell by the size of the files that InnoDB created (`ib_logfile0`,
`innodbdata`, etc.) that InnoDB tables will take up significant disk space.

USING INNODB TABLES

Transactions in MySQL

The more robust database applications, such as Oracle, support the concept of transactions in which SQL queries are executed as a two-step process. First you run the query (or queries) to see what the results will be. Then, if the results were acceptable, you enact the queries; otherwise you undo its effects. With InnoDB (or BDB) tables, you can now use transactions in MySQL as well.

Transactions bring increased reliability to your databases. If you have a sequence of SQL queries that should either all work or not work at all, you can now trust that you'll never get stuck halfway through the sequence. In fact, you could say that transactions bring an undo feature to your database applications. To this end, transaction-safe tables such as InnoDB are more secure and easier to recover should the server crash (since queries are either completely run or not at all). On the downside, transactions can be slower than standard queries would be and your databases will require a more advanced API to adjust for the transactional nature.

To start a transaction, you use the SQL term BEGIN. Then you proceed with all of your queries as you otherwise would. If you like the results of the transaction, enter COMMIT to enact the queries. Otherwise, enter ROLLBACK to retract their effect. As a simple example of this process, I'll begin adding directors and movies to the *movies_db* database. Because the *director_id* in the *movies* table depends upon the *director_id* in the *directors* table, with transactions you can guarantee that both tables are successfully modified when adding records.

To use transactions:

1. Log onto the mysql monitor.

   `mysql -u root -p`

2. Select a transaction-safe database.

   `USE movies_db;`

   Remember that transactions can be used (in current versions of MySQL) only on InnoDB and BDB table types.

3. Start a transaction (**Figure 11.9**).

   `BEGIN;`

   Every query from here until I enter `COMMIT` or `ROLLBACK` will be part of one transaction, even if unrelated.

4. Insert a new director and movie (**Figure 11.10**).

   `INSERT INTO directors (first_name,`
   `→ last_name) VALUES ('Martin',`
   `→ 'Scorsese');`

   `INSERT INTO movies (title, director_id)`
   `→ VALUES ('The Age of Innocence',`
   `→ LAST_INSERT_ID());`

   Because the `director_id` value is related between the `movies` and `directors` tables, I want to be sure that each is updated correctly before making the changes permanent. In such instances, transactions will help guarantee the integrity of the database.

5. If the queries worked, commit the changes (**Figure 11.11**).

   `SELECT * FROM movies, directors`
   `→ WHERE movies.director_id=`
   `→ directors.director_id;`

   `COMMIT;`

   With my `SELECT` query, I'll check the tables to see if the information was properly entered. When performing transactions, any changes you make will be reflected in your `SELECT` queries even before you commit them, which is why this statement works.

Figure 11.9 To start a new transaction, type `BEGIN;` and press Return.

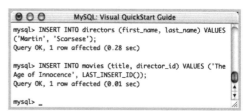

Figure 11.10 You can perform as many queries as you'd like as part of one transaction, including INSERTs, UPDATEs, and DELETEs.

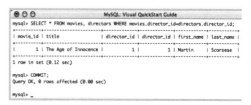

Figure 11.11 Entering `COMMIT;` and pressing Return will enforce the transaction.

TRANSACTIONS IN MySQL

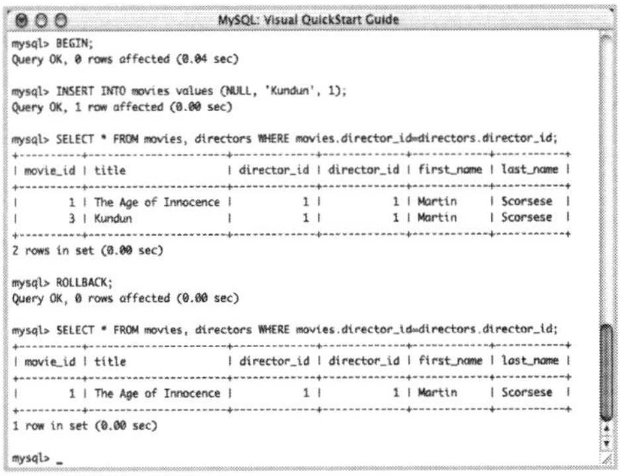

Figure 11.12 This sequence of queries reveals how rolling back a transaction negates any effects it might have had.

6. If you do not want to enact the changes, revoke the queries (**Figure 11.12**).

```
BEGIN;
INSERT INTO movies VALUES (NULL,
→ 'Kundun', 1);
SELECT * FROM movies, directors
→ WHERE movies.director_id=
→ directors.director_id;
ROLLBACK;
```

Just to demonstrate how you roll back transactions, I'll add another movie but then cancel the transaction. You can see how the change is reflected by SELECT queries during the transaction but, should you use ROLLBACK in lieu of COMMIT, the same SELECT query would no longer display those changes.

✔ Tips

- If the connection to the database is lost (whether it comes from a script or a mysql client), all of the transactions are rolled back.

- Many SQL commands will automatically commit and end a transaction, including ALTER, DROP, BEGIN, and TRUNCATE.

- When using tables that support transactions, if you fail to use the BEGIN command, the queries will be automatically run as they are on non-transactional tables (in other words, queries will be automatically committed).

Locking Tables

Transactions allow you to protect the data and integrity of a table by restricting actions, but they will work only on transaction-safe tables. For other table types, including the default MyISAM, your only option for protecting tables during a sequence of queries is to lock them. The syntax for doing so is

```
LOCK TABLES tablename1 LOCKTYPE,
→ tablename2 LOCKTYPE
```

When locking a table (or tables, as you can lock several at the same time) you can specify a READ or WRITE lock as the LOCKTYPE. A read lock restricts everyone to only reading from a table (in other words, the table's structure and contents cannot be altered). A write lock restricts everyone but the issuer of the lock from reading or writing to a table. An important aspect of locks is that they are related to the connection that issued them. In other words, if a mysql client session issues a lock, every other mysql client and/or script connecting to the database would be locked out.

To unlock a table, the issuer (in other words, the same connection that locked the table) must enter

```
UNLOCK TABLES
```

Because of the secure way that MySQL works, locking tables is generally unnecessary, although there are certain situations (such as backing up the database via SQL) where it's a good idea. Another common example is when you perform an update based upon the immediate result of a SELECT query, in which case you would not want the information to change in the interim.

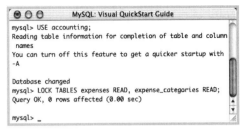

Figure 11.13 Use the LOCK TABLES SQL command to prevent a table from being altered while you perform other actions.

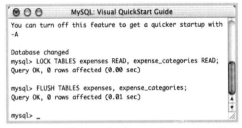

Figure 11.14 Before you back up a table, you should run the FLUSH TABLES query on it.

To lock a table:

1. Log onto the mysql monitor.

   `mysql -u root -p`

2. Select the *accounting* database.

   `USE accounting;`

   Since there is little cause to use locking on a transaction-safe database (such as *movies_db*, created earlier in the chapter), I'll use the *accounting* database for locking purposes instead.

3. Lock the tables you will be using (**Figure 11.13**).

   `LOCK TABLES expenses READ,`
   `→ expense_categories READ;`

   While I'm backing up these two tables, I'll lock them to prevent alterations from affecting the integrity of the backup.

4. Flush the tables (**Figure 11.14**).

   `FLUSH TABLES expenses,`
   `→ expense_categories;`

   Before backing up the tables, with the **BACKUP TABLE** command, it's best to perform a FLUSH on them so that the tables will be backed up in their most current form.

   continues on next page

LOCKING TABLES

5. Back up the tables (**Figure 11.15**).

```
BACKUP TABLE expenses,
→ expense_categories TO '/tmp';
```

This query will send the structure and contents of these two tables to the /tmp folder. The BACKUP TABLE query will work only on MyISAM tables. See Chapter 10, "MySQL Administration," for more information on backing up databases with SQL.

6. Unlock the tables (**Figure 11.16**).

```
UNLOCK TABLES;
```

This command will unlock every locked table (there's no need to itemize). Do not forget this step or else other users (including your scripts) would be locked out!

✔ Tips

- A second LOCK TABLES command entered by the same issuer will automatically unlock previously locked tables.

- You can set different locks on different tables at the same time:

```
LOCK TABLES table1 WRITE, table2 READ
```

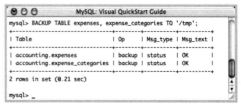

Figure 11.15 Here I've used the BACKUP TABLE syntax to perform a backup within the mysql monitor.

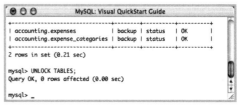

Figure 11.16 The final step is to unlock every table so the database can be used as normal again.

LOCKING TABLES

Full-Text Searching

MySQL, since version 3.23.23, supports a technique called full-text searching. With full-text searches, you can find occurrences of words within values stored in columns. The syntax for using full-text searching is

```
SELECT * FROM tablename WHERE MATCH (column)
→ AGAINST ('string');
```

The result of the query will be the rows returned in order of relevance from most to least. In other words, the rows in which *string* most matches the values in *column* will be listed first. To view the relevance of a row returned by a match, you would select it:

```
SELECT column_id, MATCH (column)
→ AGAINST ('string') FROM tablename
```

If you want to match against multiple words, you can do so, separating the words by spaces:

```
SELECT column_id, MATCH (column)
→ AGAINST ('word1 word2') FROM tablename
```

With a query like this, rows that contain both words will rank higher than those that contain only one or the other (which would still qualify as a match).

You can take your full-text searching one step further by using its Boolean mode (as of MySQL version 4.0.1). This allows you to enter multiple keywords and weight them:

```
SELECT column_id, MATCH (column)
→ AGAINST ('+word1 word2' IN BOOLEAN MODE)
→ FROM tablename
```

continues on next page

In Boolean mode the words are preceded by special characters (**Table 11.1**) to indicate how their presence should be weighted with regards to relevancy.

There's one last catch with full-text searching: Before you use it in a SELECT query, you'll need to establish a full-text index on the appropriate column or columns. You do so with

```
ALTER TABLE tablename ADD FULLTEXT
→ indexname (column1, column2)
```

Full-text searching is most important in situations where people will be entering in keywords that must be searched against specific fields in a table, such as search engines.

Special Boolean Mode Characters

CHARACTER	MEANING	EXAMPLE	MATCHES
+	Word is required	+punk rock	*punk* is required and *rock* is optional
-	Word must not be present	+punk -rock	*punk* is required and *rock* cannot be present
" "	A literal phrase	"punk rock"	Occurrences of the phrase *punk rock* is weighted
<	Less important	<punk +rock	*rock* is required and *punk* is less significant
>	More important	>punk +rock	*rock* is required but *punk* is more significant
( )	Creates groups	(>punk roll) +rock	*rock* is required, both *punk* and *roll* are optional, but *punk* is weighted more
~	Detracts from relevance	+punk ~rock	*punk* is required and the presence of *rock* devalues the relevance (but *rock* is not excluded)
*	Allows for wildcards (use at the end of word)	+punk +rock*	*punk* and *rock* are required, but *rocks*, *rocker*, *rocking*, etc., are counted

Table 11.1 These characters are specifically used to weight the importance of terms in full-text searches.

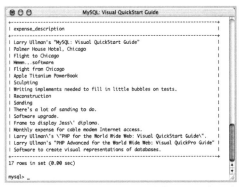

Figure 11.17 Once my *expenses* table has a number of records stored in it I can begin to perform full-text searches in it.

Figure 11.18 To create a full-text index on an existing table, I use the ALTER TABLE syntax.

Figure 11.19 The most basic full-text search will retrieve every record that contains the one matched word.

To use full-text searching:

1. Log onto the mysql monitor.

   `mysql -u root -p`

2. Select the *accounting* database.

   `USE accounting;`

3. Make sure the *expenses* table is well populated (**Figure 11.17**).

   It doesn't really matter what SQL you use during these steps as long as you add records with good descriptions to the *expenses* table. Full-text indexing and searching becomes more useful and accurate the more records a table has.

4. Create a full-text index (**Figure 11.18**).

   `ALTER TABLE expenses ADD FULLTEXT`
   `↪ (expense_description);`

   Before I run any full-text searches on a table, I must create a full-text index on the column or columns involved.

5. Do a full-text search using the word *visual* (**Figure 11.19**).

   `SELECT expense_id, expense_description`
   `↪ FROM expenses WHERE MATCH (expense_`
   `↪ description) AGAINST ('visual');`

   This query will return the *expense_id* and *expense_description* columns wherever *visual* has a positive relevance in the *expense_description* values. In other words, any record that contains the word *visual* will be returned.

   continues on next page

6. Run a full-text search using the words *visual* and *guide* (**Figure 11.20**).

SELECT expense_id, MATCH
(expense_description) AGAINST
→ ('visual guide') AS rel,
→ expense_description FROM expenses
→ WHERE MATCH (expense_description)
→ AGAINST ('visual guide');

This query differs from that in step 5 in two ways. First, I'm also selecting the MATCH…AGAINST so that the calculated relevance number is displayed. Second, I've included a second term to match. Those records with both terms will score higher than those with just one.

7. If you are using version 4.01 or higher of MySQL, practice full-text searches using the Boolean mode.

✔ Tips

■ Full-text searches are case-insensitive.

■ If you match against a term that appears in more than half of the records, no rows will be returned because that term will be treated as not specific enough.

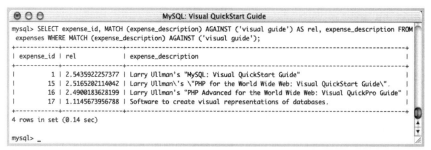

Figure 11.20 When you use multiple keywords in a full-text search, those records containing every word will be listed first (but any record containing at least one of the terms will be returned).

Special Regular Expression Characters	
CHARACTER	MATCHES
.	any single character
q?	zero or one *q*
q*	zero or more *q*'s
q+	at least one *q*
q{x}	*x* instances of *q*
q{x,}	at least *x* instances of *q*
q{,x}	up to *x* instances of *q*
q{x,y}	between *x* and *y* instances of *q*
^q	starts with *q*
q$	ends with *q*
(pqr)	grouping (matches *pqr*)
q|z	either *q* or *z*
[]	character classes (e.g., [a-z], [0-9])
\	escapes a special character (\., *, etc.)

Table 11.2 Here are the different special characters you can use when writing regular expressions.

Regular Expressions

In Chapter 4, "SQL," I discussed and demonstrated how you can use the terms LIKE and NOT LIKE to match a string against the values in a column. Furthermore, you could use the single (_) and multiple (%) wildcard characters to add flexibility to what is matched. For example,

SELECT * FROM users WHERE first_name LIKE
→ 'John%'

Thanks to regular expressions, which MySQL also supports, you can take this concept one giant step forward. With regular expressions you can define more elaborate patterns to match and then use REGEXP and NOT REGEXP (or RLIKE and NOT RLIKE).

SELECT * FROM users WHERE first_name REGEXP
→ '^(Jo)h?n+.*'

This query differs from the LIKE query above in that it will match *John, Johnathon, Jon, Jonathon*, etc., whereas the earlier one would match only *John* or *Johnathon*. Since this may not make much sense to you if you are unfamiliar with regular expressions, I'll go over how patterns are written in more detail.

To define a pattern, you use a combination of literals (e.g., 'a' matches only the letter *a*) and special characters (**Table 11.2**).

To match a string beginning with *ab*, you would use '^ab.*': the literal *ab* plus zero or more of anything (represented by the period). To match a string that contains the word *color* or *colour*, you would write 'col(or)|(our)': the literal *col* plus either *or* or *our*.

Obviously, the hardest part of using regular expressions (in MySQL or elsewhere) is coming up with accurate and useful patterns. Defining this pattern is frequently a matter of finding a balance between one that is too lenient and another that is too strict.

To use REGEX and NOT REGEX:

1. Log onto the mysql monitor.

   `mysql -u root -p`

2. Select the *accounting* database.

   `USE accounting;`

3. Find which clients have a toll-free number (**Figure 11.21**).

   `SELECT client_name, client_phone FROM`
   `→ clients WHERE client_phone REGEXP`
   `→ '(800)|(888)|(877)';`

   Toll-free numbers (in the United States and Canada) have an 800, 888, or 877 area code. The pattern in this regular expression will match any column whose value contains one of those three.

4. Retrieve all of the valid contact email addresses (**Figure 11.22**).

   `SELECT client_name, contact_first_name,`
   `→ contact_email FROM clients WHERE`
   `→ contact_email REGEXP '[[:alnum:]]`
   `→ +@.*\.[[:alnum:]]{2,3}';`

   The pattern defined here for recognizing usable email addresses is very basic and perhaps overly lenient but should suffice for testing purposes. You can always make your patterns more (or less) exacting, per your needs.

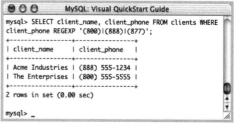

Figure 11.21 Regular expressions can add flexibility to your queries...

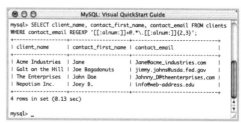

Figure 11.22 ...or assist in validating column values.

REGULAR EXPRESSIONS

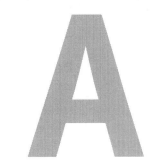

TROUBLESHOOTING

Like any software, MySQL can occasionally cause those bang-your-head-against-the-wall moments, so this book includes a troubleshooting appendix to help address the most common problems. On the bright side, once it gets going, MySQL tends to run for extended periods of time with little to no issues. On the other hand, sometimes getting the server itself to start, before you even attempt to connect to it, can be unduly troublesome. This section of the book will address the most frequently witnessed problems, giving a sense of what the cause is and what can be done to remedy the situation. As you might expect, you can always turn to the MySQL manual for a more complete list of problems and solutions.

Installation

For better or for worse, you won't discover most installation-related problems until you go to run the software. That being said, four issues to be aware of when configuring and installing MySQL are

♦ Be sure to use the `--prefix=/path/to/mysql` parameter when configuring MySQL if you are installing from the source.

♦ You must run the `mysql_install_db` script (found in the `mysql/scripts` directory) to set up the users and privileges tables, unless you are copying over existing databases (**Figure A.1**).

♦ When installing a new version of MySQL from the source, first delete the previous configuration by typing `rm config.cache` followed by `make clean`.

♦ On Windows platforms, install MySQL in `C:\mysql` (the default location) if at all possible.

✔ Tips

■ For more information on configuration issues, see www.mysql.com/doc/C/o/Compilation_problems.html or type `./configure --help` (**Figure A.2**).

■ For more information on the `mysql_install_db` script, see www.mysql.com/doc/m/y/mysql_install_db.html.

■ Instead of clearing out a previous configuration as a two-step process, you can run `make distclean`.

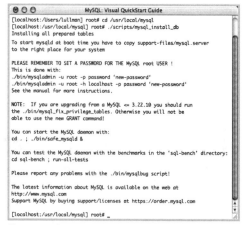

Figure A.1 The `mysql_install_db` script establishes the *mysql* database that is used to grant access to users.

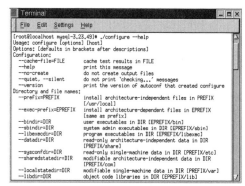

Figure A.2 The configuration step (when installing from the source files) has dozens of parameters that can be adjusted for your server.

INSTALLATION

MySQL: Visual QuickStart Guide
[localhost:/usr/local/mysql] root# ./bin/safe_mysqld --user=mysql --debug &
[1] 372
[localhost:/usr/local/mysql] root# Starting mysqld daemon with databases from /usr/local/mysql/data
[localhost:/usr/local/mysql] root# _

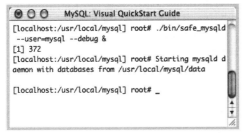

Figure A.3 The --debug option will help you determine why mysqld will not start properly.

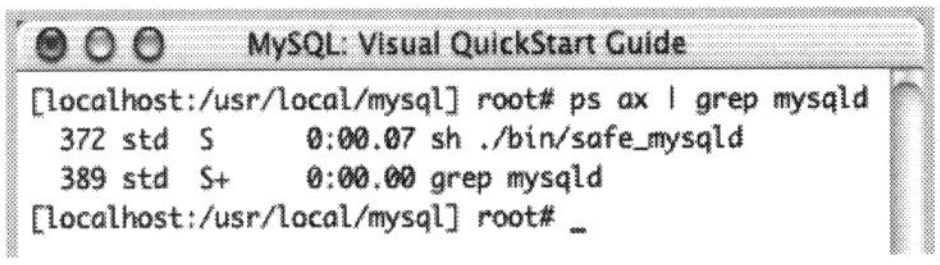

MySQL: Visual QuickStart Guide
[localhost:/usr/local/mysql] root# ps ax | grep mysqld
372 std S 0:00.07 sh ./bin/safe_mysqld
389 std S+ 0:00.00 grep mysqld
[localhost:/usr/local/mysql] root# _

Figure A.4 The command `ps ax | grep mysqld` should show that safe_mysqld and mysqld are running.

Starting MySQL

Here are some common problems and solutions for starting MySQL:

- If MySQL cannot find the data directory, set the value when you start mysqld using the `--basedir=/path/to/mysql/data` option.
- If you are using Windows, keep your operating system as up to date as possible. MySQL on Windows NT requires service pack 3 or later.
- If MySQL claims that it cannot find `host.frm` or `mysql.host`, it means that it cannot read the grant tables in the *mysql* database. Check that you ran the `mysql_install_db` script and that MySQL has permission to access the *mysql* files.

As a further method of debugging, you can start MySQL with `--debug` (**Figure A.3**), which will create a file called `mysqld.trace` that records errors. (You can view `mysqld.trace` in any text editor.)

✔ Tips

- On Windows, you can have difficulty starting MySQL as a service if there is a space in the path name, e.g., `C:/program files/mysql` or if part of the path name is too long.
- On Unix and Mac OS X, to check if MySQL is already running, type `ps ax | grep mysqld` in a shell (**Figure A.4**).
- For more information, see www.mysql.com/doc/P/o/Post-installation.html.

Accessing MySQL

Once you know that MySQL has been successfully installed and is running, getting access to a database can be the next hiccup you encounter. The three most important variables for connecting to MySQL are host name, user name, and password. These values will be matched against the records in the mysql database to approve access.

Next, MySQL will check to see if the user has the permission to run specific queries on specific databases (see Chapter 2, "Running MySQL," for more information). However, an inability to connect to MySQL as a whole is a far more common issue than an inability to run a particular query.

Common problems and solutions to access denied errors are

◆ Reload MySQL after altering the privileges so that the changes take effect. Use either the mysqladmin tool (**Figure A.5**) or run FLUSH PRIVILEGES in the mysql monitor.

◆ Double-check the password used. The error message *Access denied for user: 'root@localhost' (Using password: YES)* normally indicates that the password is wrong or mistyped. (This is not always the cause but is the first thing to check.)

◆ Use the PASSWORD() function when setting privileges or updating a password.

◆ If you are having trouble using a host name, try omitting the host name, using a different host name (such as *localhost* if you are working directly on the computer), running mysqladmin flush-hosts (**Figure A.6**), starting mysqld with --skip-name-resolve, or changing the host setting for the user within the *mysql* database.

Figure A.5 After changing any user/privilege setting, use mysqladmin (or SQL) to enact the changes.

Figure A.6 If you are having particular difficulty with a host name, flush MySQL's host cache with the mysqladmin tool.

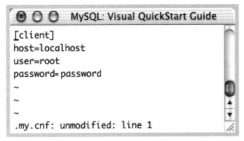

```
  ⦿ ○ ○     MySQL: Visual QuickStart Guide
[client]
host=localhost
user=root
password= password
~
~
~
 .my.cnf: unmodified: line 1
```

Figure A.7 Settings in a .my.cnf file can affect access to a MySQL utility without your awareness.

◆ If you are using a .my.cnf file to establish parameters for client programs, don't forget to check these settings (**Figure A.7**). Also inspect any my.cnf or my.ini files.

◆ The error message *Can't connect to...* (error number 2002) indicates that either MySQL is not running or is not running on the socket or TCP/IP port tried by the client. First check that MySQL is running, then attempt to connect using a different port or socket.

✔ Tips

■ Use the Task Manager on Windows NT operating systems to confirm that MySQL is running.

■ For more information on access problems, see www.mysql.com/doc/A/c/Access_denied.html.

ACCESSING MYSQL

mysql.sock Problems

The mysql.sock is the socket that clients use to access the mysqld server on Unix and Mac OS X systems (MySQL on Windows uses TCP/IP). Should the client application—for example, the mysql monitor—be unable to find the socket (it is normally stored in the /tmp directory), you'll encounter problems accessing MySQL.

Like most computer problems, this one can be frequently solved by rebooting the computer. This does not always work, nor is it necessarily the best solution. There are two other, more permanent solutions: Protect the directory where the socket is stored so that it will not be deleted, or create a symbolic link to the socket in a different location.

To protect the /tmp directory:

1. Access your server as the root user in a Terminal.

2. Add a "sticky bit" to the /tmp directory (**Figure A.8**).

   chmod +t /tmp

   Adding a sticky bit to a directory means that all of the files therein can be deleted only by the owner of the file or by a super-user. One of the reasons MySQL may not be able to find the socket is that it has been inadvertently deleted by another user or application. This step will prevent that from occurring again.

3. Restart MySQL.

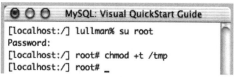

Figure A.8 On Unix and Mac OS X, the chmod command can be applied to the /tmp directory to protect the mysql.sock socket.

Figure A.9 MySQL needs to be able to find the `mysql.sock` socket in order for clients to connect to the server.

To create a symbolic link:

1. Access your server as the root user in a Terminal.

2. Locate the mysql.sock socket (**Figure A.9**).

   `find / -name "mysql.sock"`

   This command will search through the entire server to find mysql.sock. If it is stored in an unusual location, MySQL will not be able to find it and a symbolic link will need to be created instead.

3. Create a symbolic link from where MySQL thinks the socket should be to where the socket actually is.

   `ln -s /path/to/actual/mysql.sock/tmp/`
   `→ mysql.sock`

   A symbolic link will trick MySQL into thinking that /tmp/mysql.sock is the real socket, even when it is not.

✔ Tips

- To test that a socket's location is acceptable, try running `mysqladmin --socket=/path/to/socket` version from a command line.

- On some installations, the socket will be in `/var/lib/mysql` instead of `/tmp`.

- You can specify the socket's location by using either the `my.cnf` file or the `--socket` parameter when mysqld is started.

MYSQL.SOCK PROBLEMS

Resetting the Root Password

I know it happens, because I've done it myself: You go to log into MySQL as the root user and access is denied. You cannot remember the correct password or get a new password to work. Effectively you've locked yourself out of MySQL and all hope is lost. Luckily, there is an easy enough work-around when (or if) this does occur: You need to reset the root password.

Resetting an access password involves starting MySQL without the user/privilege system in use. Then anyone can access the database, make the alterations, and restart MySQL.

To reset the root password:

1. Stop the MySQL server by issuing the following command as Unix root user or mysqld user.

   `kill cat /path/to/mysql/data/`
   `→ hostname.pid`

   You may have difficulty stopping MySQL without a root user password. Try to stop MySQL using the standard methods, if you can. If you can't, use this strong-arm technique (for Unix and Mac OS X).

2. Start mysqld with `--skip-grant-tables` (**Figure A.10**).

   `./bin/safe_mysqd --user=mysql --skip-`
   `→ grant-tables &`

   The `--skip-grant-tables` option tells MySQL to run without concern for user and access privileges. While this is an obvious security issue, it's the only way to reset the root password.

Figure A.10 Using the `--skip-grant-tables` option when starting MySQL allows you to circumvent the user/privilege system.

Figure A.11 After starting MySQL without the grant tables, you can stop it without a user name and password.

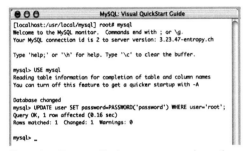

Figure A.12 To manually change a password, use the UPDATE SQL with the PASSWORD() function on the *mysql.user* table.

3. Update the root password using mysqladmin.

`mysqladmin -u root password 'newpassword'`

This step is exactly the same as the one used to first establish a root password (see Chapter 2, "Running MySQL"). No password is required to make this change since the grant tables were skipped.

4. Stop mysqld again (**Figure A.11**).

`mysqladmin shutdown`

Since mysqld is currently running without verifying access, you'll need to stop and restart the daemon rather than just flush the privileges.

5. Restart mysqld as normal.

`./safe_mysqd --user=mysql &`

6. Access the mysql monitor using the root user name and the new password.

`mysql -u root -p`

✔ Tip

- To reset the root password using the mysql client, follow steps 1 and 2 above, then enter mysql, select the *mysql* database, and run UPDATE user SET password=PASSWORD('newpassword') WHERE user='root' (**Figure A.12**). Finally, restart mysqld as normal.

Resetting the Auto Incrementation

Having automatically incremented fields in a table, like a primary key, is the perfect way to add a unique index. MySQL generally manages these values easily so that you never need to consider them. However, if you delete records at the end of a table, the auto-incremented values will get out of sync. For example, if you have ten rows of data, and then you delete records with IDs of 9 and 10, the next row added will still use an ID of 11, even though 9 would be available. To correct for this, you'll need to adjust the auto-incrementation counter.

To reset the auto incrementation:

1. Access the server through the mysql monitor.

   `mysql -u username -p`

2. Select the database.

   `USE databasename;`

3. Update the appropriate table (**Figure A.13**).

   `ALTER TABLE tablename AUTO_INCREMENT=1;`

   This command forces `AUTO_INCREMENT` to use the specified number for the next row, or the next highest available number. In the example above, it would tell MySQL to use 9 as the next record entered.

✔ Tips

- You can accomplish the same effect using the myisamchk tool:

  `myisamchk --set-auto-increment`

- Like most queries, you can also run the `ALTER … AUTO_INCREMENT` SQL through any programming script or application.

- Even though I set `AUTO_INCREMENT` equal to 1 in my example, you can set it to any integer, per your needs.

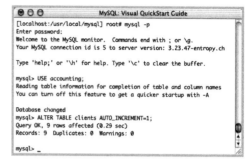

Figure A.13 The `ALTER` command can also be used to adjust an auto-incrementation setting.

A Word of Caution

I've included the steps for resetting the auto incrementation value here, as it's a frequently asked question from beginning users. In my opinion, there are times when doing this makes a lot of sense, for example, after you've completely emptied a table and want the counting to begin at 1 again.

But it is also true that if you are over eager in adjusting the auto incrementation, you could adversely affect the integrity of your data, for example, if the auto-incremented column acts as a foreign key in another table. While it's useful to know how to adjust the auto incrementation setting, you should also be aware of any adverse affects doing so could have.

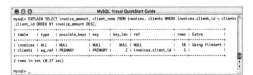

Figure A.14 The SQL term EXPLAIN shows what information MySQL uses to run a query.

Queries That Return Strange Results

A problem many MySQL users come across, particularly when accessing the database from a PHP, Perl, or Java script, is that a query does not give the intended results. Beginning developers might errantly assume that it's a programming issue, when it really comes down to a matter of SQL.

To debug strange query results, try these steps:

1. If using a programming language to create an SQL query, print out the query so that you know exactly what is trying to be executed.

2. If possible, run the query on the database via another method, such as using the mysql monitor.

3. Use EXPLAIN to see how MySQL is handling the query (**Figure A.14**). See the MySQL manual for more information on how EXPLAIN functions.

4. Alter the query so that you are selecting only the columns used in a WHERE clause, ignoring extraneous information.

5. Rewrite the query in its most basic form. Then keep adding dimensions back in until you discover which clause is causing the problem.

SQL AND MySQL REFERENCES

This appendix should stand as a quick reference for your SQL and MySQL needs. In this section you'll find tables from elsewhere in the book—sometimes in a more complete form—along with other terminology and function listings. The tables and references here have been loosely grouped based on the subject, which generally follows the same outline as the content of the book as a whole. For information not listed, or to see the most current specifications for a newer version of MySQL, check the MySQL manual.

Basic SQL

MySQL aims to have full ANSI SQL92 and SQL99 support, although some considerations are made in the interest of performance. This section of the appendix deals with SQL-specific standards, whereas the other sections refer to more MySQL-specific issues. To start, **Table B.1** lists the most common SQL terms.

Here are some examples as to how these queries would be used:

◆ CREATE DATABASE database_name

(Creates a new database.)

◆ CREATE TABLE table_name (column_name1
→ column_definition, column_name2
→ column_definition)

(Creates a new table, structured according to the column definitions.)

◆ DELETE FROM table_name WHERE
→ column_name = 'x'

(Removes every record from the table where column_name is equal to *x*.)

◆ DROP TABLE table_name

(Deletes the table and all of its columns, rows, and data.)

◆ DROP DATABASE database_name

(Deletes the database and all of its tables, columns, rows, and data.)

◆ INSERT INTO table_name VALUES ('x',
→ 'y', 'z')

(Inserts the values *x*, *y*, and *z* into the three columns of a new row in *table_name*. This syntax will work only if the number of values specified exactly matches the number of columns.)

SQL Terminology

TERM	USED FOR
ALTER	Changing the structure of a table
CREATE	Creating a table or database
DELETE	Deleting records from a table
DROP	Deleting entire tables or databases
INSERT	Adding records to a table
SELECT	Retrieving information from a database
SHOW	Displaying information about the structure of a database or table
UPDATE	Modifying a database entry

Table B.1 These terms are the eight most common SQL keywords to use in queries.

◆ INSERT INTO table_name (column1_name,
→ column3_name) VALUES ('x', 'y')

(Inserts the value *x* into the first and the value *y* into the third column of a new row. This syntax will work as long as the specified columns exist.)

◆ INSERT INTO table_name VALUES ('x',
→ 'y', 'z'), ('a', 'b', 'c')

(Inserts two rows into the table. This is a MySQL addition to the SQL standard and will not necessarily work in every database application.)

◆ SELECT * FROM tablename

(Returns every column of every row.)

◆ SELECT column1_name, column2_name FROM
→ table_name

(Returns just the two columns for every row.)

◆ UPDATE table_name SET column_name = 'x'

(Sets the value of *column_name* to *x* for every row in the table.)

BASIC SQL

ALTER

While every SQL term can be used in many ways to accomplish different goals, ALTER may be the most complex. In general, ALTER is used to change the structure of a table: by changing its name; by adding or deleting indexes; or by adding, deleting, or modifying its columns. **Table B.2** lists some of the common ALTER clauses, all of which would begin with the phrase ALTER TABLE tablename.

ALTER TABLE Queries

CLAUSE	EXAMPLE	MEANING
ADD COLUMN	ADD COLUMN column_name VARCHAR(40)	Adds a new column to the end of the table.
CHANGE COLUMN	CHANGE COLUMN column_name column_name VARCHAR(60)	Allows you to change the data type and properties of a column, including its name.
DROP COLUMN	DROP COLUMN column_name	Removes a column from a table, including all of its data.
ADD INDEX	ADD INDEX indexname (column_name)	Adds a new index on column_name.
DROP INDEX	DROP INDEX indexname	Removes an existing index.
RENAME AS	RENAME AS new_tablename	Changes the name of a table.

Table B.2 The ALTER keyword is used to change the structure of an existing table.

Operators and Comparators

OPERATOR	MEANING
+	addition
-	subtraction
*	multiplication
/	division
%	modulus
=	equals
<	less than
>	greater than
<=	less than or equal to
>=	greater than or equal to
!=	not equal to
%	multiple wildcard character (used with LIKE)
_ (underscore)	single wildcard character (used with LIKE)
IS NOT NULL	has a value (including an empty string or zero)
IS NULL	does not have a value
BETWEEN	within a range
NOT BETWEEN	outside of a range
IN	is one of a listed set of values
NOT IN	is not one of a listed set of values
OR (also ||)	where at least one of two conditionals is true
AND (also &&)	where both conditionals are true
NOT (also !)	where the condition is not true
OR NOT (also ^)	where only one of two conditionals is true
LIKE	where the value matches a string
NOT LIKE	where the value does not match a string
REGEXP	where the value matches a pattern
NOT REGEXP	where the value does not match a pattern
MATCH AGAINST	where the values matches against a series of words

Table B.3 These operators and comparators can be used in conjunction with parentheses to create different expressions in SQL queries.

Clauses

On your queries, primarily when using SELECT, UPDATE, or DELETE, normally you will want to use clauses to limit the information returned. The four common clauses are WHERE, GROUP BY, ORDER BY, and LIMIT. Examples:

◆ SELECT * FROM tablename ORDER BY → column DESC

(Retrieves every column and every record from the table, sorted by column in descending order.)

◆ SELECT * FROM tablename ORDER BY column → ASC, column2 DESC

(Retrieves every column and every record from the table, sorted by column in ascending order, then by column2 in descending order.)

◆ SELECT * FROM tablename LIMIT 10

(Retrieves every column of the first ten records from the table.)

◆ SELECT * FROM tablename LIMIT 100, 50

(Retrieves every column of the 101st through 150th records from the table.)

You can also, and frequently will, use multiple clauses in the same query. Clauses can be applied just to a column name or they can be used in conjunction with parentheses and operators to create more elaborate conditionals. **Table B.3** lists the operators and comparators you'll commonly use in a WHERE clause.

BASIC SQL

Administrative SQL

Besides the SQL used to manage data, there are several terms used explicitly for managing the database as a whole. These were introduced in Chapter 10, "MySQL Administration," and are also included in **Table B.4**.

Administrative SQL

TERM	EXAMPLE	MEANING
ANALYZE	ANALYZE TABLE tablename	Inspects MyISAM and BDB tables.
BACKUP	BACKUP TABLE tablename TO '/path/to/backup/directory'	Stores the structure and data of a MyISAM table as text files.
CHECK	CHECK TABLE tablename	Inspects MyISAM and InnoDB tables.
FLUSH	FLUSH PRIVILEGES	Enacts user privilege changes made to the *mysql* database.
OPTIMIZE	OPTIMIZE TABLE tablename	Improves the efficiency of a fragmented MyISAM or BDB table.
REPAIR	REPAIR TABLE tablename	Repairs damaged MyISAM tables.
RESTORE	RESTORE TABLE tablename FROM '/path/to/backup/directory'	Rebuilds a MyISAM table based upon text files created by BACKUP.
SHOW	SHOW GRANTS FOR user	Displays the privilege information for a user.

Table B.4 The various SQL terms in this table are all used for administrative-level tasks.

ADMINISTRATIVE SQL

Privileges

PRIVILEGE	USER LEVEL	APPLIES TO
SELECT	browser	tables
ALTER	manager	tables
DELETE	manager	tables
INSERT	manager	tables
UPDATE	manager	tables
CREATE	DB admin	databases, tables, or indexes
DROP	DB admin	databases or tables
FILE	DB admin	file access on server
INDEX	DB admin	tables
GRANT	MySQL admin	databases or tables
PROCESS	MySQL admin	MySQL server
RELOAD	MySQL admin	MySQL server
SHUTDOWN	MySQL admin	MySQL server

Table B.5 MySQL users can be allowed to have or not have any of the privileges listed in this table.

MySQL Privileges

The user privilege system built into MySQL dictates who can do what within each particular database. The *mysql* database—created when the `mysql_install_db` script is run at installation—stores the specifics in terms of users, passwords, hosts, and databases. It also records what individual, allowable actions particular users can do—in other words, what SQL commands they can run on the database. **Table B.5** lists these privileges. I've added a rough "User Level" column to give a sense of what type of user would be given each privilege: *browser* (a person viewing records), *manager* (a person adding and updating records), *DB admin* (a person creating the database itself), and *MySQL admin* (the person managing the server and the MySQL software as a whole). These are entirely artificial distinctions of my own making but should help give you a sense of how to assign privileges. As a rule, always give each user the minimum required privileges on a database.

MySQL Data Types

Selecting the proper column type for your tables is key to a successful database. **Tables B.6**, **B.7**, and **B.8** define the different string, number, and other types you can use, along with how much space they will take up on the server's hard drive. When choosing a type for each column, you should use the most efficient (i.e., the most size-frugal) data type based upon what the largest value of the column could be.

MySQL String Data Types

TYPE	SIZE	DESCRIPTION
CHAR[Length]	*Length* bytes	A fixed-length field from 0 to 255 characters long.
VARCHAR(Length)	String length + 1 bytes	A fixed-length field from 0 to 255 characters long.
TINYTEXT	String length + 1 byte	A string with a maximum length of 255 characters.
TEXT	String length + 2 bytes	A string with a maximum length of 65,535 characters.
MEDIUMTEXT	String length + 3 bytes	A string with a maximum length of 16,777,215 characters.
LONGTEXT	String length + 4 bytes	A string with a maximum length of 4,294,967,295 characters.

Table B.6 These six data types should be used to define columns that will contain string values.

MySQL Number Data Types

TYPE	SIZE	DESCRIPTION
TINYINT[Length]	1 byte	Range of -128 to 127 or 0 to 255 unsigned.
SMALLINT[Length]	2 bytes	Range of -32,768 to 32,767 or 0 to 65,535 unsigned.
MEDIUMINT[Length]	3 bytes	Range of -8,388,608 to 8,388,607 or 0 to 16,777,215 unsigned.
INT[Length]	4 bytes	Range of -2,147,483,648 to 2,147,483,647 or 0 to 4,294,967,295 unsigned.
BIGINT[Length]	8 bytes	Range of -9,223,372,036,854,775,808 to 9,223,372,036,854,775,807 or 0 to 18,446,744,073,709,551,615 unsigned.
FLOAT[Length, Decimals]	4 bytes	A small number with a floating decimal point.
DOUBLE[Length, Decimals]	8 bytes	A large number with a floating decimal point.
DECIMAL[Length, Decimals]	*Length* + 1 or *Length* + 2 bytes	A DOUBLE stored as a string, allowing for a fixed decimal point.

Table B.7 The most important consideration when choosing number types is whether the values will always be integers or could contain decimal points.

MYSQL DATA TYPES

I've not included BLOBs (Binary Large Objects) within the string types even though they are technically the same as the TEXT data types. The only difference between the two is that BLOB values will be handled as case-sensitive and TEXT is case-insensitive. Regardless, I've separated out BLOBs since they are normally used for binary data.

Further, I should mention that MEDIUMINT, SET, ENUM, as well as the different-sized BLOB and TEXT column types are all MySQL-specific extensions of the SQL defaults. The same applies to the terms AUTO_INCREMENT, NULL, UNSIGNED, and ZEROFILL, which are used to add attributes to a column's description.

Finally, when it comes to defining columns, remember that any column type can be NULL or NOT NULL, integers can be UNSIGNED, and any number can be ZEROFILL. As of MySQL 4.0.2, you can also use UNSIGNED to describe a floating-point column.

MySQL Date and Other Data Types

TYPE	SIZE	DESCRIPTION
DATE	3 bytes	In the format of *YYYY-MM-DD*.
DATETIME	8 bytes	In the format of *YYYY-MM-DD HH:MM:SS*.
TIMESTAMP	4 bytes	In the format of *YYYYMMDDHHMMSS*; acceptable range ends in the year 2037.
TIME	3 bytes	In the format of *HH:MM:SS*.
YEAR	1 byte	In the format of either *YY* or *YYYY*.
ENUM	1 or 2 bytes	Short for enumeration, which means that each column can have one of several possible values.
SET	1, 2, 3, 4, or 8 bytes	Like ENUM except that each column can have more than one of several possible values.
TINYBLOB	String length + 1 byte	A binary file with a maximum length of 255 characters.
BLOB	String length + 2 bytes	A binary file with a maximum length of 65,535 characters.
MEDIUMBLOB	String length + 3 bytes	A binary file with a maximum length of 16,777,215 characters.
LONGBLOB	String length + 4 bytes	A binary file with a maximum length of 4,294,967,295 characters.

Table B.8 If the values being stored in a column are not strings or numbers, one of these miscellaneous types should be used.

MySQL DATA TYPES

MySQL Functions

Pre-formatting the results returned by a query makes your data more usable and can cut down on the amount of programming interface required. To do so, you make use of MySQL's built-in functions, first introduced in Chapter 5, "MySQL Functions." **Table B.9** shows those used for strings. **Table B.10** has most, but not all, of the number-based functions. **Table B.11** lists date-related functions. **Table B.12** has the formatting parameters for the DATE_FORMAT() and TIME_FORMAT() functions. **Table B.13** is the aggregate or grouping functions. **Table B.14** is the catchall for miscellaneous functions. Most every function can be applied either to the value retrieved from a column or to a manually entered one (e.g., SELECT ROUND (3.142857, 2)).

Text Functions

FUNCTION	USAGE	PURPOSE
LEFT()	LEFT(column, x)	Returns the leftmost *x* characters from a column.
LENGTH()	LENGTH(column)	Returns the length of the string stored in the column.
LOCATE()	LOCATE(substring, string)	Returns the first instance of *substring* in *string*, if applicable.
LOWER()	LOWER(column)	Turns the stored string into an all-lowercase format.
LTRIM()	LTRIM(column)	Trims excess spaces from the beginning of the stored string.
REPLACE()	REPLACE(column, find, replace)	Returns the column value with every instance of *find* substituted by *replace*.
RIGHT()	RIGHT(column, x)	Returns the rightmost *x* characters from a column.
RTRIM()	RTRIM(column)	Trims excess spaces from the end of the stored string.
STRCMP()	STRCMP(column1, column2)	Returns *o* if the strings are the same, *–1* or *1* otherwise.
SUBSTRING()	SUBSTRING(column, start, length)	Returns *length* characters from *column* beginning with *start* (indexed from o).
TRIM()	TRIM(column)	Trims excess spaces from the beginning and end of the stored string.
UPPER()	UPPER(column)	Capitalizes the entire stored string.

Table B.9 These functions are used for manipulating string values, in columns or otherwise.

Numeric Functions

FUNCTION	USAGE	PURPOSE
ABS()	ABS(column)	Returns the absolute value of *column*.
CEILING()	CEILING(column)	Returns the next-highest integer based upon the value of *column*.
FLOOR()	FLOOR(column)	Returns the integer value of *column*.
FORMAT()	FORMAT(column, y)	Returns *column* formatted as a number with *y* decimal places and commas inserted every three spaces.
LEAST()	LEAST(x,y,x…)	Returns the smallest value from a list.
GREATEST()	GREATEST(x,y,z…)	Returns the greatest value from a list.
MOD()	MOD(x, y)	Returns the remainder of dividing *x* by *y* (either or both can be a column).
POWER()	POWER(x,y)	Returns the value of *x* to the *y* power.
RAND()	RAND()	Returns a random number between 0 and 1.0.
ROUND()	ROUND(x,y)	Returns the number *x* rounded to *y* decimal places.
SIGN()	SIGN(column)	Returns a value indicating whether a number is negative (-1), zero (0), or positive (+1).
SQRT()	SQRT(column)	Calculates the square root of the column.

Table B.10 Here are some of the numeric functions MySQL has, excluding the trigonometric and more esoteric ones.

Date and Time Functions

FUNCTION	USAGE	PURPOSE
HOUR()	HOUR(column)	Returns just the hour value of a stored date (in 24-hour time).
MINUTE()	MINUTE(column)	Returns just the minute value of a stored date.
SECOND()	SECOND(column)	Returns just the second value of a stored date.
DAYNAME()	DAYNAME(column)	Returns the name of the day for a date value.
DAYOFMONTH()	DAYOFMONTH(column)	Returns just the numerical day value of a stored date.
MONTHNAME()	MONTHNAME(column)	Returns the name of the month in a date value.
MONTH()	MONTH(column)	Returns just the numerical month value of a stored date.
YEAR()	YEAR(column)	Returns just the year value of a stored date.
ADDDATE()	ADDDATE(column, INTERVAL x type)	Returns the value of *x* units added to *column*.
SUBDATE()	SUBDATE(column, INTERVAL x type)	Returns the value of *x* units subtracted from *column*.
CURDATE()	CURDATE()	Returns the current date.
CURTIME()	CURTIME()	Returns the current time.
NOW()	NOW()	Returns the current date and time.
UNIX_TIMESTAMP()	UNIX_TIMESTAMP(date)	Returns the number of seconds since the epoch or since the date specified.

Table B.11 The different date functions are for doing calculations and formatting this unique data type. Table B.12 lists the parameters for the DATE_FORMAT() and TIME_FORMAT() functions.

MySQL Functions

DATE_FORMAT() and TIME_FORMAT() Parameters

Term	Usage	Example	Term	Usage	Example
%e	Day of the month	1-31	%Y	Year	2002
%d	Day of the month, two digit	01-31	%y	Year	02
			%l (lowercase "L")	Hour	1-12
%D	Day with suffix	1st-31st	%h	Hour, two digit	01-12
%W	Weekday name	Sunday-Saturday	%k	Hour, 24-hour clock	0-23
%a	Abbreviated weekday name	Sun-Sat	%H	Hour, 24-hour clock, two digit	00-23
%c	Month number	1-12	%i	Minutes	00-59
%m	Month number, two digit	01-12	%S	Seconds	00-59
			%r	Time	8:17:02 PM
%M	Month name	January-December	%T	Time, 24-hour clock	20:17:02
%b	Month name, abbreviated	Jan-Dec	%p	AM or PM	AM or PM

Table B.12 The DATE_FORMAT() and TIME_FORMAT() functions make use of these special characters to format a date or time.

Grouping Functions

Function	Usage	Purpose
AVG()	AVG(column)	Returns the average of the values of the column.
COUNT()	COUNT(column)	Counts the number of rows.
COUNT(DISTINCT)	COUNT(DISTINCT column)	Counts the number of distinct column values.
MIN()	MIN(column)	Returns the smallest value from the column.
MAX()	MAX(column)	Returns the largest value from the column.
SUM()	SUM(column)	Returns the sum of all of the values in the column.

Table B.13 The grouping functions are frequently tied to a GROUP BY clause to aggregate values in a column.

Other Functions

Function	Usage	Purpose
CONCAT()	CONAT(column1, ' - ', column2)	Combines the elements in parentheses into one string.
CONCAT_WS()	CONCAT_WS('- ', column1, column2)	Combines the elements with the one common separator.
DATABASE()	DATABASE()	Returns the name of the database currently being used.
ENCODE()	ENCODE('string', 'salt')	Returns an encrypted version of *string*, which can be decrypted.
ENCRYPT()	ENCRYPT('string', 'salt')	Returns an encrypted version of *string* using *salt* (requires the Unix crypt library).
DECODE()	DECODE('string', 'salt')	Returns a decrypted version of *string*.
LAST_INSERT_ID()	LAST_INSERT_ID()	Returns the previous auto-incremented value.
PASSWORD()	PASSWORD('string')	Returns an encrypted version of *string*.
USER()	USER()	Returns the name of the user of the current session.

Table B.14 These various functions are for everything from encryption to concatenation.

Special Characters

CHARACTER	MEANING
\'	single quotation mark
\"	double quotation mark
\\	backslash
\n	newline
\r	carriage return
\t	tab
\%	percent character
_	underscore

Table B.15 To insert certain special characters in a database, you'll need to escape them as they are shown here.

Other References

The last three references for this appendix include **Table B.15**, how to store special characters in a database; **Table B.16**, how to weight keywords in a binary mode full-text search; and **Table B.17**, significant characters for regular expressions.

Special Boolean Mode Characters

CHARACTER	MEANING	EXAMPLE	MATCHES
+	Word is required	+punk rock	*punk* is required and *rock* is optional
-	Word must not be present	+punk -rock	*punk* is required and *rock* cannot be present
" "	A literal phrase	"punk rock"	Occurrences of the phrase *punk rock* is weighted
<	Less important	<punk +rock	*rock* is required and *punk* is less significant
>	More important	>punk +rock	*rock* is required, but *punk* is more significant
()	Creates groups	(>punk roll) +rock	*rock* is required, both *punk* and *roll* are optional, but *punk* is weighted more
~	Detracts from relevance	+punk ~rock	*punk* is required and the presence of *rock* devalues the relevance (but *rock* is not excluded)
*	Allows for wildcards (use at the end of word)	+punk +rock*	*punk* and *rock* are required, but *rocks*, *rocker*, *rocking*, etc., are counted

Table B.16 As of version 4 of MySQL, you can perform full-text searches in binary mode, using these symbols.

Special Regular Expression Characters

CHARACTER	MATCHES	CHARACTER	MATCHES
.	any single character	q{x,y}	between *x* and *y* instances of q
q?	zero or one *q*	^q	starts with *q*
q*	zero or more *q*'s	q$	ends with *q*
q+	at least one *q*	(pqr)	grouping (matches *pqr*)
q{x}	*x* instances of *q*	q|z	either *q* or *z*
q{x,}	at least *x* instances of *q*	[]	character classes (e.g., [a-z], [0-9])
q{,x}	up to *x* instances of *q*	\	escapes a special character (\., *, etc.)

Table B.17 When using REGEX and NOT REGEX, you'll need to define patterns with the characters listed here.

RESOURCES

Because a book can only be so thorough and so current, I like to include a list of useful resources in each one I write. Here you'll primarily find links to Web sites I consider valuable along with other, miscellaneous resources such as book titles and mailing lists.

Your first reference for MySQL-related issues should be MySQL's official Web site, located at www.mysql.com. After that, I hope you will frequent this book's home page, found at www.DMCinsights.com/mysql. The site was designed with the express intention of supporting this book and thus you will find there:

- More Web links (nearly 200 at last count)

- Sample scripts not demonstrated in this book

- Extra tutorials (as I create them)

- A support forum for questions and issues arising from this book

- An errata page, listing printing errors (which does unfortunately happen)

All of the resources listed in this chapter are items I have come across that may be useful to the average reader. Referencing something here does not constitute an endorsement nor does it imply that each of these is the best possible resource or tool for your needs.

MySQL

The absolutely very first resource you should consider is the MySQL manual, available through the company's Web site (www.mysql.com) in many different forms. The main online version has the added advantage of being searchable, while another online version includes user-submitted comments that are occasionally helpful. I also keep a copy of the manual on my hard drive for whichever version of MySQL I am running (since the manual reflects the current version of MySQL, it's smart to retain older copies).

Once you've performed an exhaustive search through the MySQL manual, you can consider turning to one of several MySQL-dedicated mailing lists (there are no official MySQL newsgroups). Each list has a different subject:

- Announcements
- General
- Java
- Windows
- ODBC
- C++
- Perl

All of these but the announcements are available in a digest form so that you can receive two large emails per day rather than 50 individual ones. Plus these lists are available in other languages. For more information, see www.mysql.com/doc/M/a/Mailing-list.html.

Through another link at the MySQL site—http://lists.mysql.com (**Figure C.1**)—you can perform searches through the mailing list archives. Doing a quick search here before posting a question to a mailing list (and presumably after you've scoured the MySQL manual) will save you time and the potential flaming from the list denizens.

The Danish Web site Bit By Bit has some good MySQL resources, including the MySQL FAQ, created and maintained by Carsten Pedersen. You can find it at www.bitbybit.dk/mysqlfaq (**Figure C.2**).

Figure C.1 You can access information from the MySQL mailing lists by subscribing or by searching the respective archives.

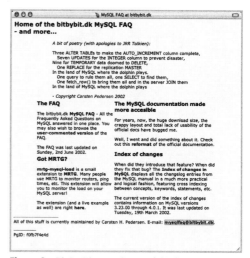

Figure C.2 Bit By Bit contains useful information for the beginning MySQL developer.

Figure C.3 DeZign, by Datanamic, is a tool that assists in creating a database scheme (or *entity-relationship* plan) for your application.

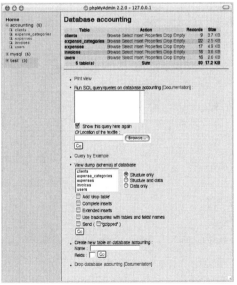

Figure C.4 The phpMyAdmin software, developed by phpWizard.net, is an excellent way to interact with MySQL.

Third-Party MySQL Applications

The MySQL Web site maintains a list of various third-party MySQL applications and tools, ranging from simple Perl scripts to elaborate interfaces to the MySQL software. You can find the links to these through www.mysql.com/downloads/contrib.html.

As I mentioned in Chapter 3, "Database Design," you can use dedicated applications to help you with your database scheme. Two such programs are Dezign (www.datanamic.com/dezign/index.html, **Figure C.3**) and Tabledesigner (www.tabledesigner.com). While applications like these may be written with a particular database in mind, the processes may still be useful for MySQL.

For an easy-to-use and powerful database administration tool, one of the hands-down favorites is phpMyAdmin, created by the talented people at phpWizard.net (www.phpwizard.net). It requires that you have a Web server and PHP installed but allows you to interact with MySQL through a Web browser, rather than the mysql client (**Figure C.4**).

Finally, EMS's MySQL Manager (http://ems-hitech.com/mymanager/) is an affordable and potent all-around MySQL administrative tool.

SQL

Since SQL is used by MySQL and other databases, you can find an endless supply of resources for this language. While generic SQL references will not necessarily show you how to get the most out of a MySQL database, they should teach you the fundamentals. A few online SQL references include

◆ SQL Course, www.sqlcourse.com

◆ W3Schools.com, www.w3schools.com/sql/default.asp (**Figure C.5**)

◆ A Gentle Introduction to SQL, www.sqlzoo.net (**Figure C.6**)

◆ SQL Course 2, www.sqlcourse2.com

Many bookstores stock books dedicated to the language. Two recommended titles are *The Practical SQL Handbook* by Judith S. Bowman and *Mastering SQL* by Martin Gruber. You may find, however, that an entire book on SQL is more knowledge than all but the advanced database developer requires. Further, you'll see that MySQL does not support a number of features that would be discussed in an all-purpose SQL text.

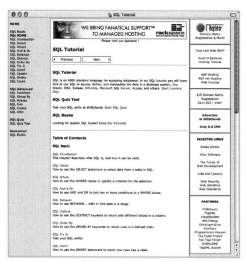

Figure C.5 The W3Schools site includes tutorials on lots of subjects, including SQL.

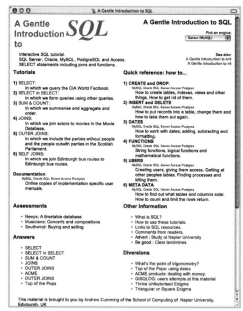

Figure C.6 Andrew Cumming's A Gentle Introduction to SQL is a user-friendly discussion of the language.

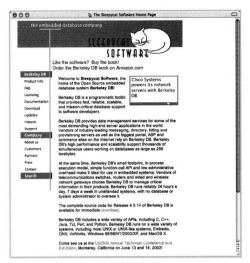

Figure C.7 Sleepycat developed and maintained BDB databases, which you can use with MySQL.

General Database

Much like the SQL resources, which are not MySQL-centric, there are any number of general database Web sites and books that you could find useful when working with MySQL. Two good Web sites are SearchDatabase (www.searchdatabase.com) and the Web Developer's Virtual Library (http://wdvl. internet.com/Authoring/DB/Relational/).

Three other sites related to MySQL are

◆ ANSI, www.ansi.org, which maintains the SQL standard

◆ InnoDB, www.innodb.com, the creators of the InnoDB table type

◆ Sleepycat, www.sleepycat.com (**Figure C.7**), the creators of the Berkeley DB (BDB) table type

One book that deals with everything about database design—from identifying the needs of the database to defining the column types—is *Database Design for Mere Mortals* by Michael J. Hernandez.

PHP

In Chapter 6, I demonstrated how to interact with a MySQL database from a PHP script. Because of its popularity, there are dozens of PHP-related sites on the Internet. The three most popular and useful are

◆ The PHP home page, www.php.net (**Figure C.8**), where you'll find the manual and more

◆ Zend, www.zend.com (**Figure C.9**), which contains articles and sample code

◆ PHPBuilder, www.phpbuilder.com, a great repository of PHP tutorials, forums, and code.

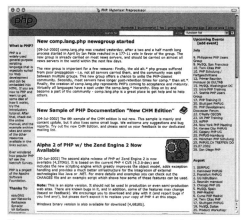

Figure C.8 PHP.net is the home page of the PHP scripting language...

Figure C.9 ...whereas Zend.com supports the language in many different ways.

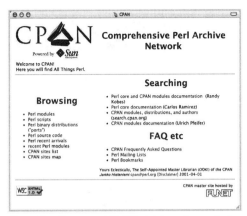

Figure C.10 To access a MySQL database from a Perl script, you can use some of the CPAN modules.

Figure C.11 The DBI Documentation pages include both Perl and general database information.

Perl

In Chapter 7, I interfaced with a MySQL database from Perl scripts. At the time, I included some URLs to visit for more information, such as:

◆ The official Perl home page, www.perl.com

◆ The CPAN (Comprehensive Perl Archive Network), www.cpan.org (**Figure C.10**), where you can get the modules necessary to interact with MySQL

◆ ActiveState, www.activestate.com, where you can download ActivePerl for running Perl on Windows

◆ DBI Documentation, http://dbi.perl.org (**Figure C.11**), which contains links to various Perl DBI resources

Java

In Chapter 8 I introduced the topic of using JDBC to access MySQL from a Java application. The corresponding Web links for that topic are:

◆ Java home page, http://java.sun.com (**Figure C.12**)

◆ JDBC home page, http://java.sun.com/products/jdbc

◆ MMMySQL Driver page, http://mmmysql.sourceforge.net

◆ Javaboutique, http://javaboutique.internet.com, which has sample code and articles

◆ JavaWorld, www.javaworld.com (**Figure C.13**), which also has sample Java code and tutorials

◆ Caucho JDBC Driver page, www.caucho.com/projects/jdbc-mysql, which is an alternative to the mm.mysql driver

Figure C.12 Sun, the makers of Java, maintain the language and its documentation.

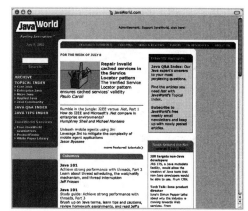

Figure C.13 JavaWorld is a good site for Java programmers of all skill levels.

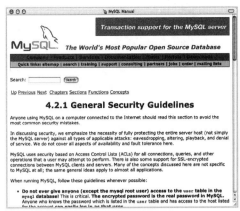

Figure C.14 The MySQL manual's section on security is a must read for every MySQL user.

Security

Database security is a topic that could merit its own book. Unfortunately, outdated information is highly detrimental when it comes to security. Thus, the best way to stay in touch with the relevant security issues of the day is to track the following Web sites:

◆ The MySQL documentation includes its own specific section on security at www.mysql.com/doc/G/e/General_ security.html (**Figure C.14**).

◆ CERT, www.cert.org, is an institution associated with Carnegie Mellon University that tracks and reports on relevant Internet security issues.

◆ SecurityFocus, www.securityfocus.com, lists security-related issues primarily for the Windows and Unix operating systems. It also tracks bugs and viruses of which developers should be cognizant.

◆ Insecure.org, www.insecure.org, was developed from a hacker's perspective. It provides different security tools and information with a Unix focus.

◆ Tripwire, www.tripwire.org, is an open source security application that runs on your server (or computer) and monitors key files. It is currently available for the Unix family of operating systems.

◆ OpenSSH, www.openssh.org, is a free application that provides for secure telnet and FTP.

◆ PuTTY, www.chiark.greenend.org.uk/ ~sgtatham/putty, is a free and popular SSH client for Windows.

I'll also add that MySQL, as of version 4.0, has the ability to use SSL (Secure Socket Layer) to connect to a database over a safer connection. The manual further describes how to use SSH to do the same. Both are worth considering wherever secure data transmission is critical.

SECURITY

Other Resources

Finally, I'll throw out a few miscellaneous resources that do not fall under the previous categories. For starters, people using Mac OS X (of which I'm obviously a big fan) should get to know

Figure C.15 Apple's Developer Connection pages are a must-use resource for more advanced OS X users.

◆ Apple Developer Connection, http://developer.apple.com (**Figure C.15**)

◆ Entropy, www.entropy.ch

E-gineer, www.e-gineer.com, is an Internet information site that has excellent information on installing MySQL and other software.

SourceForge.net, www.sourceforge.net, which I've referenced previously, claims to be the world's largest repository of open source applications (and there's good cause to believe that). Thousands of different technologies are developed through and hosted by SourceForge.net, including the mm.mysql JDBC driver.

Developer Shed, www.devshed.com, is a general development site that includes articles discussing the various programming languages and technologies you are likely to use.

WebMonkey, www.webmonkey.com, is very similar to Developer Shed, although it is broader in scope.

If you are intrigued by the open source community and projects such as MySQL, see www.opensource.org.

INDEX

G

WWW.PEACHPIT.COM

Quality How-to Computer Books

Visit Peachpit Press on the Web at www.peachpit.com

- Check out new feature articles each Monday: excerpts, interviews, tips, and plenty of how-tos

- Find any Peachpit book by title, series, author, or topic on the Books page

- See what our authors are up to on the News page: signings, chats, appearances, and more

- Meet the Peachpit staff and authors in the About section: bios, profiles, and candid shots

- Use Resources to reach our academic, sales, customer service, and tech support areas and find out how to become a Peachpit author

About

News

Books

Features

Resources

Order

Find

Welcome!

Peachpit.com is also the place to:

- Chat with our authors online
- Take advantage of special Web-only offers
- Get the latest info on new books